WORKPLACE GENIE

WORKPLACE GENIE

An Unorthodox Toolkit to Help Transform
Your Work Relationships and
Get the Most from Your Career

NATALIE CANAVOR
AND SUSAN DOWELL, LCSW

Skyhorse Publishing

Visit our website at www.skyhorsepublishing.com.

10 9 8 7 6 5 4 3 2 1

Library of Congress Cataloging-in-Publication Data is available on file.

Cover design by Rain Saukas
Cover photograph: iStockphoto

Print ISBN: 978-1-5107-1525-7
Ebook ISBN: 978-1-5107-1526-4

Printed in the United States of America

To my husband, Greg Bush, for his unwavering support, insights, and sharp critical eye. —Natalie Canavor

I dedicate this book to the memory of my late husband, Robert, whose compassion, wisdom, and integrity continue to inspire me. —Susan Dowell

CONTENTS

Chapter 1

WORKPLACE GENIE AND YOU

Today's workplace is an unhappy place for many people. Almost 70 percent of employees say they feel disengaged with their jobs. And almost always, the reason is summed up in one word: relationships. So if you feel . . .

- Unfairly treated at work . . .
- Undermined by a coworker . . .
- Paralyzed by criticism . . .
- Cowed by an abusive boss . . .
- Frustrated by your inability to advance . . .
- Victimized by office politics . . .

You're not alone! Most people feel that way at times. Even if your situation is less extreme than those on our short list, you may feel stuck in place or unsure how to speak up for yourself. Or you might feel like an outsider in the office and wonder why you don't relate to your coworkers, or you might suspect your people skills are hampering your career.

What if you had the resources to improve your relations with the boss, coworkers, and other problem people? What if you knew how to initiate change in your own situation and alter other people's perceptions of you?

You do! Most people own the inner resources to deal effectively with workplace problems and people. But they haven't developed strategies to connect with those capabilities and use them with confidence.

Workplace Genie will show you fresh ways of seeing and acting. The approaches may seem surprising and even unorthodox at first glance, given our entrenched patterns of thinking about the workplace, but they're based on sound psychological principles. We'll help you understand your own past experience so you can vanquish the ghosts of earlier situations you mishandled and no longer have to worry about repeating your mistakes. We'll give you specific techniques for taking the lead to improve your immediate work relationships. And we'll equip you to create good relationships in your future career stops, whatever direction you take.

What we won't do is give you a set of formulaic approaches that involve labeling other people as types, or tell you how to outmaneuver an "opponent." Nor will we fill you with clever responses that may make you feel good in the short run, but short-circuit your ultimate success.

Our goals for you are more ambitious. We want to:

- Open up your perceptions so you see the world around you and other people more accurately, and more deeply.
- Free you from false ideas about your own limitations.
- Equip you to assess your options realistically and creatively.
- Empower you to deal confidently with difficult people and situations.
- Enable you to bring out other people's better selves.

And most of all, we want to show you how to know and bring out your own best self.

This book gives you illuminating ideas from psychology and professional communication and shows you how to use them based on real-life experience of people you'll recognize. You'll discover strategies to access your intuition and thinking power, as well as techniques to manage and shift your state of mind, stay cool under fire, and manage your emotions. Everything in this book is based on deeply human truths, but it's all practical, realistic, and in many cases, surprisingly simple.

WHY WORKPLACE RELATIONSHIPS MATTER

Most employers place "interpersonal skills" at the top of their most-wanted lists. They have good reasons. Few jobs today exist in a vacuum. We don't accomplish much on our own. In every field and type of organization, important work is accomplished through collaboration. We need coworkers to actively support us and want supervisors to value us and help us grow.

Given more or less equal skill sets, the individual perceived as most personable will always be hired. On the job, you must keep proving yourself not just in terms of your technical abilities, but also by how you interact on a daily basis with the boss and coworkers. If you look back over your own work history, whatever your field, we think you'll agree that your own success or failure—as well as happiness—has rested on relationships.

The boss-employee relationship sets the tone and can create a positive, encouraging environment, or the opposite. A recent Gallup poll showed that *75 percent of workers who voluntarily left their jobs did so because of their bosses*. The survey also revealed that employers don't know this: 89 percent believe that most people leave to earn more money (in fact, only 12 percent quit for this reason).

WHY WORK RELATIONSHIPS ARE HARD

Typically, we're in the company of coworkers far more than that of friends and family. We work on average 8.7 hours per day, sleep 7.7 hours, and have only 7.6 hours for everything else in our lives. For most of us, the office is a second home, populated by individuals we're not related to, didn't choose to spend time with, and may not even like. Power is typically unequal, and company culture may foster fierce in-house competition.

Today's work environment multiplies these built-in challenges:

- We may be called on to do more with less and even more than one job.
- Organizations may slash jobs and benefits, reorganize budgets, and shift priorities often.
- Jobs are more specialized and technical, demanding more collaboration.
- Today's diverse workplace presents us with deep differences in how we see the world, communicate, and assign value.
- Progress in addressing gender issues and cultural differences makes the work environment more hypersensitive.
- Many leaders remain oblivious to the impact of untrained supervisors put in place for the wrong reasons, and fail to provide support structures for conflict resolution.

Because the stakes are high and the environment is basically impersonal, workplace emotions are often highly intense. We have a lot at stake and the many levels of daily interaction can easily tap into our insecurities. Once generated, bad feelings tend to escalate because it's hard to express them to people we only relate to in a business setting. So we usually muffle them. Even a small misunderstanding can linger to sour a relationship. Resolving interpersonal issues in our private lives may be daunting enough, but it's even harder at work.

It's impossible for us to approach the office setting as a clean slate. Because we're the same individual in both our work and personal lives, we bring our own personalities, needs, pressures, insecurities, anxieties, and response patterns with us. And typically, we also carry in the emotions generated at home. A fight with a spouse, a money problem, or a sick child can start the workday badly and continue to cloud our perspective, making it more difficult to address the obstacles we encounter at work.

HOW *WORKPLACE GENIE* CAN HELP

As a result of the many challenges of today's workplace, only 30 percent of employees surveyed by Gallup describe themselves as engaged, and therefore productive, as well as happy with their work.

Workplace Genie cannot fix the enormous set of problems this suggests, of course. But we can show you how to diagnose your own work situation and relationships so you can better understand what you're dealing with, assess your options, and make decisions.

Our central message: Your workplace now—and those you encounter in the future—may seem like intractable worlds where you are boxed in, the victim of circumstances. So you may come to feel unengaged, frustrated, dead-ended. But here's the big "but": you have a surprising degree of power to make your own role more satisfying and create better, more supportive relationships. *Workplace Genie* will help you understand your experience, take charge of your own responses, and assume the initiative in building a more satisfying environment.

WHAT YOU'LL DISCOVER

To help you accomplish these goals, we'll show you a variety of techniques drawn from psychology, such as reframing, visualization, and role-playing, as well as practical communication strategies. When helpful, we'll include examples of their use to solve typical problems, with analyses of what works, why, and what might have been more successful. Each chapter will also suggest stimulating activities to help you practice the ideas.

Here are some of the basic principles on which we base our advice, along with the goals that we hope resonate with you.

1. *Don't believe everything you tell yourself.* Contrary to what you may think, you are *not* the best authority on yourself. That's fortunate, because most of us share a human characteristic that leads us to give negative experiences far more weight, credence, and longevity than the positive ones. We hardly pay attention to our successes, but forever agonize over our mistakes and failures. We put them in our mental forefront, distorting our perceptions. We take our own self-criticism far more seriously than we usually should. And we are each a storehouse of false assumptions—like "I can't handle so much responsibility" or "I can't learn this program" or "She'll never listen to me."

   Goal: Don't set limits on your own capacities. We'll show you how to better value your strengths, move past self-negating ideas and self-criticism, and encourage yourself to keep growing.

2. *Don't be blinded or distracted by your emotions and personal patterns in dealing with other people.* We often let our insecurities and feelings get in the way of reacting appropriately to other people, as well as ourselves. Anger, fear, anxiety, assuming that we'll be rejected or disrespected, expecting the worst—all these things block both our intuitive and rational thinking. Then we misinterpret behavior, misunderstand meaning, respond inappropriately, miss opportunities, and invite mistreatment by people who tap into our insecurities.

   Goal: Learn to manage your own state of mind. We'll show you ways to say no to your impulses, control your negative patterns, and shift into observer mode. You'll know how to recognize the kind of behaviors and situations that trigger your emotions, as well as how to resist the trap of other people's strong emotions. We'll help you figure out when to stand your ground, when to reconcile, and in some situations, when to plan your exit.

3. *Critically examine the situation that challenges you.* Is the boss's recent coldness a sign that she is unhappy with your work, or is she coping with problems in her role? Is your contribution ignored because you're not valued, or is the company in crisis? Are you reporting to a supervisor who is at times moody or unfair, or to one who consistently abuses you—a bully? Assessing the realities makes a big difference in how you handle situations.

Goal: Assess and understand before you act. Don't rush to assumptions about other people or ascribe motives—they may be far offtrack. We'll give you ways to see other people's perspectives and scan the scene more objectively. It's important to differentiate between a truly toxic environment and a temporary problem in a climate that is open to adjustment. We'll give you the clues.

4. *Recognize that you—and everyone else—have not just one self, but many.* You have a five-year-old self, and a grown-up one. A confident self, and an insecure one. An assertive self, and a timid one. A social one, and a reclusive one. You even have a future wise self who can be called on for advice! At the same time, everyone you encounter has multiple selves. More easily than you may suspect, you own the power to call on the self you need and draw out another person's better self.

   Goal: Rather than "know yourself," choose to "know your selves." Instead of seeing yourself—and other people—as constant and unchangeable, discover that they are complex individuals who are different people at different times. Learn how to draw on your best self for the occasion—and how to draw out another person's more forgiving, or generous, or flexible self.

5. *Believe that* you *have the power to take the lead and make things happen.* Don't wait for a hope to materialize. You can build a positive relationship, warm one up, and at times accomplish a reset. You can create allies. Take the initiative to become both more valuable and more valued. Recover from a serious mistake. Create your own happiness at work—or make a good decision about your next step and take it in your own time frame, not someone else's.

   Goal: Realize that you own 50 percent of the responsibility for how you are treated and are in charge of how you act and react. Be open to recognizing your role and the many options available to you for creating better outcomes. Learn to practice empathy and compassion, and you'll be able to build more supportive relationships, even with those to whom you don't naturally relate.

When you bring *Workplace Genie's* strategies to work, the rewards may come faster than you expect.

ABOUT CHOOSING TO CHANGE

Having read this far, you know that our main mission is to help you achieve your work goals. You can opt for "quick fixes" and adopt the various practical tools to plan conversations, come up with better answers, and counter negative actions from other people. We also want you to use the tools on a deeper level: to change yourself in ways that make you more open, empathetic, and creative. This kind of change demands commitment. It's also the most rewarding effort you can make for your career, and for becoming the person you want to be.

It's not an impossible dream. If you have the commitment, we have the tools and techniques. *Workplace Genie* gives you a wide array of strategies to draw from according to your own nature and need, adapted from the authors' combined toolkits.

We invite you to undertake the deeper journey.

HOW TO USE THIS BOOK

Ideally, read through all of *Workplace Genie*. We've built in a natural sequence to help you expand your perception, thinking, and skills. You may find helpful ideas and examples throughout the book and can combine different strategies to handle a given challenge.

We recommend dedicating some time to the activities that resonate with you. There are a number of choices. Reading can be a passive experience, and we want to orient you for *action*. We've developed the practice activities specially for this book based on our joint experience in psychology and communications.

Begin right now with your first set of exercises: questions to help you define your goals and orient yourself to the discoveries ahead. It's best to write out your answers, as with most of the activities throughout the book. Writing promotes an analytic frame of mind, and you'll be surprised at how much you know.

INTO ACTION

1. *Which relationships with a supervisor, coworkers, or other individuals at work challenge you the most, or are not serving you well?* And what would the ideal relationship in each case look like? For example, you might want a boss to give you more attention or praise. From a coworker, you may want more respect, consideration, or communication. Write down a specific analysis of what you want to change.

2. *Where do you think these problems originated?* Who do you believe is responsible? Do you see any ways in which you contribute to the problems?

3. *What kind of options do you give yourself to solve work problems*: Do what you're asked and live with it, like it or not? Minimize your engagement? Ask for what you want? Abandon the scene?

4. *If a current problem is not "fixed," how could it affect your career?* Might it undermine your hard work and career ambitions? Are the stakes high in another way?

    Keep your notes! At different points in working through this book, check back and see if you've changed your ideas about your own capabilities and how you can achieve your goals.

Chapter 2

FIND THE POWER IN KNOWING YOUR PERSONAL PATTERNS

Y*ou* have more power than you realize: the power to take charge of how you're treated, how you build relationships, and how you handle tough situations in your workplace.

Especially under stress, we often discount or distrust our own resources, intuition, and perceptions. This chapter shows you how to begin tapping into your intuition and deeper knowledge. Absorb these ideas and adapt them to your work life, and you'll find yourself opening up to new possibilities. These strategies are not just special-occasion tactics: they will help you interact with other people more realistically and more comfortably on an everyday basis, not only solving problems, but also preventing them.

The first step is to identify the roadblocks you unconsciously place in your own way—the personal patterns that lead you to interpret and react to challenging situations in deeply entrenched and often-counterproductive ways. You'll find that techniques for recognizing what's shaping your responses and holding you back will meld into action strategies to create the changes you want.

IDENTIFYING YOUR PERSONAL FILTERS AND PATTERNS: WHY AND HOW

Did you ever take an art class where everyone in the room drew the same object, whether a flower or a human model? If so, you probably noticed that each drawing differed distinctly from the others, but all resembled the original subject in some way. Some may have seemed more "true to life" than others—probably because they looked closer to your own vision of the original. But each was an interpretation.

Similarly, we constantly interpret the events, words, and actions we encounter. For example, you're at an industry event and spot a client across the room. Instead of acknowledging you, she turns and walks out of sight. What does it mean?

- You're sure she's angry at something you overlooked. You return to your office and wonder all day how you failed and how to remedy the situation.
- You conclude that she doesn't like you, doesn't appreciate all the work, is probably looking elsewhere, and your firm will lose the business.
- You note the action and think that maybe she's focused on making a connection with someone else right now.
- You think that maybe she just didn't notice or recognize you.

Rationally, without knowing the facts behind what happened, it's clear that the third and fourth interpretations are the most useful. Either might lead you to seek her out a bit later to say hello and reinforce the relationship. But if your pattern is to interpret mystery actions to reflect badly on yourself or others, you follow what feels like instinct, limiting your ability to react in your own interests.

We need to manage the expectations and assumptions that influence our perspective, which determines how we see, think, and act. But where does individual perspective that shapes our patterns come from?

Every one of us carries our own way of seeing and experiencing the world. It's created by our early family life, personal experience, and all the rest of our unique history. We bring this personal filter into the workplace and every other part of our lives. It acts as a private frame of reference and can produce blind spots, limiting our ability to understand other people and interpret their actions objectively. It may block us from accessing exactly the resources we need to field a challenge or solve a problem. It leads us to channel others into behavior we don't want.

This is especially apt to happen because human beings have an innate predisposition toward the negative. It's estimated that the human brain generates fifty thousand to eighty thousand thoughts per day—of which 95 percent are repeats, and 80 percent are negative. We have no idea whether these claims are scientifically valid, especially because there's no clear definition of "a thought." But most of us can agree that it feels like our brains are constantly puttering away with inner conversation, whether we want them to or not, and that many of our thoughts are negative.

In workplace contexts we are variously prone to think things like:

- I'm fat (or short or skinny or young or old), so no one will respect me.
- I'll make a serious mistake on this.
- I'll be exposed for not knowing such and such.
- Nobody here likes me.
- If I speak up, they'll be angry.
- I'm not going to get this opportunity.
- I never get credit for my hard work.

The problem is that when ideas like these are in our mental forefront, or when even a minor incident triggers them, powerful emotions can take over. As we lose perspective and restrict our perceptions, our bodies reflect the negative feelings and further lock us into them. Thus, we respond to the emotion rather than the situation in front of us. We may turn a neutral interaction into a negative one, or handle a real threat less ably than we could.

When you're conscious of your reaction patterns, you can bypass your own filters and start to separate your perceptions from reality. You can identify your personal triggers: the specific actions or words that set off unproductive responses that repeat, over and over again, in your work and personal life. Once you're aware of them, you'll be better able to break unproductive patterns, understand other people, and respond in positive ways.

But how to see what's generally invisible to us? Here's a set of ways.

Find your patterns by analyzing your emotions

Emotions in themselves provide major clues to our patterns. Think about a time when you felt misunderstood and bring back the moment. Where do you feel tension? How does your body feel?

The impact of emotions on the body differs among individuals. Maybe your chest gets tight, or your stomach hurts, or your heart speeds up. You may sweat. You may find yourself digging your nails into your palms or generally stiffening. These are symptoms of anxiety. Or you might experience symptoms of anger, or sadness, or other emotion. Instead of letting them pull you down, see these emotions as cues that you need to resist your negative response and focus on what's important to you.

For instance, our acquaintance Margaret, though quite successful in her career, found herself endlessly anxious in her new job. She had held her previous position for almost a decade and become comfortable with its demands. But now she found herself challenged to adopt more advanced technology systems, so old insecurities about her competence surfaced. This nervousness hampered her learning curve. She was sure everyone was marking her insufficiencies. So when her boss made a neutral remark or asked a question—such as "When will this report be ready?"—she responded defensively with long, unnecessary explanations about the problems and delays. This undermined her in the boss's eyes and made her annoying to talk to. He began avoiding her.

Unaware of her role in this downward spiral, Margaret felt, and behaved, increasingly indecisive. She sought frequent reassurance from those around her. One day a coworker burst out: "You know, Margaret, you're driving everyone crazy asking for so much help all the time! Isn't it time you stood on your own feet?"

Margaret was jarred into considering her own behavior. Why, despite her considerable professional achievement, did she feel like she couldn't master new ways of working and needed to depend on other people's opinions so much? She began to glimpse that she was living an old pattern that had cropped up in her life before, and that it probably related to her earliest experience. Margaret had grown up in a family with high expectations and ready criticism when those expectations were imperfectly met, so she was prone to feeling anxious and unsure when faced with a new task. In her previous job she'd initially been treated as a beginner. But now she was expected to function on a sophisticated level out-of-the-box and her technical deficit had triggered insecurities she thought she'd left behind. This in turn put her in an emotional turmoil.

Margaret began gradually understanding that her personal pattern led her to misperceive events and misread other people's actions. She assumed they were as critical of her as she was of herself.

Did understanding this "cure" Margaret of the internalized pattern? No—of course it's not that easy. But the realization caused her to take note of her own negative assumptions. Now, when she feels herself becoming anxious and defensive, she consciously hits "stop" and asks herself, did something happen here or am I reacting to my own distortions? Seeing more clearly also prompted her to take practical steps. She easily found learning opportunities to develop skill with the new technology.

Find your patterns by considering common possibilities

While in many ways we are each unique, a number of response patterns are common. See if you recognize any of the following behavioral patterns. Do you . . .

- Frequently feel overlooked or unappreciated?
- Personalize it when an idea is turned down or you're left out of a conversation?
- Blame yourself for everything that goes wrong?
- Dwell on what you might have done differently when something doesn't work out?
- Tend to be critical of others and diminish them?
- Shy away from standing up for yourself?
- Rescue people from mistakes habitually even when it's not your role?
- Avoid taking responsibility for your mistakes?
- Close your ears to disagreement or automatically reject criticism?
- Try to avoid the limelight?

These patterns represent just a handful of ways people consistently interpret events and react to them. Do any of the descriptions resonate with you? Do they suggest other personal patterns close to your own?

It's important not to cast blame on yourself. We all have patterns like these. We guarantee that even the people you most admire and respect have just as many powerful personal patterns that could work against them if given free rein. Instead, highly successful people learn to work with their own patterns by noticing when they're triggered, staying conscious of their response, and managing their behavior.

Of course, context matters. A constant rescuer, for example, may provide valuable help, but offering good advice that's welcome is different from intervening to show off.

Notice how patterns also carry habitual and recurring consequences. Someone who's uncomfortable with success might repeatedly hold himself back from reaching a goal. Someone who is always ready to feel rejected may not follow up if someone doesn't return a phone call or instantly agree to a request. Imagine how hard it might be for a self-blaming person to weather the small daily storms of office life. And an "I-won't-listen" or "it's-never-my-fault" pattern tends to backfire on the job and contribute to a quick exit.

Find your patterns by listening to what people tell you

Listening for a grain of truth in what other people say doesn't mean taking every criticism to heart and vowing to change with every negative remark. First consider the source: Is he or she well-meaning? If it's your boss who is generally a nice person, the criticism might be constructive.

Also take seriously a criticism you've heard often, or from different managers or coworkers. Criticisms from your personal life are just as relevant. Someone we know, Jenny, was often told by her husband: "You close your mind and never want to hear another side to anything!" She saw this as a response pattern particular to their relationship and her partner's own reactions when they disagreed.

Then at work, she made a major error in the early stage of a project that would cost her days of headache to correct. Hearing her vent, another team member observed mildly, "I could have told you that the data was questionable, but I knew you'd just argue with me."

Jenny paid attention to the echo she heard between her work and personal lives and put herself on alert for occasions when she might be closing out things she needed to hear. While there was no quick fix to her tendency to shut out unwelcome input, awareness put her a big step ahead. Take note when you hear the same message—whether an observation, criticism, or suggestion—from two or more people in different ways and different kinds of situations.

Find your patterns by embracing positive input

While it's important to consider criticism, it's also crucial to accept positive and supportive input—especially given that we are often prone to negative patterns, which we'll discuss in some detail later on in the chapter. Give credence to compliments and resist rushing to discount them. Many of us are far too ready to accept negative input as more "true" than the positive kind, and let it make a much bigger impression on us. Some of our associates who present workshops professionally may get input that is 90 percent favorable, but obsess over the 10 percent that is not. This keeps them focused on what they didn't do perfectly, but they might actually learn more from knowing what did work and what the participants most valued. If you have a pattern that makes you uncomfortable with praise, think: What might be different if you allowed yourself to absorb it? What do you need to do to hear compliments and accord them more weight?

Receiving praise helps you know how well you are aligned with other people's needs, expectations, and values. Pay attention to specifics of what someone says. Here's a story we heard from an assistant office manager, Alex. For months on the new job, he had consciously tried to please his supervisor—staying late, troubleshooting the computers, proofing documents. One day the boss said, "Hey, Alex, thanks for handling the IT guys so well yesterday. You must have a real knack—they fixed the problem fast for a change."

Alex thought about this. In appreciating his interpersonal skills, rather than the technical ones he took pride in, the boss gave him an important clue to an unconsidered strength and higher potential value in his role.

It's hard to see our own assets in perspective, because we tend to take a natural ability for granted. We can be similarly blind to our best personal qualities. Ask a colleague or friend what she admires about you and you will probably be very surprised. Her list of your strengths may be quite different from yours and should be taken to heart.

Organizations have learned to ask similar questions of customers. "What do you like best about working with us?" often elicits an answer that bears little relation to the leaders' expectations and may highlight an asset they have not especially valued. This discovery process gives them a firmer foundation for building on strengths and communicating about the company.

Find your patterns in your own history

It's useful, as Margaret found, to build your awareness of how your background develops the patterns you may take with you through life. Think about other members of your family. It's easier to detect patterns in people other than yourself. In every family, we train ourselves to read responses based on patterns of action and response. One family may greet an achievement exuberantly with warm hugs, and later in life, we feel disappointed when we experience this lack of physical affection.

Or a family might not value a particular skill or asset, shaping a long-term expectation of being unappreciated. Your parents and siblings might have rarely listened to you—or might have paid rapt attention to every word. Siblings might have been supportive or behaved jealously. Either situation instills built-in expectations.

Think about the emotional patterns in your family, or talk about them with another member or a trusted friend familiar with your early home. You might ask:

- What complaints did family members make about one another?
- What was the family trait or habit most difficult or uncomfortable for you while growing up?

- Was there someone in the family whose extreme behavior dominated family interaction and communication (e.g., bullying, demanding, whining, criticizing)?
- Were there traumatic events or a single big event that affected the family interaction?
- Do you feel you had a specific role in the family dynamic (e.g., the popular one, the studious one, the good-looking one, the victim, the caretaker)?

Another good way to tap into your history is to monitor your own more recent repeat experiences. Do you find yourself saying internally, "It's happening again—I'm being bypassed for the best assignments," or "I'm being ignored again at business events," or "This colleague doesn't like me, either"? Ask yourself: Is this an old story, something that's happened to me many times before?

One of us recalls hearing from an acquaintance, Lou, about an argument with his wife. In the heat of the moment she threw at him, "The problem with you is, you're never willing to admit you've made a mistake!"

"Can you imagine?" Lou said. "She made the same criticism my first wife used to make all the time! What's wrong with women?"

It didn't occur to Lou that he should consider this reiteration as a response to his own behavior and patterns of interaction. There's a lot to learn by reviewing our full range of life experience and noticing any recurring situations we get caught in.

HOW TO START BREAKING PATTERNS THAT WORK AGAINST YOU

Once you begin noticing your patterns, you can identify the ones that get in the way of enjoying harmonious personal and work relationships. Negative patterns and the negative expectations they carry often take the form of habit. As we all know, breaking a habit isn't easy, but the payoff here is big: the more attuned you are to the process, the more you are able to change your life.

Think back to when you were in high school. You desperately wanted to join the tennis team, the debate club, the school newspaper—you fill in the blank. But with at least some of your aspirations, an internal skeptic kept reminding you of your limitations, how much more qualified other people were, and all the other reasons not to get your hopes up.

We bring the same tendency to the workplace. Think about times when you've taken negative thoughts as facts—for example, my boss will never adopt any of my ideas because they're not good enough; or my clients will never let me raise my prices because they don't value what I give them that highly. Ask yourself: If someone else said to you, "Your colleagues will never accept your suggestions because they're just plain dumb" or "Your work isn't good enough for you to charge more," would you be affronted? You should be!

We often downgrade our own capacities without being conscious of doing so and ignore how powerful this self-denigration can be. When the denigrations come from someone else, we can often recognize that they are just opinionated insults. We often don't show ourselves the same skepticism. But being aware of this tendency frees us to interrupt an insidious pattern of self-doubt. *Pattern interruption is a major doorway to change.* The more we encourage ourselves to open our minds to positive reality, the harder it is for us to keep insulting ourselves.

Pay attention to the tone of voice inside your head when you're undermining yourself. Is it abrupt? Impatient? Are you giving yourself negative labels, like "I'm an idiot," "I'm hopeless," or "I never stand up for myself"? "I always lose"?

Counter your self-diminishing labels

The labels you give yourself can literally stop you in your tracks. They interfere with realistic perception and prevent you from responding effectively to what is happening. This is unlikely to advance other people's opinion of you and may well damage it.

Negative self-labeling makes it harder to connect with your confident part, too. It prevents you from thinking well on your feet. Suppose, for example, you're giving a presentation and are not happy with how it's going. If you think to yourself, "Oh my God, it's not working, I'm a loser," it's all over but the cleanup. But if you say to yourself, "Oops . . . this piece didn't go over very well. I'll shift direction now," you support your own success.

Train yourself to be mindful of when you slip into negative self-talk and pessimistic predictions. When you're starting to feel engulfed by such thinking, pause. Breathe slowly and deeply—this quickly slows the heartbeat and pulse and helps release anxiety, panic, and anger. Take a quiet moment to consider the important dynamic you're experiencing. Ask yourself:

- Am I jumping to conclusions?
- Is my interpretation of this incident colored by a negative pattern and the emotions it provokes?

- Are other interpretations of what's happening possible?
- Am I closing my mind to evidence or opportunities to know the facts?

The more open you are to recognizing that you're succumbing to negative expectations, the faster you can master the techniques to counter them.

Resist negative assumptions about other people

- "The boss won't listen . . . he'll never understand . . . he doesn't value me."
- "She'll be so angry at me for bringing this up that I'll only make the situation worse."
- "If I tell the group I found a big problem with the plan, they'll think I'm a troublemaker."
- "My coworker doesn't like me, so why try to be friendly?"

Making such assumptions about other people is often unfair, and they stand in your way. People tend to meet your expectations. For example, if you want to address an unreasonable workload with a supervisor, expecting her to discount what you say works against you. It shapes your argument and how you present it. If you hold back an informed opinion because you assume the group will ignore it, you hurt the common goal and lose an opportunity to contribute.

Assumptions may be based on your own distorted perceptions and may not reflect the total reality. Here, too, our strong emotions can act as filters that prevent us from seeing the full picture.

Notice that when you're angry with someone, you start remembering every other incident involving that person that provokes similar feelings. You may also bring to mind and dwell on situations in which other people caused you to feel mistreated. When your mind floods with this general kind of resentment, *notice that your eyes narrow—and so does your perception.* Remind yourself to withhold judgment in such moments, perhaps with a practical reminder, like consciously widening your eyes to counter that closing down tendency.

Recognize how you create patterns of expectation in others
One of Newton's laws of motion says that for every action, there is an equal and opposite reaction. This holds true for the world of human behavior as well. With people we spend time with, we quickly create

patterns of expectations, and vice versa. If you've reported to a supervisor for more than a few weeks, she'll have expectations about what she may ask of you, the nature of your skills, your strengths and weaknesses, your temperament, and your probable reaction to many circumstances. And you've drawn similar conclusions about her.

In addition to being careful not to make negative assumptions about other people, be aware that your own behavior may have created negative assumptions in how they see you. You may have earned them by the quality of your work, the attitude you've communicated, the way you speak to the person. Of course, factors beyond your control are often involved as well. Even a simple interaction can be highly complex because every individual brings to it his own perspective, assumptions, and set of patterns.

For the factors that are within your control, keep in mind: *constancy creates expectations.* If you're a reliable and resourceful hard worker, you may find yourself with a disproportionate share of the work. If, on the other hand, you've demonstrated that you can only be counted on for a limited amount of work, of a certain kind, that expectation becomes entrenched and you are unlikely to be promoted.

In either case, you probably want to remedy the situation. Both efforts demand that you take the initiative, but the second one—changing someone's poor opinion of your capabilities—is harder to accomplish. *Others see us as we have been—not as we want to be.* So, along with techniques for becoming the person you want to be, we'll share tools to help people see you in a different light.

Here's an immediate approach for starters: What one small thing might you do to break a pattern of negative expectation that works against you? For example, instead of going straight to your desk every day, could you pop your head into your boss's office and say "good morning"? Could you be the one to ask someone who was out sick how she feels today? Could you return a grumpy remark with a cheerful smile? Could you come in earlier for a week at crunch time?

Now we hope you will practice what you've learned so far. The activities are designed to help you absorb your new insights so you can use the techniques ahead to connect with your own best resources.

INTO ACTION

1. *Hear your negative self-talk.* This activity will show you the full impact of how you talk to yourself and launch you into the process of conscious rethinking.

A. Go down the list and notice which statements resonate with you. If other ideas are closer to your experience, add them.
   - I don't get things done when I should.
   - I let people put me down.
   - I can't figure out how to get my boss to listen to me.
   - I am not good at standing up for myself.
   - I always hold myself back.
   - I speak up too often.
   - I'm always worried about letting people down.
   - I can't think on my feet.
   - I'm not creative.
   - I'll never be able to handle that assignment (or client, or colleague, or problem).
   - I can't stop people from picking on me.
   - I never get the credit I deserve.
   - People always take advantage of me.
   - I'll never learn that.
   - I'll never be comfortable in social situations.
   - I'll never get what I want.
   - I'll never get over feeling angry (or jealous, or nervous, or inadequate, etc.).

B. Rephrase the wording of those statements to sound like the critical language you use with yourself. Record yourself saying each of these statements with all the emotion, tone, pauses, and inflections that you usually feel when you speak to yourself. Pause after each one for two minutes and then listen to what you said and how you said it: Was your tone self-denigrating? Accusatory? Does this give you any insights into how you treat yourself? Take written notes of everything you notice in listening to yourself.

C. Reshape the negative statements. Review the negative self-talk you identified and change the phrasing to shift your perspective in a more productive direction. For example, if your statement is "I always hold myself back," you might shift to "I often choose not to speak up when I have good ideas, though my ideas would be helpful and appreciated. So I'll say to myself in these situations, 'I have a good idea and right now is the time to share it and find out what people think.'"

D. Record yourself saying the new positive statements. Replay them in your mind whenever you can: walking, relaxing, cooking, driving to work.

2. *Identify your personal patterns.* Do any of those mentioned in the chapter feel familiar? Do they suggest other possible patterns? As fully as you can, write about the patterns you feel apply to you.

   Then think:

   – Might they at times create problems—what kind? Can you cite an example?

   – How important is it to you to change the pattern?

   – Can you perceive what triggers the pattern and associated emotions (e.g., what someone says or does, a type of event, challenge, or situation)?

3. *Rethink a past incident.* Envision a specific interaction that provoked your negative assumptions. For example, someone spoke to you rudely or forgot to include you in an invitation. What questions might you have asked yourself after recognizing the *uh-oh* moment and pausing your response? Write them down. Can you now think of other interpretations or explanations of what happened?

4. *Think about how to change a pattern of interaction.* Do you dislike how your supervisor asks you to do something, or how a coworker talks to you, or how a client deals with you? Can you think of one thing to do differently that might change the dynamic and move the meter even a tiny bit?

5. *Collect positive thinking.* Ask three friends what they most value and like about you and note down their answers. Then ask three colleagues with whom you get along well what they value and like about working with you. Review all the responses: What do they have in common? Are the colleagues' comments different from your friends'? What surprised you: Did people pinpoint qualities you were not especially aware of? Were there any that you thought would be named but were not?

Chapter 3

MANAGING YOUR EMOTIONS AND OPENING YOUR PERSPECTIVE

Other people may seem inconsistent and at times unpredictable to us, but most of us feel that we are very consistent people. This is an illusion. Despite the personal patterns that we follow, we are mobile and malleable creatures composed of many moods, emotions, and feelings.

You probably know intuitively that mood influences outcome in your various life arenas. One of us (Natalie) recalls that when shopping in a specialty food store after work, she was sometimes waited on quickly. But at other times, she seemed to be ignored. Eventually she noticed that what happened tied in with her frame of mind: a good day at work left her in an up mood, and she was attended to quickly, but on a bad day her negative cloud was sensed by other people and they avoided interacting with her.

We communicate different states through our facial expressions, posture, tone of voice, and ways of walking. People pick all this up and respond accordingly. Your behavior can end up reinforcing your own negative feelings even when you don't realize it. And when you're down, you may perceive other people in a very narrow light, misread their state of mind, and make bad decisions.

This pattern is especially risky in work settings. When we don't know people on a personal level, we tend to take them at "face value." We're often judged on the visible cues we present as well as how we react. Moreover, a boss or coworker is much less likely than a friend to forgive and forget a bad mood or related misstep.

Psychologists and neuroscientists agree that our bodies and brains interweave. New research tools chart how our nervous systems, specific parts of the brain, hormones, and senses interact to produce thoughts and physical responses. Science is also exploring how emotions affect the body. This perception is, of course, not new. It's built into our language—frozen in fear, hot under the collar, limp with relief, a heartfelt sigh.

CONTROL YOUR MOODS AND FEELINGS? YES, YOU CAN!

While we know that our emotions create physical effects, what's less commonly recognized is that we can reverse the process by making a simple physical change. The power of smiling is one example, as Natalie found at the grocery counter. In organizations that depend on telephone communication, frontline people are trained to smile before they pick up each call because facial expression controls voice mechanics. It's very hard to sound angry, resentful, or overwhelmed if you're smiling. Try it.

Then try the following activities to see for yourself how much your emotions can be influenced by changing your facial expression and posture. *If you feel uncomfortable with any of these exercises, as with those throughout the book, don't rush into them.* You'll find plenty of other activities to learn from, so take a pass on any you don't like. And don't be concerned if the experiments generate different responses than those we mention. We are different from one another and respond differently: there is no right or wrong, just knowledge.

Mind-body experiment: Force a smile

Can smiling shift your mood as well as your voice? That question has been the subject of many experiments. Here is an often-cited one.

Place a pencil or chopstick in your mouth lengthwise.

You may not notice a shift in your feelings, but investigators proved that people forced to smile in this way found humorous material funnier than control groups who were not made to smile. The difference was even stronger compared to people forced to frown by holding the pencil's end in puckered lips, without touching it with their teeth.

Later research found that induced smiling, even if the person does not feel happy, seems to reduce the body's stress response and help the heart under stress. Additional studies show that a genuine smile releases biochemicals that make us feel good, changes an individual's mood, and attracts other people.

Suggestion: Experiment with beginning your day or an important interaction with a smile. Try creating a smile when you're under stress. It may begin as a grimace, but stay with it and observe your experience.

Even if it doesn't make you feel good immediately, notice whether you find yourself feeling more confident and in charge. Even better, experiment with producing a genuine, natural smile. Smile at someone you care about and vice versa, and notice how it feels. The more that you practice, the more natural it will become for you to approach a challenging situation in this manner.

Notice how people respond when you shift to a smiling demeanor during a problem or confrontation. The more you pay attention to the impact of this behavior, the more it enhances your comfort.

Grain of salt: We don't claim this can magically transform a highly problematic boss, coworker, or client. But in many cases, it helps achieve greater engagement with the other person and sets a more positive tone.

Mind-body experiment: Alter your posture

Like many people, you may be unaware that posture instantly communicates how you feel about yourself in a given situation. This in turn affects other people's perceptions of you, how they hear you, and how much value they accord to what you say.

Stand in front of a full-length mirror and take a good look at your natural stance. Think about different experiences you've recently had and allow your body to assume different postures. Or just think of different moods—I'm sad, I'm angry, I'm peaceful—and take a minute to reflect that in how you stand. Are you communicating the different states of mind without saying a word? Now, perhaps with a friend to gently prod you, assume a posture of confidence. Center your neck over your spine, find your own center of gravity, relax your arms, place your legs slightly apart in just the right way for a stance that is balanced and comfortable.

What do you notice about your feelings when you stand in that way? We bet you feel more energetic, confident, capable, a little more assertive. How familiar does this posture feel to you? How you feel affects how you stand, but how you stand also affects how you feel. Assume a confident stance and you shift your mindset.

One of us participated in a voice class where the instructor poked and prodded a young man into a different posture. He normally stood with shoulders narrowed and hunched, head forward, stomach out, arms dangling awkwardly. His appearance was at best unimpressive.

When the teacher stepped back, the class saw an erect young man with an air of self-esteem and consequence. He looked alert, authoritative, and a touch assertive. Alas, he could only hold the pose for a minute. Those watching wondered how different his life might be if he practiced the new posture frequently enough for his mind to get the message, and considered the benefits he might gain from a sustained effort to change.

Suggestion: Practice your confident posture and experience the difference in how you feel, act, and talk. As *Workplace Genie* progresses, we will give you tools to help you better redirect your emotions . . . and maintain your preferred posture.

Mind-body experiment: Shift your emotional states

Try these three ways to experience how your emotions determine your body's behavior. In the process, think about the impact of each on your ability to perceive and think, and the strength of the signals these physical states send to everyone nearby.

Anger

Stand relaxed with feet apart, hands at sides. Bring your eyebrows down hard—as strongly as you can. Notice to what extent you sense the following: head tips down, eyes squint, lips compress, neck and shoulders stiffen.

You might feel an energy run through your body from feet to head or vice versa. You may feel yourself breathing faster. You may feel more pugnacious or even hostile.

Say something simple, like "I'm glad to see you." How does it sound? Convincing? We expect not. Try walking: notice your stiff-legged gait, often a threat signal in animals and humans.

Did you start to feel an emotion? What impact does that feeling have on what you see around you and on how you might greet someone? Do you recognize the feeling? When something occurs that angers you, is this how your body naturally reacts? Observe how the different physical components—eyes, head, shoulders, eyebrows, posture, voice— automatically connect with each other to embody an emotional state, communicate it to other people, and reinforce your own state of anger.

Serenity

Stand relaxed. Think of a "happy place" or thing: a landscape, favorite object, pet, memory, or someone you love and are secure with. Live in that place for half a minute and then smile.

What do you notice about your shoulders? Where do you feel comfort most in your body? What is your breathing like? Is it slow and peaceful? What other adjectives might you use? Say, "I'm glad to see you." What do you notice most about the quality of your voice now?

Do you feel serene, hopeful, and generally positive? Do you feel more open and accessible? Do you feel that good things will happen? How do you recognize that feeling internally? Notice what it feels like when you are walking in this state of mind: the difference in the simple way that you move forward, in the way that you would greet someone.

Sadness

Stand relaxed. Pull the inside of your eyebrows—the parts nearest the nose—as high as you can so they point upward. Feel your brow furrow? Feel yourself blinking more? Do your shoulders droop? Are you breathing a bit more anxiously? Try saying, "I'm glad to see you." What does your tone of voice convey? Try walking: Do you feel diffident? Self-effacing? Needy?

This configuration comes with sadness. Notice that when sad, we tend to dwell on more sad thoughts and negative ideas. In that state, we appear to be insecure, dejected, self-conscious, withdrawn. It's easy for other people to pick this up and experience their own reactive emotions—perhaps sympathy, but in a work environment, more likely annoyance or frustration.

When you feel like this on a workday, how do you think it might affect your workplace relationships?

CHOOSING YOUR STATE OF MIND

These activities demonstrate how strongly our faces and bodies express our emotional states. Remember four points:

First, these states drive how you look, sound, and behave to other people, and they play a major role in how others react to you.

Second, your state of mind influences how you experience the world and people around you. A negative state limits your perceptions and skews your behavior. It may lead you to make inaccurate conclusions about how you're treated and misinterpret what you hear. Then you may respond inappropriately or ineffectively.

Third, your state of mind is not fixed. Many states of mind are potentially available to you, and often you can move fluidly from one to the other. The brain's "plasticity" is an important tenet of modern psychology, as well as medicine. You have the ability to learn how to change your state of mind in small ways—and big ways. Knowing your own malleability brings you closer to more consciously managing your own emotional state.

Fourth, everyone else has many states of mind, too! Taking account of this makes you more empathetic and receptive to human variability.

You're able to notice that each person is different at different times and in different circumstances. This opens up all kinds of possibilities for reaching out to someone else's "better angels" in particular situations.

The fact that modern medicine has only recently come around to affirming the mind-body connection doesn't mean people haven't leveraged it forever. Actors consciously control face and body to mirror personality and inner states. Salespeople attune to customers this way. A trial lawyer we know routinely molds his own face, posture, and body language to mimic prospective jurors so he can select those most sympathetic to his cause. "Assume someone's persona, and his thoughts will come to you," he explains.

And, of course, everyone adopts "outside" ways to influence their own mood, depending on the circumstances and individual preference: music, caffeine, meditation, a walk in the park, playing with the dog, not to mention alcohol and drugs.

While external ways of altering your mood can be immensely helpful, discovering your internal resources and abilities will lead to deeper and more lasting results. Understanding your own fluidity—your variable moods and emotions, and their relation to your physical self—is a major step toward learning how to control your behavior far more than you may assume possible.

EMOTIONS AND THE WORKPLACE

It's all too easy to fall into negative emotional patterns in the workplace. You make a mistake, or someone throws a casual negative remark your way, or a challenge materializes that calls up insecurities or past "failures." A powerful emotion takes over. You instantly feel inadequate, or anxious, or angry, or all of these at once. Your emotional state is expressed and communicated by your body, further freezing you into an isolated and self-absorbed state. Perspective recedes along with your ability to accurately perceive.

When we respond to the emotion rather than the situation in front of us, we risk turning a small incident into a damaging one, and handle real threats much less ably than we could. We allow the intensity of our feelings to make decisions for us, bypassing our rational mind.

Learning to manage your emotional responses and keep your perspective open is an important part of self-change. In the sections below, we'll address both immediate strategies for dealing with particularly intense emotions, like anger, in the moment they arise and longer-term strategies for reframing your perceptions and altering your emotional patterns. Once adopted, these techniques can be mainstays of your personal resource toolkit.

ON-THE-SPOT TOOLS FOR MANAGING INTENSE EMOTIONS

Many strong feelings are elicited by the everyday workplace. Some are positive and good to express: enthusiasm, cheerfulness, happiness, perhaps passion (of the professional kind). But communicating intense negative emotions is risky and can be very damaging. For many people, anger presents a particular problem. Therefore, we'll start there, but the approaches apply to all potentially destructive emotions that you want to control.

Anger is a hot emotion—literally. Many phrases associated with it reflect this characteristic: red in the face, boiling over, letting off steam, seething with rage. In the moment's heat, it easily overpowers your cognitive process, leading you to toss your well-honed social skills out the door and say things, or do things, you would ordinarily avoid.

When your self-censorship skills are not in gear, you are unable to think strategically. Notice that an angry person's eyes narrow, a signal that little light is being let in. In this state, we often justify our angry behavior by blaming others. Someone else is treating you disrespectfully, for example, or has hurt your feelings, or sloughed off her responsibilities onto your shoulders.

Your imperative: remind yourself that *you* are still in charge of *you*. No one can "make" you feel a certain way without your permission. When you become caught up in an escalating cycle of anger and self-justification, it's all too easy to attack other people and generally inflict a great deal of damage on yourself. You risk losing more than an argument—other people's good will and trust, for example, and ultimately your own self-respect.

The first step in learning to deal with anger is to acquaint yourself with your own hot buttons, your patterns, as we discussed in the last chapter. Think about situations where you lost your objectivity and said or did things you wish you could take back. Remember how you felt and what happened, or was said, to trigger your reaction. Did someone speak disparagingly or criticize you? Use a certain tone of voice? Or say something that reminded you of a family member's admonition?

Assemble a written list of at least three personal triggers. Once conscious of them, you can actively begin to anticipate challenging situations and handle yourself more effectively.

Here's a good strategy for disrupting your own negative energy.

Order yourself to take a break: the Power Pause

When you're aware that an intense emotion like anger is building, give yourself a Power Pause. Refraining from an instant response allows your rational brain time to recuperate. Count to thirty, fetch a glass of water, tell your boss or coworkers you need to stretch your legs and walk around for a few minutes—whatever is practical. Deliberately slow your breathing. Consider: Am I being fair? Or might I be coming to conclusions that may not be merited? You can save yourself a lot of unwarranted anguish and uncertainty about other people's motives by reserving judgment when you don't like what they say or do.

Once you start gifting yourself with the Power Pause, you'll be amazed to find how seldom an immediate response is necessary. Silence is often a golden response because it gives the other person time to recover his balance as well. Psychologists find that human beings are predisposed to take action more often than they need to, and that "no action" can sometimes produce better outcomes. Reporters and law enforcement personnel know how powerful the pause can be.

To see for yourself how an emotion like anger can affect you, try this. Think of a pleasing encounter you recently had with a boss or coworker: an acknowledgment of your good work, a compliment, or just an encouraging smile. Recreate the moment of pleasure. Do you remember how the exchange affected your work for that part of the day, or your thinking about projects you were engaged with? Jot down this memory.

Now bring up a situation where you were angry with someone, at work or at home. Close your eyes and bring up the scene in your mind. Relive the negative exchange and the feelings it provoked. Now think about a project you need to finish, or upcoming work. Does it feel different? Jot your thoughts down and compare them with the "positive" set. Notice that when you put a negative experience in the front of your mind, it biases what you perceive and what you expect. In a positive mind frame, you tend toward optimism and enthusiasm. When a negative mindset takes over, you expect negative outcomes.

Determine to use the Power Pause when you're experiencing anger or other strong emotions that can do you harm. You may be surprised to know that research says venting to a friend or partner, let alone at work, is not a good method. It's like creating a groove for ourselves that reinforces the anger and hostility. Rather than dampening the flames, it fuels the fire.

A better option is to follow up your on-the-spot pause by writing a letter. Express your feelings in as much detail as you want and assign blame to your heart's content. This safely clarifies what's upsetting you and restores your perspective. Just be sure not to send your message! If you write it as an e-mail, leave the space for the name blank.

You can also try to use the pause to practice a calming technique, like Square Breathing.

Square Breathe your way to calm

When we are in the grip of strong emotions, we tend to take short, rapid breaths. In the case of a perceived emergency, the body prepares us to respond physically by directing oxygen away from the brain, which shuts down our perceptions and rationality. Reversing this works just as effectively: deep, slow breathing sends oxygen to the brain, slows your heart rate and pulse, and activates the system that calms your nerves. It opens up your perceptions and enables you to speak in a strong, steady voice. Actors, meditators, athletes, and many more people depend enormously on controlled breathing. You can too, and it's an excellent technique when you experience anxiety, panic, and even depression, as well as anger.

One powerful calming technique is Square Breathing. People find it helpful for everything from preparing for a job interview to making a rough decision to handling conflict. Some people like it for falling asleep. Once you learn it, you can do it almost anywhere, without anyone noticing. Practice it first in a comfortable, distraction-free place.

1. Sit in a chair with your feet on the ground.
2. Place your right hand over your heart and feel its warmth, the comfort of the connection.
3. Visualize a square shape—it can be a familiar object like a picture frame, or just an abstract square of any color you choose.
4. Focus on the upper left corner of the square. Breathe in slowly and hold to the count of four.
5. Move your gaze smoothly to the upper right corner of the square. Exhale to the count of four.
6. Bring your gaze to the lower right corner and inhale to the count of four.
7. Move your gaze to the lower left corner and exhale, counting to four.

8. Complete the cycle by moving your gaze to the upper left corner and repeat.

Do this exercise for as long as you like, maintaining a quiet even pace, focusing on the square, feeling the breath coming in and moving out peacefully.

The goal is to empty your mind of thought, focusing only on the easy, comfortable rhythm of your breath and the warm hand-to-heart connection you feel. Adding eye movement to the deliberative breathing makes this technique work especially well. Practice Square Breathing and you'll be able to call upon it at heated times as well as quieter ones. In a peopled environment, forgo the hand over heart.

Turn it down with the Emotion Thermostat

Stress when your computer crashes. When your boss yells at you. When you know you'll miss a deadline. When someone quits and his work is dumped on you. When a team member fails to contribute, or you hear the department will be trimmed. We don't need to furnish you with ways to imagine stress—it has many sources, big and small, and can be debilitating.

If you find yourself dwelling on work worries to the degree that they interfere with getting things done or your life in general, consider whether a conversation might at least partly alleviate the cause of your emotional response. Before spending sleepless nights on an unreasonable deadline, for example, ask your supervisor about priorities and practical realities. Use Square Breathing. Here is another tool to help you modulate worry and anxiety as well as anger.

The Emotion Thermostat is a visualization tool for managing your distress, anxiety, anger, and other strong emotions by diminishing their intensity. It takes advantage of the fact that you can use mental imagery to connect with your emotions.

Set aside some quiet time without distractions. Create a mental image of a thermostat, the kind you use to adjust the temperature of your home. You might like to draw the control on paper or a tablet. A good way to imagine it is with color: blue on the left half, red on the right half. Put a needle on the thermostat that moves from one side to another when you operate a small lever, or a dial, as you prefer. This lever connects with your body's "emotion central," where intense feelings are housed.

When your thermostat is ready, practice with a trial run. Think of a situation that thoroughly roused a strong emotion like anger. Relive the experience. How far up the red side does your emotion register? All the way, or partly? Now slowly, incrementally, mentally move the lever toward the blue. As you do this, keep breathing deeply and slowly. The system is attached to your emotions so as you control and cool the temperature, you control and cool your emotion correspondingly.

Try this a few times to get comfortable with the idea. When something happens that triggers intense negative feelings, pull the Emotion Thermostat out of your mental pocket—and use it.

In addition to helping you control your own overpowering emotions, it also helps you respond more effectively to other people's loss of control. If you're faced with an angry boss, for example, whether because you made a mistake or he's responding to his own anxieties, reacting with your own anger makes the situation worse. He might not be able to get his anger under control—but you can manage yours. Downshifting to bypass an instinctive response enables you to maintain your rationality and handle the interaction capably, rather than escalating it.

Now that you have these three tools to help get your destructive emotions under control, we'll move on to basic strategies for managing your response patterns and expanding your perspective through reframing.

LONG-TERM STRATEGIES FOR MANAGING YOUR EMOTIONS THROUGH REFRAMING

Reframing means shifting your perspective in a way that fits the known facts as well, or better, than your immediate view and gives you a more productive way to think and act. When we respond to an event with strong emotion, it feels "instinctive"—automatic, without conscious thought. There are times when instincts are important, as an alert system, in the case of emergencies, for example, or threats of any kind. But as explored earlier, instincts can be knee-jerk repetitions of entrenched negative patterns.

Restructuring how you see something interrupts these automatic patterns.

You can reframe how you *feel* about an event, or person, and this empowers you to *be different* and *act* in different ways than your initial instincts dictate. *Problems become more solvable and you can handle them far better by changing how you frame them to yourself.*

Reframing empowers you, for instance, to interpret other people's behavior in a way that doesn't hit your insecurities. "Jane snapped at me because she thinks I'm not important" is probably less true than "Jane seems to be in a bad mood today." You can shift self-blame into more productive territory: rather than telling yourself, "What a stupid mistake that was—how hopeless I am," it's often more relevant to think, "Well, that was a faux pas." If you are not caught up in negative self-labels, you can decide much more easily whether action is called for.

Looking for a reframe gives you an effective way to interpret events in ways that are often more accurate and productive. The process also helps to abstract you from an emotional moment by tapping directly into your analytic powers so you can process your perceptions and strategize. You can even reframe your perspective on the past and free yourself from ancient shadows—earlier experiences you label as failures that echo in your mind and, consequently, your life. (Chapter 12 offers a way to handle this problem.)

Let's look at some specific ways to employ reframing.

Reframe unwelcome challenges into opportunities

Many situations that trigger negative expectations and emotions can be reframed as learning opportunities. "I hate having to do this part of the work—I'm not good at it and it takes forever." Pause at "hate" and consider possible reframes:

- What value can I find in accomplishing this work?
- What skills can I learn?
- Who might help me figure this out?

It's often useful to resist an initial reaction to what someone else says or does based on assumptions about their motives. Is there another way of looking at it? For example, rather than "she's micromanaging me," would it be equally possible that "she's trying to coach me into handling this work to her satisfaction"?

Another scenario: A coworker notices your work-in-progress and dismissively remarks, "Hey, that's a dinosaur method—you could do it a whole lot faster if you used the new software." Your first impulse might be to withdraw into defensive silence and self-blame for not knowing how to use the new program. What if you said: "You're right, thanks for noticing. I have a problem figuring out how to apply the new software. Do you have five minutes to help?"

What do you think would happen? Most likely, your coworker will feel flattered and help you. Reframed as a learning opportunity, the situation earns you a chance to upgrade your skills, and very probably, warm up your relationship with the coworker a little. If, instead, the person sloughs off your call for help—well, you've learned something about the other person, and that has value, too.

To reverse the scenario, suppose a coworker you don't know well asks for your input on a special project. Your first instinct might be, "She's going to take credit for my work." But you can choose to reframe to: "This is an opportunity to team up and get to know this person better." Is there a risk that she will in fact unfairly take credit for what you contribute? Of course. But suspending the negative assumption and categorizing this as a collaborative opportunity lets you better evaluate gain against risk, and perhaps reduce that risk.

By considering the possible opportunities—whether to learn new skills or get to know a colleague better—you can begin to see challenging tasks in a more positive and less emotional way.

Reframe why into how

Notice what happens if you turn *why* into *how* when you have a complaint:

"Why doesn't my boss ever give me the best assignments?"

versus

"How can I show my boss I'm ready for more responsibility?"

Thinking *how* rather than *why* turns your own state of resentment into a can-do action mode that leads to better outcomes. It moves your perspective from the narrow negative state of resentment to a broader and more fruitful view of the situation. *How* leads to much better questions— "How is my boss evaluating me?" rather than "Why doesn't she give me a chance?" The more specific your questions, the clearer your options become and the more motivated you will be to find practical solutions. For example, if you want better assignments, consider the following:

- How can I improve my work in his eyes?
- What can I best contribute to the common cause?
- What skills should I improve and how can I learn them?
- How can I bring myself to her attention and demonstrate how capable I am?

Most workplaces offer ample opportunities to turn *why* into *how* on an everyday level.

- "Why doesn't Mary cooperate with me more?" can be reframed as "How can I work better with Mary?"

- "Why does it take so long to do this work?" becomes manageable as "How can I do this work more efficiently?"
- "Why do I have to work on such trivial tasks?" can translate to "How can I make myself more comfortable with this?" or "How can I make the experience more pleasant for myself?" or "How can I obtain the maximum benefit for my time?"

The approach leads you to break the work down into steps, identify roadblocks, and look for better methods.

For instance, we know that many business people—from newbies to high-up executives—"hate" writing reports. They see them as boring busywork, which leads them to create dull material that betrays a lack of thought. They fail to consider the value of this work to higher-up managers. Important decisions are often based on reports. If you're asked to account for your activities over a set period of time, the manager doesn't want a recitation of how-I-spent-my-un-vacation. He wants to know what you accomplished, your progress on a project, information that is worth sharing, any problems he should note, and perhaps even your on-the-ground observations. Not to mention, he is noticing your judgment and how well you communicate.

The useful question here is not "Why do I have to do this?" but "How will this material be used?" and "How can it communicate my abilities?" Once you properly frame a task's value, you can weigh the degree of effort it merits and perform it better.

Reframe perceived criticism as constructive support

Many of us are prone to react defensively to criticism that is part and parcel of the work scene. It's natural to want to hear only a positive evaluation of an assignment or our overall job performance. In an ideal world, managers would skillfully provide guidance in positive ways that reinforce our "pros" and lead us to improve our "cons." But few have a natural ability or training for this. Our common tendency to react emotionally to criticism—especially when it threatens our own self-perspective—further complicates the task. The boss's delivery may be lacking. Then it's up to us to evaluate criticism as objectively as we can, find the merit it hopefully possesses, and reframe it as advice that can help us do better work and be more valued.

Here is a real-life example. Ellie came to a new bank job as an assistant manager of auditing based on five years' similar experience with an insurance firm. The work was more specialized than she expected, but she dug in and worked at adapting to the new practices. However, after four months on the job, she was shocked to find on her desk a notice that she was being transferred to another department. Worse, it looked like a downward move to a nonmanagement role, with a salary cut.

She spent the night ruminating on how she might have failed and why she was being demoted. She liked her boss, Neil, and had put her full energy into the job. In the morning, she summoned her courage and went to see Neil. Not hiding the fact that she was close to tears, Ellie thrust the notice in front of her boss and choked out: "Why did you do this? What did I do wrong? I've worked so hard here. You never told me I was failing. Why?"

After a long pause, Neil said: "Ellie, do you like your job?"

"Of course!"

"But you seem to struggle with it."

"It's new, yes, and some of the work is different, I'm needing to re-orient myself, but I'm learning fast . . ."

Neil interrupted: "Ellie. Listen to me. I like you, and I see that you work hard. But I just don't think it's a good fit. If you want to move on, I'll give you a good reference. But maybe you should try the new job." That was all he would say.

Ellie thought about the situation for a few days, feeling both depressed and angry. She confided in a friend, who asked simply, "Why don't you look into the other job?" She did, grudgingly. Ellie talked to people in the other department, which handled customer relations. She found her interest piqued by the idea of working with people, rather than spending her workdays with accounting records. Yes, she'd trained for that profession and started working her way up—but maybe it was not her best skill or natural inclination.

Ellie had interpreted Neil's action as a sign that she had failed in his eyes. She responded emotionally and closed her mind to what her boss was telling her. He had assessed that she would be happier and more effective in another venue. Once she accepted the idea that Neil's perspective on the job fit need not be taken as a negative judgment, Ellie was able to free her thinking. Reframing Neil's intentions enabled her to accomplish a more important personal reframe—how she viewed her own potential talents and interests. Then she was able to see that the lower position offered entry to a field she could enjoy and ultimately excel in.

Remind yourself to keep working at a broad perspective that enables you to hear other people. As in Ellie's case, a short-term "failure" can prove to be a long-term benefit. Time is the biggest reframer of all. In the short run, of course, it's hard to accept rejection. So try to keep an open mind. Anyone with a long career will tell you how lucky it was to lose some of the most-wanted chances. Good managers are adept at identifying good matches and also poor ones, regardless of how much enthusiasm the candidate expresses.

Reframe goals to take a wider perspective

Suppose your supervisor is dumping more work on you than you can reasonably handle. You feel resentful and frustrated. To address the unfairness, you can go to the boss and tell her, "You're being unreasonable—I can't possibly do all this work, it's really unfair—especially when Maggie has almost nothing to do." This approach is likely to make you seem like a complainer and accomplish very little to improve the situation.

But suppose you reframe your goal of modifying your workload to taking a broader and more collaborative perspective of office priorities. Then you open your mind to consider an approach like speaking with the boss about a mutual challenge. This naturally suggests a conversation along these lines: "I really appreciate your showing confidence in me by giving me so much important work. But it's hard to apply my best skills to each assignment when there are so many. Can you help me prioritize so I do what's most important first and won't create delays?"

This perspective automatically sets you up for a productive conversation on a more equal level with the manager. You are tackling a problem in which you both have a stake and come across as thoughtful and goal oriented.

This kind of thinking works the other way around, too. Smart managers know that telling people how their work fits into a bigger picture is highly motivating. In leading a business communication workshop, Natalie referred to the value of writing considerate messages to subordinates. A young woman executive broke in: "Wait a minute! I'm a very busy person! If I want my assistant to do something, I write, 'John, have this on my desk Tuesday morning by 9:00 a.m.' Are you telling me I have to . . . sugarcoat it?"

The answer is yes—but when she labels the concept as "sugarcoating," she is using prejudicial language to dismiss an idea that can be of real benefit. In the broader perspective, she would have seen her goal as more than simply getting the piece of work on her desk at a specific time. Does she not want it done well? That requires motivating John. This is easy to do by explaining the goal—the reason for the rush assignment. For example, "John, I need to prepare for a new client meeting at noon and having your report on the competition in hand by 9:00 a.m. Tuesday will be a really big help. Thanks for meeting this unanticipated deadline. It's much appreciated."

Framing a request this way gets you a lot further than making a demand. Instead of feeling resentful, the other person feels recognized as a valued contributor and part of a team. He is far more likely to take pride in his work and go the extra mile for a manager who communicates that his work is important. Cheap at the price of a few words!

Regardless of how specific your particular complaint or goal might be at the moment, make it a habit to reflect often on your wide-perspective goals, as well as the long-range ones.

Reframe emotion into action

When you linger too much on negative emotions, you may become caught up in reviewing a problem over and over again without resolving the issue. And you might imagine all kinds of negative outcomes. This stands in the way of productive action.

Instead, try to replace the endless rumination by using the emotion to generate an action mindset. If you're worrying that you'll get a poor evaluation, can you find a way to ask how you're doing and how you might improve? If you worry that a presentation is lacking, can you use your worrier focus on detail to identify specific ways to improve it? If you're worried that a relationship is souring, why not come up with a plan to improve it? Try turning a worry into active curiosity, fact finding, and problem solving. Use it to expand your frame, rather than diminish it.

For example, "Alan ignored me today when I said good morning" could, on reflection, prompt you to ask Alan if everything is OK. Refocusing a worry like "I didn't get the numbers I need from accounting, and I won't meet my deadline" can lead you to request an extension on the deadline or ask the accounting staff if they can give you a partial picture sooner. Or you might be able to work on another part of your report. By focusing on the actionable aspects of the problem, you give yourself a way to move forward instead of staying caught up in the problem.

Reframe your relationship with yourself

As we explored in this chapter and the previous one, we often subject ourselves to negative ideas that lead us to feel bad about ourselves. If you tell yourself you don't have the ability to do something, you won't be able to do it, or at the least, you're set up for a hard struggle. You communicate this negative expectation to others, and they pick it up without questioning your self-judgment.

Reframing allows you to rescue yourself from negative assumptions that lead to unprofitable reactions. You can use the strategy to help you create more positive frameworks that serve you better in every situation and part of your life.

One way to do this is to counter the language you typically use with yourself. If a past "failure" overshadows your thinking, try a statement like one of these:

- "Just because I wasn't comfortable doing that before doesn't mean I can't do it now."
- "I've learned so much since then that of course I can handle this."
- "I'm a different person now than I was last year (or yesterday)."
- "I can call up another part of myself that's good at handling tough situations."

Review your personal patterns of negative thinking that you charted for chapter 2. Think about how to counter the unproductive self-talk they may trigger and invent a new mantra.

For example, if you feel your accomplishments are overlooked and undervalued: "I'm rightfully proud of meeting the sales goals, and I owe it to myself to make sure it's noticed."

If you assume other people won't take your ideas or concerns seriously: "People do listen when I present the idea in a way that considers their own perspective."

If you shy away from talking to new people: "I'll find out what interests people I don't know and encourage them to tell me about that."

If you're a frequent worrier, give yourself a general mantra to restore your perspective as needed, such as: "The sun will come out tomorrow even if I don't solve this problem today."

Positive countersuggestions work well if you repeat them often. The approach helps soften the everyday trials of working alongside negative people and weathering the day's ups and downs:

- I won't waste energy feeling angry because this is something I can't change right now.
- I'll just say no to acting on other people's emotions.
- I'll put this in my mental parking lot and think about it later.

Be patient with yourself when talking to yourself in new ways, and use all the strategies *Genie* gives you for understanding your response patterns and recasting them. It's not easy to change your relationship with yourself. *But if you cannot change your relationship with yourself, it's hard to expect that you can change your relationship with anyone else.* That is a dark thought. But when you chastise—blame—criticize—warn yourself constantly, and tell yourself that you cannot do it right or will never master the problem, you disrespect yourself. You deny yourself the opportunity to learn, grow, and do it differently.

Don't be surprised if a part of you wants to hold onto your self-limiting perspectives. Over time, negative expectations entrench themselves, leading to habitual emotional and behavioral responses. This has a physical base: in its quest for efficiency, the brain creates convenient neural pathways for often-repeated thoughts. It happens with complaining, for example. Track how often you complain about things in your everyday conversations and like most people, you'll probably be surprised.

Remind yourself that a bigger part of you wants to move forward. How do we know? You're reading this book! Absorb the techniques, practice them with the activities, and we promise—the rewards are powerful and often faster than you expect.

INTO ACTION

1. *Rethink a past situation.* Recall a scenario where you lost your temper or felt overwhelmed by another strong emotion. Think about how you might have handled the situation better by applying this chapter's tools.
   - Which might have helped you: the calming techniques, mind-body connection ideas, a reframing strategy? How could you have used them?
   - Can you see ways to change the outcome if a similar situation arises?
   - Can you imagine handling a situation that worries or upsets you now, or that might occur, in different ways?

2. *Practice shifting your perspective.* Reframe the following situations so they lead you to bypass an emotional response and handle the challenge more effectively.
   - The boss asks you to write a portion of a proposal over the weekend and deliver it on Monday. You feel . . . annoyed!

You're tempted to treat it as being worth only an hour of your personal time.

- You're new on the job and must use an unfamiliar technology. You feel . . . inadequate. You anticipate a time-consuming trial-and-error process that will embarrass you in front of your new coworkers.
- The whole team is going on retreat to a glamorous resort for two days—but you're told to stay behind and hold down the fort. You feel . . . angry. Will you play computer games most of the day and file minimal reports?
- You're continually bypassed on plum assignments and given dull ones beneath your ability. You feel . . . resentful that your talents are ignored. Will you request a transfer?

3. *Practice how to think through a problem situation.* Are you currently struggling with a work experience that provokes strong emotion and clouds your judgment? Review the following questions. Use those that resonate with you as a base for creating your own internalized checklist for future challenges. If a relevant situation is not currently on your horizon, think about one from the past. Relax first with a few minutes of Square Breathing.
    - How can I describe the problem, specifically?
    - How am I reacting? Am I making negative assumptions or responding on instinct?
    - Is a strong emotion overtaking my judgment and rational thinking? Narrowing my perspective?
    - What triggered this reaction?
    - What other ways of interpreting the event, incident, conversation, etc., can I come up with?
    - What are the ramifications beyond myself, if any? Can I see a bigger picture of why the situation matters, or doesn't, beyond my own feelings?
    - Exactly what result or solution would I like to see?
    - What are my response options? Is action called for?
    - Which course of action is most likely to achieve what I want?
    - What can I learn from this experience?

Chapter 4

BEYOND LOGIC:
USING VISUALIZATION
AND ROLE-PLAYING

I magine the following situations:

- Your new boss never seems to have time to explain what he wants, but expects you to perform flawlessly.
- The manager promotes a friend to a job you feel should have been yours. Now you report to her and grow increasingly resentful.
- You're bored with your job and feel you're not learning anything. You want your manager to recommend you for a new one in a different office.
- A coworker avoids talking to you and you hear that she's dissing you to your workmates.

If you've faced any of these scenarios, we bet you've felt the need to *do* something about it. But speaking up carries risks. You might not keep your cool when you're in the grip of strong emotions that cloud your ability to think. You might not have the confidence to carry off the conversation. You might make people angry and damage important relationships—or your career.

Good common sense may take you only so far in solving serious problems. This chapter shows you how to use your *imaginative power* to navigate difficult interactions with a major set of techniques: visualization, role-playing, and role reversal. Integrated with one another, they are very adaptable to a wide variety of circumstances and events. Do we promise they will solve every problem? No. But we're sure they will open your mind so you can better assess the challenges, find alternative perspectives, and identify new solutions.

The strategies in this chapter are change techniques. They invite you to reevaluate your perceptions and even form new mental pathways by first imagining difficult situations and problem relationships, and then rehearsing better response strategies than those you might automatically employ. Read this chapter with an open mind, participate in the activities, and embark on a voyage of self-discovery. We are sure you will find some valuable insights and some happy surprises.

THE POWER OF VISUALIZATION

When you create a conversation mentally, or rehearse something you plan to do or say, you're practicing an everyday form of visualization. *Think of visualization as imagining something that you would like to see happen and how you will get there.*

This may sound like we're talking about daydreaming, but it's very different.

Daydreaming has its own value for problem-solving in a free association manner, but when you focus on pitching a no-hitter, or singing like your favorite star, or telling your boss what you really think about him, you're fantasizing. The goal may be unachievable, or you may long for the outcome without taking into account the price of getting there: the endless hours of practice in the field or studio, for example. Or losing your job.

In contrast, when you visualize, the goal may be lofty, but you see and experience yourself working out what you must do to get there. This equips you better to accomplish the goal in real time. You can even reimagine something that happened in the past and figure out how you could have handled it more effectively. This frees you from worry about repeating a pattern you want to change. You possess most of the abilities to accomplish these things, consciously or not, and can apply them once you free your imagination.

Athletes and other high-stakes performers (including many CEOs) routinely use visualization. Fierce competitors often practice the physical experience of being successful to build confidence and project it to other people. The great boxer Muhammad Ali was famous for visualizing his moves as well as a demeanor that said, "I *know* I'll win" to each opponent.

Similarly, a ski jumper prepares by mentally reviewing the course and every small action. Actors mentally rehearse their portrayals and the physical manifestations that express character. Musicians practice difficult fingering in their heads to facilitate actual practice. Scientists imagine the progress and outcome of experiments to sift out the most promising. A patient who loses use of a limb after a stroke learns to mentally focus on controlling the physical movement over and over again. One theory of why this often works is that the brain forges new pathways to accomplish the goal.

In each case, people immerse themselves in every aspect of their own task. Athletes, for example, envision as deeply as they can how the action feels, how they're breathing, how they use their eyes and ears, how they move their bodies. They imagine every action they want to improve, anticipate problems and obstacles, plan a response, and practice it. Researchers are finding that the brain seems not to distinguish between intensely imagining an experience and real-life activity. We experience this blurring of imagination and reality in daily life. For instance, when we strongly empathize with someone else or experience a book or film that moves us to tears, the brain responds in much the same way as when we ourselves live the experience.

Putting visualization to work for you

Particularly for hypnotherapists, visualizing is among the most powerful tools for helping people move past their own blockades. Using mental imagery allows people to experiment with alternative behaviors and emotional responses, and to experience what feels and works best. Visualization can help you:

- *Connect to your own resources.* You can discover many resources you already have and even draw on your own future resources and those of other people you admire.
- *Reinforce your power to think positively.* Even when logic tells you that an outcome is unlikely, or your emotions say "I can't," visualizing enables you to see the desired result as more real and empowers you to discover creative responses.
- *Connect with helpful parts of yourself you may have been bypassing.* A part of you may feel you can't accomplish something, but another part thinks you can; another part has new ideas, another part sees the obstacles, and so on. You can integrate

these parts so they work cooperatively rather than warring with one another.

- *Move past impasses.* When you feel stuck and frozen, or can't find a way out or a way in, visualization frees you to apply solutions from other experiences or find new solutions.
- *Reduce anxiety.* When you give yourself the chance to believe you can accomplish a goal and see it happen, you feel more confident. You present as believing in yourself—which in itself contributes to more positive interactions.
- *Act strategically.* In stressful situations, you can distance yourself from emotional responses that damage your cause and instead focus on outcomes and analyses.

Psychologists also call visualizations *imaginal rehearsals.* The terminology suggests many uses. Suppose you want a plum assignment but you're not on the A-list and don't know how to approach your supervisor. First, fully visualize the project: What would it accomplish? What would working on it be like? What skills or experience does it demand? How can you contribute to the goal? With all this in mind, fully imagine the conversation with your boss starting at the end—the outcome you want. Visualize winning your goal and how it feels. Experience the success in your body. Now mentally create the steps you will take to achieve that success.

A wise friend once suggested a variation on this idea with an even bigger goal: getting your ideal job. "Take five minutes every day to think about the job you want," she said. "Define it in more and more detail: how you'd spend your time, what you'd learn, the kind of people you'd report to and work with, how the environment looks—everything you can think of. The more complete your mental picture of what you want, the closer you come to finding it." Magic? "No," she explained. "The better you define what you're looking for, the better you're able to recognize opportunities that take you in the right direction. And you'll know when you've found what you truly want."

Now try a visualization experience.

The Confidence Kick-Start

Who wouldn't like a way to call up confidence on demand? Visualization can do that! Here's how.

Set aside some private time for yourself in a comfortable setting where you can relax and not be disturbed. Sit comfortably. You may close your eyes or keep them open. Relax for five minutes with the Square Breathing technique (chapter 3) or another relaxation technique you like.

Let yourself remember a meaningful moment anywhere in your past that gave you a wonderfully good feeling. It need not be work related. Your special moment might be a meaningful compliment, congratulations on a job well done, a positive overheard remark, an accomplishment that gave you great satisfaction, a time when you were the focus of admiration, or when someone communicated caring or support—something that produced a special glow and brings a quiet smile to your lips now.

Fill your mind with the memory. See it, hear it, relive it. Feel it. Allow the warm feeling of appreciation, accomplishment, or pride to wash through you. Give yourself permission to fully experience this wonderful feeling. Luxuriate in it.

Hold the feeling and explore it in your body. Feel every sensation, starting with your breathing: the movement of muscles, the deepness, the slow and steady rhythm of air moving in and out. Experience how your shoulders feel, and your posture. Note the position of your head and the relaxed set of your features—the corners of your mouth may lift toward a smile—no tightness or tension. Notice how your hands and arms and legs feel—relaxed, loose, comfortable.

Say something aloud—perhaps introducing yourself—and feel how your voice works and how it sounds.

Hold that feeling as you stand and walk around the room. Notice your posture again, your shoulders, your gait. Feel your breathing. Do you feel a calm energy? Notice what thoughts come to you. Are they optimistic? Confident? Do other good experiences come into your mind? *Memorize the feeling and the cue you used to bring it alive in your body.*

At different times, as often as possible, repeat this exercise, centering on the same good memory, and be aware of all your body sensations. You'll find it easier and easier to recreate and deepen the feeling, ever more quickly. With repeated rehearsal, you will soon be able to trigger your own self-confident and capable self by keying off the memory.

Before a meeting or conversation or presentation, especially if it prompts insecurity, take a minute to return to your personal moment, focus, and recreate its expression in your body. Walk around, one step at a time. Maintain that feeling and walk into the situation as that self.

Here is a real-life example of how Mel, a city planner, used the Confidence Kick-Start to good effect. Soon after he was promoted to head the planning office of a municipal government, he was asked to begin reporting on his team's projects at town board meetings. He prepared exhaustively for his first such appearance. Mel was to join the action only for the portion related to his work, so he found himself pacing the hall waiting for the meeting room door to open. He reminded himself that he'd had little presentation experience. He thought about all the re-percussions of doing it badly in front of this audience. The fifteen-minute waiting time felt like hours. His nervousness grew into anxiety.

Finally he was summoned. Mel looked around at the expectant faces and realized he was breathing quickly, standing rigidly but poorly bal-anced, arms and hands immobile. He heard his own voice come out shaky and tight. He barely held onto the thread of his report and fought a foggy brain to answer simple questions.

"Nobody said anything," Mel recalls, "but I knew they were dis-appointed, and for sure I'd have to do better next time. But the more I thought about it, the more nervous I got and felt I was doomed to bomb again. It was especially maddening because I knew my stuff so well!"

Mel tried the Confidence Kick-Start. He identified his special mo-ment—accepting an award from his professional association to loud ap-plause and warm smiles. For two weeks, in addition to planning a solid presentation, he practiced reliving that personal peak moment to sum-mon his confidence.

When it was time to deliver the new report, rather than pacing the hall and allowing negative expectations to build, Mel sat quietly in a nearby room relaxed, and reexperienced his successful moment. "It put me in a frame of mind that let me remind myself how I'd built my exper-tise over many years, how well I know my field, and that I like sharing my ideas about it."

This time, Mel strode into the room with a confident carriage and easy smile. He greeted the company leaders in a friendly, strong voice. They responded with receptive expressions and the presentation sailed along successfully.

This technique leverages the mind-body connection we explored in chapter 3. Confidence is a physical state as well as a state of mind, pro-ducing a steady pulse, good oxygen flow, and release of just the right amount of adrenaline to spark you without triggering panic. This condi-tion helps our brains work better so you can think on your feet. Some people like attaching the exercise to a particular visual image, like a photograph, or a mental picture of a favorite place. Bring this image to mind when you want to reconnect with that moment of success and pride. Think of your moment or the visual symbol you chose, relax your hands, open your arms, straighten up, breathe slowly, and feel your mind open up.

USING ROLE REVERSAL AND ROLE-PLAYING

Visualization techniques work especially well when integrated with an-other set of psychotherapy staples—role reversal and role-playing. The principle of both is that we know a lot more about other people than we consciously recognize. We can temporarily move into someone else's state of mind and see the world—and ourselves—through their eyes. Role re-versal may sound like magical thinking, but it's not very different from moving from one frame of mind to another: insecurity to confidence, for example, or from a negative assumption to a more positive one.

Usually we look at other people in the third person—*he* or *she*. When we make the effort to feel as they feel—*I*—we discover much more about their perspective and response patterns. Think of it as intuition cultivated through empathy.

The Empty Chair Role Reversal

This is a simple but very effective way to bring yourself into someone else's viewpoint. Take two chairs and place them to face each other. Identify one chair as yours and the second as the "other" person's—let's say, your boss's. Begin a conversation in "your" chair as yourself and talk about whatever is on your mind—asking him how you're doing on the job is a good subject. When you've started the exchange and would naturally pause for a response, move to the other chair. Then, as closely as you can, assume your boss's posture and way of sitting; the expression on his face; his focus—on you? Elsewhere? Hear his voice, see his gestures, feel his breathing patterns. Now, drawing on your memory of your interactions with him and your intuition, envision what he says in response to your question. When that answer feels complete, move back to your chair and follow up by responding to what he said. Try questions such as:

- How can I do better or contribute more?
- What areas of improvement would you like to see?
- How can I demonstrate I'm ready for more responsibility?
- Why didn't I get the opportunity to do . . . ?
- What did you mean when you told me . . . ?

Move back and forth between chairs, listening closely, and respond as you would in the actual experience. Also notice how you feel when listening to the other person's concerns. How are you reacting: Do you feel tense? Defensive? Does your voice tighten? How does it feel to be attuned to the boss's language? Continue carrying on both sides of the conversation until it draws to a natural close.

Analyze what you learned. Did you discover anything about the boss's view of you that surprises you? Did you gain any new insight into how he evaluates you? Can you make better sense of any advice or criticism he's given you before? Do you detect any clues to making yourself more valuable? You may need to suspend disbelief the first time you try this strategy but if it works for you, even partly, you have a valuable tool to deploy in many situations where you feel at an impasse with a supervisor, coworker, or subordinate, or are experiencing a conflict. Here's an example.

Stephan, a computer specialist at a small manufacturing company, found himself at an impasse with his supervisor. On the one hand, his contributions were often praised and he was frequently asked to stay overtime to fix the inevitable computer crises. In spite of this, however, he had been regularly bypassed for promotions, and his salary increases were not as high as he felt he deserved. This was especially frustrating because he learned that several of his colleagues received higher raises.

Stephan blames his supervisor, Margot. He believes she is prejudiced because he's "foreign"—Stephan was born in Russia, retains his accent, and feels culturally isolated from his coworkers. He knows his increasing resentment is obvious to those around him and becomes even more isolated. He worries about damaging his situation but can't see a way to address it without showing how angry he is. The longer he keeps silent, the more irritated he feels. As the time for his yearly review approaches, he struggles with how to present his concerns effectively, knowing that his anger and sense of injustice interfere with his ability to think clearly and present his case.

To help Stephan communicate better with Margot, Susan suggested that he try the Empty Chair strategy and glimpse what it felt like to see himself through his supervisor's eyes. He visualized Margot sitting at her desk in front of him and noted in detail her expression, posture, breathing pattern, and gestures based on experience with her in the same setting. He listened to her voice. Then he began with a simple question: How do you see my value to this office? He switched chairs for the role reversal and assumed her physical presence. He felt her gaze. After a few minutes, he felt that he was in full connection.

Without his "mental Margot" even speaking, he could sense how she saw him and what she thought about his work, his interactions at the office, and his persistent request for raises. He could imagine what she would say and how she would say it. When he switched back to his own chair, he listened to his own response and tone of voice.

In his words: "I had a sense of insecurity in her, which surprised me. And I realized she felt very uncomfortable being questioned. Like I was disrespecting her judgment. I heard myself speaking up and was shocked by the tone of my voice—I sounded accusing and maybe even insulting. That made me realize that Margot was angry herself and making an effort to control it. I was calling her unfair and making demands. She felt cornered by my demand for explanations. We were both stuck in our positions."

Once he'd worked through his insight that his own manner was a big part of the blockade, Stephan realized, "I could actually change her perception of me and how we talked to each other." This set the stage for a better relationship that enabled him to like his job better and present his requests with a better chance of success.

If you have trouble getting into the Empty Chair technique, try it with a trusted friend playing the other role. You might also record the conversation and listen to your own voice—what you said and how you said it—a few days later.

Role-playing your Wise Future Self

What would it be like if you could take a journey into the future and talk to your Wise Future Self about your present-day problems? He or she could give you valuable advice based on your experiences, challenges, and successes seen from the future perspective. This role-playing technique is based on our premise that you possess untapped resources: skills, ideas, and solutions that derive from your entire life experience. Trust us that it's there and try out this activity. See it as integrating what you already know and freeing your creativity. It's especially helpful when you feel confused, blocked, and fresh out of solutions. Adapt the script to your need. This strategy echoes a hypnotherapy experience, as you will notice from the language.

Settle in comfortably to your quiet space and relax with a breathing technique. Square Breathing is a good choice. Take extra time to create your calm feeling. You are going to meet the "you" that is your Wise Future Self and learn something you want to know, and that he or she wants you to know. First know that your Wise Future Self is a part of you that has always been there, and always will be, when you slow down, disengage from the autopilot that usually guides you, and connect from a calm place. Your Wise Future Self knows far more than you realize you know and is able to synthesize all of it and pull meaning from it for you. Knowing this self helps you build self-awareness and expand your understanding.

Allow a question to come to mind. It may relate to something you have been pondering for a while—a problem relationship, a choice to make, a conflicted decision. You will collaborate on it with your Wise Future Self.

Now begin your journey to the meeting. Place your feet firmly on the ground, close in front of you. Close your eyes. You may take a path of your own choosing. As you proceed, you can invent the details that suit you because this is a personal journey. This description is an example.

You may see a long winding country road, or a straight one that takes you directly to the meeting place. Observe everything closely: how the path feels under your feet—is it paved, or dirt or gravel? Smooth or bumpy? What do you see at the side of the road: What kind of trees? Flowers? What does the sky look like? Do you feel a breeze? Smell a fragrance? Hear birds or other sounds? Feel your progress as you move along the path. Just ahead you see a fork in the road—choose which way to go. Instinct guides you—somehow, you know exactly which way to go. You begin to glimpse a house. Notice what it looks like—the shape, size, color, design. You move closer and closer. You realize this is where your Wise Future Self lives. He or she greets you warmly and shows you around the house, which is familiar but new, just the place you'd like to live in someday. You feel comfortable and happy. Bask in this warm feeling for a moment or two.

It is time to ask your question. You know your Wise Future Self is happy to help you answer it.

Think for a minute about your concern. Breathe deeply, relax. Then express your questions as clearly and concretely as you can. Your Wise Future Self may then ask you very specific questions. Answer. The advice will emerge out of this exchange. Embrace it, even if it does not make sense to you instantly. Trust that in time it will. It can take the form of a sudden burst of insight, or one step toward the solution you seek.

What kind of help might this visualization give you? It's very individual, but here is the illumination it brought to Rebecca.

Though she had many fine qualities and skills, Rebecca, in her midforties, was hampered in her career by an unusually stressful childhood. It had trained her to stay in the background and rarely speak, to avoid being subjected to harsh treatment. This pattern was mirrored at work.

For instance, although she frequently had ideas to support her department's sales staff, she never presented them to the manager because she could not overcome her expectation of being dismissed and belittled. On several occasions when she did share her suggestions with coworkers, they adopted the ideas and took the credit. Rebecca knew that her extreme reticence limited her ability to move ahead and be rewarded.

She took the journey to meet her Wise Future Self several times. The imagery enabled her to begin reshaping how she felt about herself and enabled her to believe that she had permission to override her parents' negativity. She started to feel entitled to exercise her creativity and leadership qualities at work—and to take credit for them. Soon, she began contributing to her office's sales strategies, and the visible results reinforced her confidence and earned her recognition. She now expresses her thoughts in a much stronger voice, at work and elsewhere.

Rebecca identifies the special meaningful advice her Wise Future Self gave her this way: "Magical things happen when you step outside your comfort zone." She made up two posters with these words, one for her office and the other to hang up in her living room.

This strategy works because we are ruled by habit most of the time. Playing the role of our own Future Self, with the ability to consider our actions from a different perspective, breaks our patterns so we can think more freely. Seeing yourself on a journey, using all your senses to visualize movement from one place to another, helps the mind feel that change is tangible and possible. Your Wise Future Self is the self you aspire to be, and it helps you see your choices and how they relate to your ultimate goals more clearly. A goal may be relatively narrow—like how to remediate a bad work relationship—or more general, like which career opportunity to choose. You might try a really broad question, like how did I get to this future place of success and peace? For many people, the experience shortcuts the process of linking to their internal reservoirs of experience and intuition. Practice this versatile strategy several times and you may find your skill with it improving, and you will reap its rewards.

Role-playing a "more capable" person

Sometimes we're faced with a challenge that feels way over our heads. It may trigger our emotions very strongly, or require a skill we don't trust ourselves to exercise. When that happens, here's a good approach: put yourselves inside the head of someone else you believe is well equipped to field the challenge, and handle it as he or she would. This is much easier to accomplish than you might think. For example, think of the best boss you've had and visualize that person fully in the way we've been describing—how he or she looks, talks, laughs, dresses, stands, breathes, and so on. Now look around, holding that posture and expression: Do you feel especially confident? Does anything look different? Think of a problem: Do you perceive the possibilities differently?

Our bodies reflect who we are, what we think, how we perceive and are perceived. The outer clues cue you into how other people react to things and the framework within which they view the world. Physically echoing someone else gives us insights into their nature because we intuitively know much more about them than we tend to credit. Practicing this technique not only helps you see yourself through their eyes, but also makes it easier to predict their actions and responses. It also makes us more empathetic.

To apply the strategy, first closely define the problem. Then think of someone you know anywhere in your life, anywhere in your history, who you feel would handle that problem in an admirable way. Then think yourself into their framework by visualizing them fully, physically and mentally. Adopt their posture, expressions, gestures, response patterns. Then do what they would do. Here's a down-to-earth example that also incorporates several other *Genie* techniques.

Meg had served as executive assistant to the head of HR for eighteen months and proved her value well. Her boss, Tom, depended on her to keep his calendar running smoothly, answer correspondence, filter applications, and more. Tom was a good supervisor who took time to mentor her. But she was bored and saw no opportunity to advance. Moreover, the experience dampened her enthusiasm for a career in the field.

She was excited to spot a company ad about a job opening that related more directly to her college degree in marketing. She felt she had a good shot at landing the new job. But how to tell her boss she was applying and gain his support? Meg knew that from his viewpoint, her departure meant giving up a known reliable employee who made life smoother and having to go through the inconvenience of hiring and training someone new. And he might feel the mentoring time he'd invested in her was wasted.

She marshaled her talking points, taking account of Tom's personality and perspective. A few ideas emerged:

1. I know that as an HR professional, Tom highly values a good employee–job fit.
2. I know Tom likes me personally and appreciates my capabilities.

Meg knew she needed more—and some guidance on how to handle the actual conversation. She asked herself: How would someone else with the right skills and savvy approach the situation with confidence?

She flipped through her mental catalog of people and to her surprise, found that the person she believed most likely to win the day was not a fellow professional but her Aunt Sally. Sally was a relentlessly cheerful, forceful person who always got what she wanted in family situations—and usually left the other person feeling good about giving it to her. To Meg's knowledge, her aunt had never held a paying job, but when she'd consulted her a few times about work problems, her advice about people was always spot-on.

Meg mentally immersed herself in Sally's persona. She quickly realized Sally would directly confront the reservations that might cause someone to say no. In this case, she needed to counter Tom's biggest resistance—his personal inconvenience. Also, Sally would find a way to forestall any resentment Tom might feel about mentoring her. So she added more talking points:

3. I will personally recruit, screen, and pre-interview candidates.
4. I will find time to fully train my successor and remain available to help.
5. I appreciate the value of your coaching, and I will carry it with me to the new role and spread your good name.

Then she thought about how Aunt Sally would begin the conversation and carry it through. When the time came, she walked in with Aunt Sally's confident, no-nonsense demeanor and wide smile. She opened with a relevant and well-deserved compliment:

"You've been such a great mentor to me, Tom, and I've learned so much from you. I really value your advice and want to consult you about my career direction."

The rest of the interaction flowed naturally, and Meg made her points, all the while maintaining Sally's cheerful, friendly, practical manner and listening style that projected positive expectations. She explained fully how she will do everything possible to minimize any bother to Tom. Rather than simply telling him what she wanted, she followed her plan and consulted him. "Here's what the marketing job asks for and why I think I'm a good fit—what do you think?" In effect, she made Tom a partner in a collaborative decision that takes his own needs into account and also appeals to his mission, fitting the right person to the job. He was also led to feel good about sending a protégé out to another department where she'd do him credit.

In assuming the mantle of Aunt Sally to figure out what to say and how to say it, Meg actually bypasses "logic" to access her own inner capabilities and intuition. Logically, she assumed the necessary skills were beyond her. In reality, she possessed the resources herself but was unaware of them. The technique is a psychotherapeutic approach for tapping into resources you may not consciously acknowledge.

You'll find that identifying a good person for the job, and figuring out how she'd accomplish the goal, is easier than you suspect—you're tapping into your own good instincts. Notice that people use this strategy in different ingenious ways. Some bloggers, for example, write under an assumed name and identity because it frees them to be more irreverent, out of the box, funny, adventurous, or whatever they choose.

An alternative way to use the strategy is to choose a famous person to solve your problem: How would Albert Einstein deal with this? Bill Gates? Your political hero? Favorite celebrity? Someone we know applied for a job but decided it didn't suit him by the time he took the personality-fit test. He decided to "become" Attila the Hun. The decision-makers agreed the fit was not what they had in mind.

Role-playing yourself in different roles

We are different people when fulfilling different roles—parent, employee, boss, medical patient, brother, son, partner, client, and many more. Every day you move fluidly from role to role, just as you move between emotional states, without noticing. When you're in the dentist's chair, you're a different person than when you're in the driver's seat. When you're shopping in a store, your role is different than when you engage in your professional work.

In the office, if you manage a team, you're playing a different role than when you're reporting to your boss. Taking account of this gives you the chance to see things from multiple perspectives. For example, you can learn from a good boss how to be an effective manager and apply that to your job of directing others. You certainly might learn what *not* to do as a manager from a current or past boss who is ineffective. And you can learn by observing your staff how to deliver a valued performance from the manager's perspective and guide your own work accordingly.

Draw insights from your nonwork life as well. If you routinely drive on a crowded highway at rush hour, you learn to control your anger in a safe way, and this skill can help when you're faced with a provocative situation at work. All sorts of situations in our personal lives, both positive and negative, teach us how to master emotions, work through problems, act persuasively, and so on.

Try this: List every specific role you can think of in your various life domains: assistant manager, coworker, team leader, mentor, dog owner, parent of a seven-year-old, jogger, gardener, soccer coach, and so on. Then identify skills and strengths associated with each role. Do you see any capabilities in any part of your life that might help you field a problem or interact more effectively with someone else?

When you can't figure out a way to approach a problem, *scan your various roles*. Perhaps you're uncomfortable presenting a new approach at work, for example. But if you're a parent, you may feel quite capable of introducing a new idea tactfully and appropriately to a child. How did you do it? What can you learn from yourself?

Here's one more way to employ your own flexibility.

Hold a "Meeting of Minds"

Sometimes we suffer from an embarrassment of riches: too many opinions and perspectives in our own heads. This inner dialog can be as disturbing as the situation itself. Especially in complicated situations, we end up thinking and rethinking every option indefinitely and become frozen in place. When you need to decipher the meaning of your supervisor's criticism, or which opportunity is best for your career, which of your voices should you listen to? All may make valid points. Here's an adaptation of a psychotherapy strategy to clarify your course.

Relax for a few minutes or longer. Then make a list of the different states of mind clamoring for attention. For example, say you need to decide what professional training to pursue that will best support your career aspirations. Create an avatar for each voice with a name suggestive of its viewpoint, like Logical Lou, Immediate Irma, People Person Pat, Language Lover Lana, Long-Range Lester, and so forth. The sillier the better.

Now envision holding a Meeting of Minds to which you invite every avatar to represent its piece of your mind. Picture the meeting room and its furnishings: how the room is set up, the shape of the tables, the chair arrangement, what's on the walls and the floor. When you've fully visualized the meeting room, look around it and consider whether its configuration suggests anything about your thinking.

Decide on a discussion format to accomplish the goal of coming to a decision. Should each part take a turn at a speaking platform or talk from their seats? How much time should be allotted? Should someone facilitate—who?

When you're ready, invite all the avatars—parts of you—into the room. Notice how they each enter, where they choose to sit, who sits next to whom, which seem to avoid each other. Let the scene unfold. Sit back and watch it as an observer. Who is listening, who interrupts? Who joins in, who retreats to a corner? Listen to what each part says as well as how each behaves. Observe the arguments that surface and any compromises. A leader may emerge to guide the group toward an agreement. You may find that things move along in ways that sometimes surprise you, and that in observer mode, you see factors come to the fore at moments when you're not consciously trying to resolve the issue.

When the interaction is played out, debrief yourself: What did you learn? Which viewpoints resonated most strongly with you? Who took the lead? What new insights can you claim?

This strategy is useful for complex decisions, like whether to make a major job change. Alex, for example, needed to choose whether to stick with his job or take a new one five hundred miles away. One interior voice told him that the new job was a great opportunity, another that it was over his head and a risk. One voice said that relocating five hundred miles away was an awful lot of trouble, another that it was worth it. Another set of voices promoted staying in place—it's safer, you're up for a promotion, and so on.

Alex visualized a Meeting of Minds and created avatars—Cautious Charlie, Ambitious Angela, Stay-at-Home Stan, and others. He imagined the scenario playing out. He watched and in debriefing himself later found he had a deeper sense of the immediate and long-range outcomes of standing pat versus making the move. The strongest voice told him to take the new job: the pros outweighed the cons for him. But Alex also realized that his deepest reservation was relocating away from family and friends. He was able to negotiate the decision with himself: he took the job and determined to visit "home" regularly and look for ways to actively engage with the new community.

Psychological research suggests that drawing on our intuition is sometimes the best way to approach complicated decisions that involve numerous factors we have trouble sorting out. A Meeting of Minds may not give you a definitive answer to your problem, but it's likely to promote clarity and highlight the relative importance of different factors.

Objectifying each part of your mind helps prevent you from end-lessly stewing in your own back-and-forth uncertainty. Translating your inner dialog into one you can watch further distances you from the conflict in question. You may emerge with both a broader perspec-tive—clues as to what matters most to you—and ways to integrate the viewpoints into a solution. Ultimately, you're using your inner resources to sort through the options, evaluate their importance, and organize your thinking.

You'll find the strategies described in this chapter referred to through-out the book, applied to a range of relationship challenges. Try them out in different circumstances. Discover which ones work best for you and with which kind of problems. Enjoy the adventure of assembling your personal resource toolkit!

INTO ACTION

1. *Role-play a movie character.* Think of a movie character that you like and admire. Pick someone who is the epitome of self-assurance, likability, and all-around capability. Now use all the techniques you've learned to mold yourself into that character's image. Attend to your carriage, facial muscles, slow and deep breathing, way of moving, air of confidence and self-reliance. Now walk around whatever environment you're in. Smile in just the right way. No need to try for words. How does it feel to walk in this character's skin? Does anything look different to you? While in character, think about someone you don't get along with. Does a way to improve the relationship come to mind? Or a different way to approach a problem? Picture yourself acting in this manner in various work scenarios. If you like how this works for you, rehearse it a number of times. Then see if you can bring the feeling up at will.

2. *Do an Empty Chair Role Reversal with your current supervisor.*
   A. Hold a conversation as described in this chapter. Then write down three things that you learned about the other person that you weren't aware of. Ask yourself how you can make use of the new information.
   B. Write down three things you learned about yourself from seeing yourself through the boss's eyes. How will you make

use of this information? Do you see anything you might change in your own attitude or communication style?

3. *Find your special moment when you felt confidence and pride.* Practice it at different times, when you're in different moods and states of mind. Repeat the experience at least five times. How does the experience differ each time? Does practice make it easier to adopt and feel the confident demeanor? Can you achieve the state faster? Think about a situation where you can use it and fully imagine the experience.

4. *Think about meeting your Wise Future Self.* What are your expectations of him or her? Your hopes? What questions do you most want this self to answer? Hold the meeting. Process what you learn. Jot down what happens even if the meaning is unclear. Do you have a clearer idea of how to get from "here" to "there"? Do the steps feel a bit more tangible?

5. *Try a Meeting of Minds.* Experiment first with a nonwork decision, like what car to buy or where to go on vacation. Review what you learn from the process. In what ways might such meetings help you with work situations and relationships?

Chapter 5

THE POWER IN UNDERSTANDING "THE OTHER"

We may resemble other people, grow up in the same family, go to the same school, or share affinities through a common experience, culture, or vocation. But we are as different from one another as our thumbprints.

Psychologists used to argue about the relative importance of "nature" versus "nurture" but now generally agree that a combination of the two determines our individual beliefs, values, strengths and weaknesses, expectations, preferences, and general worldview. This composite creates a "filter" we bring everywhere we go and everywhere we look. One common cause of misunderstanding between people is that we tend to forget about these individual filters and assume that everyone is pretty much like us.

A second factor that stands in the way of understanding other people is that empathy takes some work. Staying me-focused is the easy way to live. The trouble is it doesn't get you very far. You can't align well with others, collaborate, or lead effectively. Nor can you communicate well or ask for what you want in a way that's likely to achieve it.

Gaining insight into bosses and coworkers is especially important because the workplace embeds us with people we haven't chosen to spend our time with and with whom we may have little in common. Moreover, the hierarchical nature of most workplaces means we have less power than some others.

As important as mutual understanding is, its practice seems to be a disappearing act. Research suggests that many young people possess less empathy. Teachers often complain that students find it hard to see other viewpoints and that many don't see the value of doing so. And for complex reasons, people worldwide seem to be becoming increasingly polarized.

To bring this back to *Genie* ground level: See the world from inside other people's perspective and you give yourself extraordinary advantages. You understand how other people see you and understand yourself more fully. You know how to better leverage your own strengths and work with others in ways that will appeal to their expectations, personalities, and perspectives. You own the ability to build relationships and handle—and even prevent—difficult situations. You're equipped to stand out in your own work and:

- Gain other people's trust and support.
- Like and/or respect individuals with whom you have little natural affinity.
- Identify and absorb what you can learn from others.
- Communicate persuasively in ways that make sense to other people.
- Influence or lead others more effectively and call forth their better angels.

When the person involved is someone you report to, there's more. Understand your manager and you are better equipped to:

- Demonstrate your value—and be more valuable.
- Evaluate his criticism and receive better guidance.
- Gauge when to speak up and when to shut up.
- Address unfair treatment and other problems in the "right" terms.
- And figure out how to call forth his or her better angels.

Benefits may include improving the work environment and opening up more opportunities for yourself. When you understand other people's agendas, you're less often caught by surprise. And it may sound counterintuitive, but other people will find you more interesting because you center on them, rather than yourself. What's not to like?

Sometimes a simple consideration of other people's viewpoints makes all the difference. In conducting a seminar on communication for executive assistants, Natalie asked the participants to write a memo requesting time off during their offices' busiest period of the year, for any reason they wanted to invent.

Everyone enjoyed coming up with a reason: a daughter's wedding in Borneo, winning a safari, the surprise appearance of a long-lost relative. The sharing was fun—but not a single message mentioned how the work would be covered during this absence.

At a subsequent workshop, given the same pop assignment, the first person to share focused on her plan to minimize the impact of her time away. Many in the group did a quick and visible rethink of their own memos, because once this idea surfaced, it was obvious that their bosses would not much care about an assistant's great opportunity—but would very much care about their own inconvenience.

You owe it to yourself to practice the art of living inside "other" perspectives. In chapter 4, you learned how to use role reversal to understand someone else's perspective.

Now we'll give you some practical techniques that build on these insights.

TO INTERPRET PEOPLE, PAINT PORTRAITS IN WORDS

Creating profiles of the people who are important in your work life is a valuable addition to your toolkit. Use it to illuminate the mindset of your supervisor, coworkers, colleagues, and nonsupporters. It's wise to understand your friends better, too, because you need to reinforce and reward them in ways they value. You'll find that figuring out another person's perspective moves you out of your own limited one. As a result, ways to solve problems, maneuver impasses, and build better relationships suggest themselves to you almost magically. Once you absorb the process, you'll find yourself employing it to assess other people automatically.

To start your detective work, pick one person. Begin with the facts. What do you already know about this individual? Probably a lot more than you think. Here's a structure to help you look at the whole picture. If it seems overly detailed, it's because we're giving you the full version. Each situation tells you which factors matter; sometimes it's only a few. Practice with a few profiles and you'll quickly get a feel for the process. The more depth you attempt, the more illuminating the result.

Demographic overview

Age, generation:
- Baby boomer (born 1940s to 1960)
- Gen X (born 1961 to 1981)
- Millennial (born 1981 to 2000)
- Gen Z (born after 2000)

Gender
Education level: specific school sometimes relevant
Family status: married, partner, children, extended family
Cultural background
Position
Income
Religious and community affiliations
Hobbies and pastimes

Place in the organization

What is the person's role?
How does she rank in the hierarchy of decision-making and influence?
Does this position appear to be secure? Does she seem comfortable in it?
Does she like her job and the company?
How does she relate to her own supervisor?
How much does she appear to be valued by the company?
How does she relate to you? Other workers?
What is her function in carrying out the company mission?
What are her challenges?
What are her ambitions?

Personality facets

How would you describe his temperament: Is he even-natured, cheerful, gloomy, irascible, grumpy? Is he patient or easily frustrated?
What drives him?
What does he care about?
What is he most proud of?
What does he value: people, new technology, rules, teamwork?
What are his hot buttons?
What makes him laugh? Frown?
What is he patient with, and not so much?
What insecurities are visible?
Which people does he best relate to?
What are his strengths? Weaknesses? Do they make him a good match for the job?
Do you know about any personal history that influences who he is?
Is he socially inclined? Or shy and introverted?
Does he have a personal passion?
What keeps him up at night?
What access points for relationship building do you see?

Management style

Is he a leader (someone who inspires and innovates)?
Is he a manager (someone who organizes and administers)? Or both?
Is he fair?
Does he care about people?
Is he a good coach or mentor? A role model?
Does he give constructive criticism?
A top-down decision-maker or inclusive? A consensus-builder?
How does he make decisions: fast, slow, reluctantly, rarely?
What does he do well? Less well?
Does he often change his mind?
Is he easily influenced?

In relation to you

How well does she understand what you do?
What kind of feedback does she give?
Is she an active mentor?
Is she hard to please?
Do you feel she likes you?

Communication style

What is her preferred method of contact: group meetings, one-on-one meetings, e-mail, texting, phone?
Is she comfortable with people? Which people?
What does she like talking about?
What are her most approachable times of day?
What kind of information does she prefer and how much: technical, in-depth, impact on people, just the bottom line?
Does she listen well?
Is she a skilled communicator?

General impact

Is he engaged with his work?
Does he set a formal or informal atmosphere?
Does it look like he will stay long range or is looking to leave?
Is he rewarded for his efforts?
Is he in sync with the company?
Does she hold people to standards?
Is she too confrontational? Or not enough?
Is her door open to discuss problems?

Does she play favorites?
Does she promote harmony, collaboration, competition, or discord?

To assemble a portrait, review the questions and give your best answers to those that matter. This varies according to the nature of the situation and person. Expect to use your intuition, and trust it. Scan your answers and write a summary statement of your analysis. You may be surprised at where it takes you.

Here's a summary that someone we know, Allie, came up with to portray a CEO she had found uncomfortable to work with, to the detriment her job performance.

> Smart, autocratic Baby Boomer manager, very convinced of his own opinions, formal in manner, office and dress. Makes quick judgments—doesn't change his mind about anything—thinks of himself as highly principled. Seems to me self-righteous, in fact. Dislikes any disagreement but likes to argue. Reacts extremely to any hint of disrespect. Prefers people to function without bringing up problems.
>
> Often unfair. Uninterested in the bread-and-butter parts of the organization, which seem to bore him. Favors people who manage departments and programs of personal interest to him: invariably connected to entertainment and the arts. Plays the piano himself—probably would have liked to be a pro. Most proud of the son who is an actor, even though not very successful. Appears to feel a personal mission to further the arts, encourages creation of new programs in line with this, and is personally committed to organizations that support the arts.
>
> Comfortable and relaxed with: people in the arts/arts program managers.

This synopsis clarified for Allie why she found her former CEO difficult to relate to. Writing the profile didn't help Allie like the man better and didn't suggest to her that he was a good leader. However, a singular avenue became obvious: his identification with and passion for the arts. Allie fully sympathizes with this interest. Now she wonders why she had never talked to him about the concerts she attended, a relative who is a ballet dancer, or her own childhood training at a famous music school. "I could so easily have asked his opinion about a performer or a company, found out how he learned to play the piano, and opened up conversations that would probably have engaged him."

How much difference would it have made had Allie used this access point? Hard to say, but the chances are good that a more comfortable relationship was possible. It's a rare workplace that does not allow for more authentic connections. She missed an opportunity to share a genuine mutual interest and move past the stiff relationship. *To meet people where they live, invest in understanding what they care about.* It always benefits you.

A portrait-in-writing provides practical clues for understanding who someone is, what to expect from him, and how to best interact with him.

ATTEND TO YOUR INTUITION AND PEOPLE'S PHYSICAL CUES

Intuition may feel like an instinctive, nonrational reaction to a person, a statement, or a situation, but it's often based on internalized experience. A collection of small details triggers you to expect that history is repeating itself, for example. Your opinion of someone might emerge seemingly from nowhere, but it is actually based on noticing and integrating experience. In his groundbreaking book, *Thinking, Fast and Slow*, Daniel Kahneman distinguishes between our immediate, spontaneous responses and our analytical, more methodical thinking mode.

Both have essential roles in human survival and successful functioning, but choosing which system to use in different circumstances can be important. Intuition matters heavily in precarious situations—when you're faced with a physical threat, for example, or feel a strong foreboding. A jungle dweller, thoroughly familiar with his environment, depends on his senses to alert him to potential threats. You, as an office dweller, come to know the organization and people you work with to a degree you may not consciously recognize. You too are attuned to unexpected change—in this case someone's unusual behavior, perhaps, or a perceived shift in management rhetoric. Your intuition tells you to sit up and take notice, and you should.

Keep in mind some caveats, however. In many instances, you need to regard your intuition skeptically. Instant impressions are usually superficial. Your coworker Mary may remind you of your Aunt Sadie because her nose or voice is similar, but it's a mistake to assume that the two people are alike. That's a brand of stereotyping that blocks you from recognizing someone's individuality. Responding to Mary as if she is Aunt Sadie is a bad idea.

You also need to be mindful of your own patterns. For example, you may react defensively to a forceful person and push back, or revert to your negative assumptions about yourself.

Learn to pay close attention to your intuition, which may pick up on details beyond your conscious notice or synthesize many factors that your rational mind can't take into full account. But at the same time, practice looking for evidence—the clues that will back up your intuition or lead you to regard it skeptically. In what ways is Mary *not* like Aunt Sadie? Thoughtful observation tells you a great deal about people, both serving as a test ground for your instincts and furnishing your intuition with good material to work with. Observe and think about what you see, hear, and sense. Above all, keep an open mind.

Analyzing your subject's personal environment—like her office—is one path to understanding her. Note methodically what is on the desk, on the walls. Do you observe organized neatness, clutter, or stark-ness? Are there family photos and other personal artifacts? If there are books—what kind? Is the space well lit or darkish? Is it comfortable for visitors or just for the occupant? Does the seating structure allow for side-by-side conversation or just authoritative behind-the-desk position-ing? People express themselves in the setting they create.

People also tell you who they are by their own physical appearance. Trial lawyers train themselves to notice every small detail when selecting jurors. What is the person wearing, and how does it fit? How does he walk? Hold himself? Is he reading anything—what? What is his custom-ary expression? Frown lines or smile lines? How is he breathing? How does his voice sound? Are there signs of tension, fear, anger? Is he sitting relaxed, crossing his legs, grasping his hands? Is his gaze steady or eva-sive or shifting? These are all clues to inner landscape.

Professional interrogators, airport security personnel, and border guards are also taught to notice "micro expressions," such as signs of tension and anxiety: tightness around the mouth, perspiration, darting eyes. Lying is said to create a chemical reaction in the body that includes an itchy face, dry mouth, coughing, or throat clearing. Whole books are devoted to interpreting body language.

Portrait painters, to drill to someone's basic nature, look at the char-acter indicators that people create over time rather than the features they're born with. The corners of the mouth may speak of discontent or a cheerful disposition, the permanently furrowed brow suggests a critical perspective, a person's stance denotes confidence or the oppo-site, a self-effacing nature. Actors, naturally, observe and recreate every-thing about face and figure to "become" the person they're portraying. If you've visited a wax museum, you know that these meticulous stat-ues communicate personality in an uncanny fashion. A good sculpture similarly becomes more than the sum of its parts in conveying someone's "presence."

Consciously build your awareness of all the ways in which people tell you about themselves. We all want to be known and understood. Picking up on the physical cues and developing your portraits equips you to respect the individuality of others and relate to them much more effectively.

PRACTICE EMPATHY TO RESHAPE RELATIONSHIPS

Remind yourself often that me-centeredness may lead you to entirely overlook another person's reality. Take the trouble to see people as they are rather than just as cogs in your personal world, and you can transform how you interact with them.

We often overlook the power of our own critical perspective and actions. We're quick to resent and criticize how someone interacts with us but often fail to consider the tone we may be setting ourselves. When you cause someone—especially a supervisor—to feel disrespected or inadequate, *you* are responsible for the results. Try to understand "the other's" perspective at the outset to avoid creating problems. If one already exists, you can still take the trouble to understand the other person and come up with a plan to remedy the situation.

Find the positive in others and acknowledge it

Here's a strategy that often works nicely for relating better to someone you don't respect. *Find something positive you feel comfortable saying and can say with complete sincerity.* Never offer a false compliment. It will only hurt you. People are very intuitive and will invariably sense the emptiness and feel manipulated.

To put energy into understanding other people is more than a problem-solving strategy. It's an imperative to relationship building and therefore to success. Often, we don't have the luxury of working for or with people who deserve our admiration and deep respect. It's nevertheless our job to help them function well and be the best they can. It's also more human to appreciate other people's challenges and take account of where they're coming from—it helps us be our own better selves.

Don't view this kind of compliment-finding as a manipulative technique. The need is to look past your own perspective and understand someone else's. Take from that understanding something true and genuine. Acknowledge that truth to yourself and you are open to more positive communication.

Think you can't come up with something positive? Psychologists know that *when you give yourself permission to find the positive . . . you will.*

Sometimes you'll need to really dig for something that is authentic and appropriate. You want to make the other person feel appreciated and recognized in a way that relates to the job or situation. Not "I love your dress," but "I admired the way you handled the database glitch." Or "I appreciate the time you take to share your insights about trends in the field." Or "I notice when I go to industry meetings how well respected you are."

Showing empathy for your boss or colleague is an important skill that does not mean you're compromising yourself. Offering a sincere compliment never belittles you. It gives you a new way of relating. *Shifting your own perspective opens the door to alternative patterns of interaction.*

When you take responsibility for making relationships better and practice a generous spirit, you are sure to learn, grow, and be valued. Not to mention how good you feel about yourself when you defuse a potential negative and shift it toward the positive, even if by a small increment. Often that's all you need. This was the case with Cassie, a fundraiser for a regional nonprofit.

Eight months in, Cassie was disaffected with her job. She'd been happy until her supervisor left and a new department head took over. Cassie and her cohorts immediately found their new boss inefficient, incompetent, and unfriendly. Cassie felt particularly disliked and grew ever more frustrated with her boss's attitude and bad decisions. Close to quitting, she spoke to Natalie.

After listening to Cassie's litany of complaints, Natalie led her to assess the situation more objectively. The first thing she did was ask Cassie to tell her about Mary. As is often the case, Cassie knew and intuited far more about her boss than she realized. The information quickly led to Mary's profile—a woman in her late forties, belatedly promoted after many years with the organization, apparently working over her head and lacking leadership skills, pressured to produce by superiors. To all evidence, no family of her own and not much of a social life.

A few questions about Cassie's own situation and her colleagues elicited this portrait of Mary's staff—a group of five young women in their midtwenties starting careers, with busy personal lives, excited about their futures, bonded with each other and sharing contempt for Mary.

From these two profiles, it was a short leap to intuit the basic interaction and confirm it with Cassie:

- Do you think Mary feels you like her? No.
- Do you show her respect? No.
- Does she get support she needs from the people she reports to? No.
- Do you think she feels isolated? Yes.
- Do you talk to one another about what a bad boss she is? Yes.
- Do you resent what she asks you to do? Yes.
- Do you think she feels surrounded by a bunch of mean girls? Well, yes.

To see how things feel from her boss's perspective, Cassie was asked to imagine the situation reversed—would she like it? Cope with it better? She saw that her supervisor confronted a distasteful set of pressures. From above, she was expected to produce more, and from below, to direct a judgmental set of younger people who visibly showed disrespect for her and her decisions. Understanding this, Cassie acknowledged that to keep her job and like it better, she must take responsibility for improving the relationship.

Mary had reason to feel insecure, disrespected, and disliked. It was up to Cassie to assume the initiative and address this dissonance, but she needed to stay honest with herself, and Mary, for it to work. Asked to think about a sincere compliment she could offer Mary, Cassie interpreted the advice in a way that she found comfortable. She walked into Mary's office and said, "I've been thinking about it and realize that it's your role to see the big picture. The rest of us just see our own little piece and often aren't aware of how much responsibility your role as department head involves. So we don't always understand your decisions."

Mary uncrossed her arms and smiled. Cassie had achieved a relationship reset in a heartbeat.

Thereafter, she took care to treat Mary respectfully. She didn't think Mary became better at her job, or more likable, but understanding her boss's position and her own role made it painless. Because Mary now felt more comfortable with Cassie, she treated her as a favorite. This made it more natural yet to "be nice" to the boss. Cassie was able to perform her job in a more congenial climate, long enough to outlast the supervisor.

Take the lead to mend fences

Every one of us sometimes unknowingly, or carelessly, sets off syndromes of dislike or disrespect. An inappropriate response, a remark that overlooks a sensitivity, an inadvertent snub—often that's all it takes. We can also evoke envy or resentment for no reason but our own successes or skill or position. Or for no discoverable reason at all, because it's not always about you, remember? Even if you cannot figure out the source of the tension or understand the other person's position completely, you can draw on empathy to recognize that both you and "the other" are in an unproductive situation or dynamic. Once you make that step, you will be more motivated to think of a better way forward.

Often, it isn't easy to remedy bad feelings. You can't control other people and some of them hold grudges or enjoy making others uncomfortable. A negative spirit may entrench itself over time and feel intractable. But when you take the initiative to remedy a relationship that is harming you, or is distasteful to live with, you will be surprised at how often you find a way to succeed. Very rarely will you lose face by taking the initiative to find common meeting ground.

Jen, head of a company's creative services department, found herself uncomfortably at odds with Leslie, another department head. Organizational factors beyond her control fostered a silent mutual dislike. The two were positioned to compete with each other for the same portion of funding and once begun, bad mutual feelings grew over time. Leslie's dislike of Jen led her to make negative comments about her to other staff members. Jen reacted with chilly disdain.

One evening, they found themselves sitting side by side, pointedly ignoring each other at an executive meeting. Another colleague gave a presentation that began badly and proceeded downhill. Impulsively, Jen turned to Leslie and whispered her thought: "This is so embarrassing. You do these presentations so much better!"

Leslie looked shocked. She said nothing, but thereafter the hostility vanished. While the relationship did not blossom into friendship, the two women were able to work together cordially and even negotiate a fair disposition of the funding. In sincerely acknowledging her enemy's skill, Jen ended a situation that benefitted neither person.

Jen chanced on this use of the compliment technique. She hadn't analyzed Leslie's behavior or framed a strategy. Had she chosen to take the initiative, the portrait-building exercise might have suggested a similar path. Finding a way to project respect, approval, or even a hint of liking can entirely transform another person's view of you.

It's hard to like someone who appears to dislike you, and hard to respect someone who shows you disrespect. Extending yourself to understand other people enables you to see what you can do to repair relationship damage. Also, if you try to empathize with them, you can "instinctively" avoid people's hot buttons in the future. That doesn't mean muffling your opinions and responses when it's appropriate to express them. Rather, take initiative and build awareness of other perspectives and you'll find yourself making fewer faux pas and more friends.

BRIDGING THE GENERATION GAP CHALLENGE

Making broad generalizations about groups of people is touchy for us, the authors. On one hand, we counsel you throughout this book against limiting your view of other people to stereotypes instead of seeing them as three-dimensional, complex individuals. On the other hand, the tables that marketers like to draw up, outlining the attitudes of Baby Boomers versus Generation X versus Millennials, are hard to dismiss.

Most of us cannot separate ourselves from the culture we grow up in. We take for granted our perspective and values. The language we speak, the people who raise us, and our shared experience with others who are much like ourselves shape our thinking and expectations.

The time period you are born in is part of your unconscious culture. So we encourage you to take a serious look at who you are, what you want, and how you think. See whether the generalizations illuminate any of your actual experiences and suggest clues to facilitate better relationships.

Baby Boomers: Born between mid-1940s and 1960

Who they are: Baby Boomers are a large group who remain the power movers in most traditional companies, professions, consultancies, government agencies, and nonprofit organizations. They dominate most boards. While many have delayed retirement because of economic conditions, a good number would not voluntarily depart their field anyway because they typically define themselves by their work and may be workaholics.

How they function: Boomers are highly competitive and motivated by recognition, high levels of responsibility, challenge, and accomplishment. They see their confidence as well earned over time. They're comfortable with confrontation and take pride in pioneering change in many fields. During their tenure, the great movements for equal rights—both minorities and women—took place, and many Boomers remember the hard fight and how their own careers were affected. But they are also comfortable with hierarchical structures.

What they expect: Boomers want those who report to them to "pay their dues" and "come up the hard way" like they did. They feel their position and experience merit respect and that they need not explain themselves to subordinates, help motivate them, or help them figure things out.

Communication and decision-making style: Boomers like face-to-face interaction, both one-on-one and via meetings. They use e-mail heavily but are less likely to engage with Facebook and other social media, preferring to keep their personal lives private (and preferring their subordinates do the same). Many are still happy with top-down management, especially given that they are often at the top, but many others have adapted to a "flatter" hierarchy.

Generation X: Born between 1961 and 1981

Who they are: Gen X is a relatively small cohort that has also been called the MTV generation. Many of its members occupy middle management positions and are on track to upper management, or already there. They find themselves literally in the middle, intermediating between those they report to and the younger people who report to them. People in this age group were the first to grow up in homes where both parents worked or divorced, leaving them on their own a lot of the time. (They're also referred to as the Latchkey Generation.) This group is highly educated compared to predecessor generations.

How they function: Reflecting their early environment, Gen Xers value independence, freedom, resourcefulness, creativity, and self-sufficiency. They take pride in these qualities in themselves and seek it in those they hire and supervise. They are entrepreneurial in spirit, results-oriented, and want work to be meaningful. But they're also skeptical of institutions and organizations, having lived through their parents' disappointments.

What they expect: This generation is ambitious and works hard. More than most Boomers, they want work-life balance and prefer organizations that are hospitable to that kind of flexibility. The ambition-on-all-fronts tendency is especially hard on women, who still experience difficult choices between career and home.

Communication and decision-making: Gen Xers accept the hierarchy of many organizations but will battle for better systems and decisions—respectfully. They tend to be hands-off managers who expect subordinates to figure it out on their own, like they did. They are adept with new technology but typically less dedicated to it than their younger counterparts, and would prefer it to "stand still" rather than demanding ever-more learning. Gen X may engage in social media, but often not with the same enthusiasm as Millennials, and tend to take LinkedIn more seriously.

Millennials: Born between 1981 and 2000

Who they are: This largest-ever cohort is entering the job market in droves and its members are often surprised by what they find there. Older people are also surprised by the attitude and expectations of these new employees, making for an intrinsic culture clash, especially in large, traditionally organized enterprises.

How they function: The group is also called the Connected Generation for good reason. "Native users" of new technology, they relate to the world in great part through their smartphones and social media. They are often well traveled, virtually blind to gender and color differences, and believe thoroughly in live-and-let-live (the watchword: "whatever"). They like challenge, welcome change, and dislike repetitive work. They naturally integrate their career and personal lives given the right environment. Highly nurtured in their upbringing, most arrive already confident of their skills, ability to learn, and the value of their own opinions. However, they have particular trouble seeing viewpoints other than their own and are impatient with other perspectives. They do not respect people based on seniority or experience.

What they expect: Millennials want work situations where they can learn and keep learning; where their opinion is taken seriously from their first day on the job; and where they receive constant feedback, approval, and reward—quickly. They expect flexibility with working hours and time off, but will work long hours in compatible environments. They are fast to leave situations that do not fill these needs and have scant company loyalty. They value interesting experiences, often more than financial reward.

Communication and decision-making: Many Millennials shy away from direct confrontation and argument. They use their mobile phones more often for texting, photography, and online socializing rather than conversation, and these youngest employees come to the workplace unprepared to use e-mail effectively. They don't see the point of meetings, in the workplace or out of it, preferring to rely on e-communication for networking. Few see the point of face-to-face interaction via professional associations and other venues. While most are not at a decision-making level, except in some digital businesses, they expect to be part of decision-making and to understand the purpose of everything they're asked to do.

Gen Z: Born after 2000

This youngest cohort is just starting to join the workforce and while still an unknown quantity, differences are already being observed. One viewpoint is that having been raised with an unusual degree of protectiveness due to the more intensely perceived dangers of everyday life, they may be more cautious than Millennials and tend to more conformity.

How to think about generational differences

It's easy to find exceptions to generalizations like the foregoing. Someone can be Gen X but behave more like a Boomer or a Millennial, of course. There's even disagreement about precise time frames and further subdivision. But these broad strokes help explain a lot of workplace dissonance and, we find, the personal experience of many people.

Consider the contrast between a Gen Xer's belief that employees are best left on their own to sink or swim and the Millennial desire for affirmation and approval shaped by helicopter parenting. Or a Boomer's demand for automatic respect versus the Millennial assumption that even those in authority must earn it. Or a Millennial's preference for texting and social media as opposed to e-mail or more formal messaging systems. Whichever part of the generational spectrum you belong to, awareness of common differences, plus a willingness to take the initiative and find meeting grounds, can make your work life a lot happier.

Handle generational conflicts and misfires proactively

Generational preferences offer clues to interacting with other people more effectively. An older person sees a well-written e-mail as a sign of respect as well as competence, and probably doesn't appreciate hearing about your personal life or being friended. A Gen X supervisor wants to know that you've done your homework toward solving a problem and appreciates an employee who identifies a need to fill and does so.

Smart companies are looking for ways to mediate among the generations. Every business depends on new blood! So the Boomers and Gen Xers in charge are learning to understand, and to a great extent accommodate, younger people: more flexible hours, opportunities to work at home, more systematic mentoring, receptive ears for their ideas. If you're a Millennial, you might be surprised at how many workshops your supervisors are attending to find out how to relate to you!

And smart managers are setting systems in place to better leverage the assets of all groups. One way is to encourage mutual mentoring relationships where, for example, a Millennial teams up with an older person who needs help with technology, and in turn is mentored on navigating the company culture.

If you're a Millennial, it's smart to find opportunities like this. Yes, you know more about the digital world than many of your older coworkers, but they know a lot more about people, management, and the ways of the workplace. Show an interest in learning from them and offer your own expertise in a low-key way (never be condescending about your tech skills!) and you may well find a productive partnership.

We say more about working with generational differences later on, but suggest that taking these differences into account—just as with all the differences among people—will lead you to betters ways of establishing trust, making requests, communicating, and more. It's an important tool for your not-just-about-me repertoire.

Here's an example of a cross-generation misunderstanding similar to many we hear about.

Craig, twenty-four, holds his first career position after college and two years in retail jobs. He'd been grateful to land a spot as management assistant with a small manufacturing firm but a lot less happy to work under fifty-five-year-old Ted, who heads the four-person department.

Craig's complaint:

> I just get these trivial assignments that don't seem to have any meaning and are way below my skill level. Sometimes he gives them to me late afternoon and says he needs it the next morning, so I have to stay late to get it done. Or work over the weekend. And does he say thank you? He just takes for granted that I have no personal life, like him. And he knows how hard it is to get a job these days so he doesn't have to be careful how he treats me.
>
> He nitpicks how I dress, how I write, coming in ten minutes late. He fixates on all my small mistakes, like anything I leave out in a report. I don't even go to team meetings. So I'm not learning anything, and I have no idea how decisions are made or why. He doesn't listen to my ideas for doing things better. And the outdated technology I have to use! Boring. Frustrating.

Craig needs the income and sees only one option: do the work adequately, knowing it won't lead anywhere, and put his energy into finding a better opportunity.

Unfortunately, Ted picked up on this attitude after only a few weeks and Craig found himself on notice to improve his work ethic and product, or move on.

The problem is that Craig interprets his boss's words and actions within his own limited perspective and does not extend himself to see Ted's viewpoint. This produces a mismatch of expectations made worse by differing communication style and values.

Craig assumes that his boss is simply wielding power to make him miserable. Like many people, he had given little thought to the "generation gap idea." If Craig looked at Ted more dispassionately and built a portrait taking account of Boomer perspective, he would understand that his boss wants respect for his own position and experience. And he may interpret "respect" on a subordinate's part as hard work and care with appearance, communication, and level of commitment.

Craig could say it's not his fault that he and the boss misunderstand each other, and he doesn't want to adopt Ted's lifestyle and outlook just to please him. But he's in the subordinate position, so if he chooses to keep his job, it's up to him to improve the relationship.

Clearly, Craig needed to understand Ted better and see himself from Ted's point of view. But he had trouble seeing past own perspective and feelings of frustration. A friend a few years older than Craig listened to his venting and suggested trying a role reversal (chapter 4), which he had learned about in a psychology course. He offered to play the boss's part. The friend had not met Ted and knew him only through hearing Craig's work gripes.

Craig was prompted to imagine himself in Ted's office sitting opposite to him, and to initiate a conversation about his work problems. The interchange, in condensed form, went something like this.

Craig: Ted, I want to talk to you about how I'm feeling about my work. I'm really not happy with how things are going. I often feel bored and frustrated.

"Ted": Well, I guess you make that pretty obvious. What exactly don't you like?

Craig: I don't see the point of most of my assignments. They seem very trivial, and I don't feel like I'm learning anything.

"Ted": I give you the work I need done. Maybe you don't like it, but you're telling me you don't take it seriously. Why not?

Craig: Because I'm capable of much more. And when I'm interested, I work harder. I'd do a great job. I have a lot of ideas about how to do things better.

"Ted": How would I know you'd do a great job? Why would I expect you to do more important things better? And why would I be interested in your ideas when you've only been here four months?

Craig: Well, I *would* do a great job on the assignments you give me if you bothered to tell me why it mattered. Instead you just criticize me all the time.

"Ted": What criticisms bother you?

Craig: You point out every little carelessness and typo, even in an e-mail. You complain when I leave something out of a write-up—usually because it was just too boring to concentrate on. You complain when I'm just a little late in the morning or back from lunch. You give me dirty looks when you see I'm on Facebook for a few minutes.

"Ted": Hmm. Do you disagree with any of that? Have you paid attention to any of it?

Craig: But it's nitpicking! I never get the chance to do anything important or interesting!

"Ted": Like what?

Craig: Like going to leadership meetings and sitting in on decisions. By working on team projects. Then I'd be learning!

"Ted": So? Do you think your education is my priority?

Craig: It's mine! And it should be yours because I'd feel a lot better about my job and do a lot more for you if you noticed what I'm doing and rewarded me rather than always criticizing.

"Ted": I do notice what you're doing. And you seem to agree that I give you plenty of input.

Craig: But you don't give me a chance to be my best. What would it take to make you recognize that I'm more worthwhile than the work you give me?

"Ted": I don't know. That's for you to figure out.

Craig was surprised at where this role-playing took him and not very appreciative to hear "Ted's" perspective. But the exercise made him aware that the situation might not be totally one-sided. He was able to start observing Ted a bit more objectively, as well as his own responses. The result was not so comfortable. He began to glimpse that to his boss, he was an inexperienced trainee, unenthusiastic about what he was asked to do and visibly resentful of his position. He acknowledged to himself that he might share the responsibility for not getting the opportunities he wanted, and for not opening Ted's eyes to his value.

He continued to believe that Ted was wrong in not thinking of him more highly—but he asked himself the important question: How can I show Ted I'm as good as I know I am? His conclusion: "I'll listen more carefully to what Ted says. I'll try to see his criticism as advice and act on it even if I don't agree. I'll avoid showing disrespect because it annoys him and ends up getting in my way. I'll take more care with the work, even when I don't like it. Ted doesn't know me very well. Maybe we got off on the wrong foot. I'll find ways to demonstrate how good I can be rather than assuming it's self-evident."

Resist seeing this strategy, and others in *Workplace Genie*, as capitulating to something you disagree with or don't believe in. Rather, view it as achieving a more open and less judgmental attitude toward other people so you can better manage a situation. You can decide to take the lead by understanding other people's realities and then accommodate them to whatever degree you wish. Is Craig better off responding to Ted's viewpoint or staying inside his "me" attitude and finding himself jobless?

When you understand other people and act on that understanding, you give yourself choices. Craig can decide to look for another job, but meanwhile, he is doing better work, learning, and feeling quite positive about taking charge of his own circumstances and initiating a change that benefits him.

What if Ted was motivated to try a role reversal exercise to see how he looked in Craig's eyes? The situation is not at all far-fetched. In many workplaces, supervisors acknowledge a big stake in helping the Craigs succeed. Hiring and training take time and energy, and replacing people is expensive. Many organizations are fully aware that young people are their future and that they need to accommodate their employees' desire for active learning, encouragement, and engagement.

If Ted lost a series of assistants in a short period of time, he'd be forced to recognize his need to better understand, and respond to, Craig and his peers. How would a role reversal work out in this case?

Ted might well realize how uncomfortable it is to work in an atmosphere of apparent indifference and fear of criticism, even if mostly unspoken. He might recall his own early career and that while for his generation "paying your dues" was necessary, he had not enjoyed it at all. He might feel retrospectively that he would have liked to speak out and ask for explanations and more positive guidance. He might bring to mind his own children, or other young people of Craig's age familiar to him, and accept that Craig very probably has value that could be nurtured.

There are indeed two sides to every story—two perspectives. Whether you are a Craig or a Ted, taking the initiative to understand "the other" can make an enormous positive difference. Besides, life is arranged so that we shift roles as we move along. Today's Craig is tomorrow's Ted. The new generation's expectations and needs will morph into a new reality once again, and Craig will need to figure out how to guide and motivate newbies with ideas and expectations different from his own.

INTO ACTION

1. *Perform a compliment check.* How often do you compliment your coworkers? Your supervisor? How might things be different if you did it more often?

2. *Seek coworker advice on a difficult person.* If you have trouble coming up with a strategy for connecting to your boss, or a difficult coworker, notice who does get along with that person. Try asking: "What is it you do to get along with this person? I admire how you do that. Can you give me some tips?" Alternatively, ask someone who is generally good with difficult people of a similar type.

3. *Use* Genie *strategies to plan an important conversation.* Think of something specific you would value that your manager isn't giving you. A "job well done" comment, a compliment, an offer

of support, specific feedback, or informal chat time, for example. Review what you know about her by creating a written portrait to gain insight into her perspective. Now close your eyes and visualize yourself walking into her office and sitting down comfortably.

Connect to your confident self. Take a minute to look around at the office in your mind's eye. Notice the personal effects, the colors, the overall feeling of the physical environment, and anything you hear. Now see your manager behind her desk and observe what she's wearing, how she looks, how she's regarding you as she waits for you to begin.

Focusing on her, what comes to you as a way to open the conversation? And what response do you anticipate? Frame the language to explain what you want. Take the natural tone that comes to you but avoid sounding whiny or complaining. Make your request in the way that feels most likely to succeed—in your boss's own framework. Notice her reactions as you speak and refine what you're saying in response. Perhaps she questions you: What does she ask? What objections does she make? How can you answer them in a way that makes sense to her?

Pre-living a conversation with an imaginal rehearsal, as discussed in chapter 4, can take you a long way toward creating a productive interaction.

Chapter 6

DELIVER YOUR MESSAGE! COMMUNICATION TECHNIQUES THAT BUILD RELATIONSHIPS

C an you imagine building meaningful relationships without words? It's pretty tough. Given all the pitfalls of communicating across cultures, language, geographic regions, personality, gender, family background, and our individual filters and idiosyncrasies, it's sometimes a wonder we can communicate at all. It's hard to say what we mean and to know if other people are saying what they mean. As a result, more than half of all workplace mistakes are attributed to communication breakdown or just poor everyday interaction and writing.

Successful organizations run on good spoken and written communication. Work is done better when there are fewer misunderstandings, misinterpretations, and mistakes. When proposals win, reports are clear, e-mail is straightforward, and online material is magnetic. Just in the past few years, the importance of this skill set has moved to the fore because its close connection to the bottom line is more widely recognized. When it comes to both hiring and promoting, business is on record: a number of surveys put good communication at the top of the "must have" list.

Because communication skills are in short supply, they offer a key opportunity for you to stand out. Good communication enables you to be perceived as more capable, credible, authoritative, knowledgeable, and influential. It gives you better ways to collaborate. You'll find many managers who don't communicate very well, but very few leaders.

While all of *Workplace Genie* is at heart about communication, this chapter focuses on practical communication techniques and strategies.

Consider them as primary tools for your relationship-building resource kit. The good news is that you've already done the groundwork. Understanding yourself and other people—which we've been working on throughout *Genie*—is the basis of good personal communication. All the techniques you're learning apply and put you way ahead of most people.

Communications is of course a huge topic, and we encourage you to seek out ways to improve your speaking and writing skills. We'll concentrate here on basic guidelines that apply across media, situations, and goals, plus some recognized trouble spots.

NAVIGATING COMMUNICATION IN THE COMPLEX WORKSCAPE

Language and history shape how we perceive, think, and relate to people and circumstances. This is clear to businesspeople who move back and forth between countries and discover the differences in thinking, style, and communication protocols among cultures. For example, in face-to-face interaction, other people think Americans smile too much and for the wrong reasons. Cultures differ in how much "small talk" is appropriate and degree of formality.

Then there are regional differences even within the United States. A friend who relocated told us he had trouble adapting to the different way people speak to one another: "People find New Yorkers abrupt and abrasive, even rude. In the Pacific Northwest people are more polite, more pleasant—but I can't help feeling that they're evasive and less straightforward. And they talk to friends in the same way as strangers!"

Family culture also influences what we talk about and how. We may grow up in homes where emotional feelings are constantly expressed or where they are considered unmentionable. Direct questions may be encouraged or seen as intrusions. Nonverbal cues to show interest may be expected or dampened.

Members of different generations also exhibit broad differences. Older people are often reticent about their feelings, for example, while many Millennials enjoy talking about themselves, their opinions, and at times, personal matters that embarrass older folks. It's interesting to note that anthropologists find that in developing countries, teenagers are moving toward the me-centered attitudes of Western cultures, so perhaps in the future, people globally will be more alike.

For now, many of these barriers to understanding meet in the workplace—and most are invisible. How to maneuver them all?

Here's our best advice to guide your communication across so much variability: *Remind yourself often that important differences exist even when you can't immediately see them.* Look at every individual as unique and assume that he or she doesn't necessarily think, assign value, or negotiate as you do. Use *Genie* tools and techniques to put yourself inside other people's frameworks, and you will instantly become a better communicator.

One useful tool is to build profiles of individuals (chapter 5). To develop better insight into your current workplace, or a past one, try the following. See if it helps explain any workplace problems or dissonance you've experienced and offers any clues to improve your interactions.

Write a communication-style portrait of your department

List the people in your working vicinity and then note the following for each:

- Family origins and where they were brought up
- Primary language if not English
- Education level
- Gender
- Age
- Communications style: reticent or outspoken, formal or spontaneous? Comfortable with discussing personal matters or not?
- Preferred forms of communication: face-to-face, group meetings, writing, telephone, messaging, social media, other?

Review what you wrote:

- Do you find more differences among your coworkers than you expected?
- Do you think these differences account for any problems or issues that come up?
- Do you see any ways to listen to and communicate with other members of the group more productively?

You probably found that your coworkers have a range of preferences in how HQ and coworkers communicate with them. Some workplaces accommodate a variety of media, usually in response to generational differences, as outlined in chapter 5. Both e-mail and social media might be employed, for example. But you may have to adapt to the local culture and learn to work well with channels you don't favor.

RECEIVING AND SENDING MESSAGES WELL

If you haven't experienced a lot of misunderstanding in your personal relationships, you are most unusual. The challenges multiply in work situations because so many people with different perspectives, agendas, cultural backgrounds, sensitivities, and personal triggers are squashed together in close quarters, metaphysically if not physically. Here are some techniques that will allow you to communicate more effectively across the differences you might have noted in your department profile.

Choose the right channel

In choosing *how* to communicate, take account of company culture and apply common sense. It may at times seem easiest to write rather than talk, especially when you want to get across something that's hard to deliver. But don't duck face-to-face communication. If it's appropriate to the situation, and the other person is open to it, welcome opportunities for personal contact because it's by far the best way to make yourself "real" to those you work with, rather than just existing as a name. This gives you an edge when you need a "yes" of any kind. Every salesman and negotiator aims for face-to-face presence.

Every "live" exchange is a chance to understand another person better and respond to what you see, hear, and sense. Facial expression, body language, and tone of voice show you how you're being received and enable you to adjust direction, consciously or not, to achieve your goal. Situations that involve a give-and-take of any kind are much better done in person.

Conversation via telephone, Skype, or other digital means works when personal contact isn't practical. But remember the pitfalls of talking when you can't observe expression and body language. The telephone may in any case be a disappearing act. Recently, a call for help was posted on a site for college teachers: Did anyone have a curriculum for teaching telephone skills? Her students didn't know how to use the telephone and realized this could be a problem in their prospective workplaces. On the other hand, Millennials are puzzled by some Boomers' resistance to social media for business communication and awkwardness with texting.

Remember that when you write anything, from an e-mail to a blog comment, it can be launched worldwide with the flick of a finger. It may be seen as an official record and is often easily retrieved even if you erase it. So for purposes other than formal reviews or legal issues, it's not wise to put personal information, criticism, and complaints in writing. Find an in-person option when possible.

Definitive, life-changing actions like firing someone—either from your professional or personal life—should never be done by writing or texting. It's just bad human relations. Taking a cowardly route may reverberate, especially since the different parts of our lives are increasingly integrated—and public.

Listen, listen, listen

Consider:

1. When someone else is talking, do you spend much of the time thinking about what you'll say next?
2. Do you look fully and attentively at the person or multitask in your head, or scan e-mail?
3. Do you ask for an explanation when you don't understand something or let it pass as unimportant? Do you ask questions to prompt the conversation?
4. Is your body language welcoming and open? Or do you fiddle with papers, frown, act impatiently? Cross your arms? Do you lean back, indicating disinterest?
5. Do you listen in silence or use conversational cues to show interest and encourage people to open up? (For example, "And then what happened?" "Really!" "Why?" "How did that work out?" "Uh-huh")
6. Do you consider time spent with people a waste of time better spent on your technical work?
7. Do you carefully remember what someone tells you and follow up later as suitable? ("How *was* your vacation?" "Did you get that project done?")

The "correct" answers are self-evident. Really good listening is a skill, perhaps even an art. Listen with your whole self—ears, eyes, brain, intuition—and you will find yourself rewarded tenfold. Train yourself to make and maintain eye contact: this alone will change people's perceptions of you. Most of the people we describe as magnetic are those who focus on every conversational partner as if she were the only person in the world. They communicate an authentic interest in understanding, not just hearing.

Listening is also the most effective way to defuse angry and upset people. Invariably, someone in the grip of these emotions wants to be acknowledged. And careful listening may tell you how to fix the problem.

Finally, remember that listening well is the fastest way to build trust and rapport. A good salesman encourages a prospect to talk about himself because this tells him who the person is. The best salesmen are genuinely curious, and you should be too. People are interesting. Try to follow the journalist's creed: there are no boring people—only bad listeners.

Learn to ask good questions

Better questions earn better answers and lead to more effective and productive relationships, especially if you combine these questions with attentive listening. Developing this ability will help you at every stage of your career, from getting a job in the first place to managing your own team or even company. It will equip you to . . .

- *Work better with specialists.* From IT experts to insurance agents, people give you better advice if your questions are on target.
- *Gain more help.* When you're clear in asking for guidance and information, people go out of their way more.
- *Frame your own work.* Scientists often begin their research by developing good questions and clarifying the challenge; you can do the same.
- *Make friends and influence people.* Everyone appreciates thoughtful questions about themselves, their work, their interests, and shared goals. They help you become someone people want to talk to.
- *Frame yourself.* To maintain and expand your perspective, make a habit of asking yourself questions that illuminate the bigger picture, as well as your goals and options.

Whatever the context, do your homework: don't ask questions you can answer yourself with a little in-house research, conversation, or googling. Opt for open-ended questions, because a "yes" or "no" answer is rarely useful. If you want a raise, for example, "May I have more money please?" is a conversation stopper that invites a quick "Certainly not." Better go with something like "I'm interested in a raise. Can we talk about how you see my performance the past six months?" The latter approach is certainly less direct, but it produces a lot more information on how your boss regards you, and if your request is turned down, you know how to qualify next time.

Some versatile power questions

Good questions are surprisingly adaptable to different occasions. Here are some that may be useful for your everyday conversations with supervisors, coworkers, specialists, and prospective employers.

- What is the goal? How will we measure progress?
- How will this help solve the problem (or contribute to the team, project, or goal)?
- Can you give me an example?
- Can you explain that in a different way?
- Why is this important? What's most important?
- How did you learn that (or figure it out)?
- How can I learn more about this?
- How do you see the next steps?
- How will you know when I'm succeeding?
- Is there a specific way I can improve?
- Can you help me understand why my idea/suggestion wasn't accepted?
- If my work on my last task wasn't satisfactory, can you explain how I can do it better next time?
- How can I contribute more, or show that I'm ready for more responsibility?
- What else should I know in order to do this well?
- What would you like to see changed?
- What's been tried before? How did it work out?
- What else should I have asked?

Make use of nonverbal communication

Naturally, you also want to be listened to yourself. No one wants to wonder if they are like the tree that falls in the forest and makes no sound because no one hears it. Can an idea be great if no one listens? Requests, suggestions, and wonderful contributions all need to be communicated or they stay in the forest, or rather, your own mind. It's useful to see communication as transferring ideas from one to mind to another, or to many others.

There's a lot of help available for honing your communication skills. We'll focus on some ways to open up your thinking. First, realize that effective communication goes well beyond your choice of words. In fact, nonverbal communication often plays the deciding role in how we are understood, how we understand others, and how we respond. Most of us are usually unaware of this principle.

How well do you think you can use your body language and voice to communicate your ideas and feelings without words? Here is an interesting experiment to try. Do it with a partner if you can.

Each person thinks of an important current work relationship. If you have a problem with a supervisor or coworker you find difficult to approach, focus on that.

Accept that your entire vocabulary consists of a single syllable: Ra. Now interact with your partner as if he's the problem person. Communicate your feelings and ideas through the tone and intensity of your voice, body language, gestures, and facial expression—and Ra. Express your concerns, present your request, make your explanations, offer suggestions with only this single sound. And then invite your partner to respond, using the same language of Ra in a way that communicates his or her feeling about what you said.

After each of you has taken a turn as first speaker, debrief each other. Share what you each came to understand about the situation and the person involved. See if you are surprised by how much information was conveyed in this wordless way. It's also illuminating to talk about past times where your nonverbal communication may have created problems.

You can also try this experiment on your own. Play out your interaction with the problem person using your voice and body. See if focusing away from the words gives you some clues about how to approach the conversation. Then fill in the language.

An approach similar to this technique has been used in the newscast business. A top cable network executive was known to turn off the sound when watching audition tapes of on-air reporters. If he liked how they came across without the words, he'd turn the sound up and listen to their voices.

Beyond giving you a way to approach a difficult conversation, Ra will build your awareness of nonverbal impact and power, making you not only a more compelling speaker, but also a more sensitive listener.

ADOPT THE TOOLS OF PERSUASIVE COMMUNICATION

Do you ever wonder why some writers are able to challenge your ideas or even alter them with something as brief as an op-ed piece? Why some people seem to be naturally great oral presenters? Or why politicians, CEOs, and other high-profile people are so quick on the draw when interviewed or otherwise put on the spot?

Talent certainly plays a big role, but training and practice count heavily. Fortunately, some excellent learnable techniques are available to you. You may be familiar with principles of argument if you've studied rhetoric in school. Its teachings have a lot in common with the know-your-goal-and-audience approach *Genie* recommends. Here are some specific tools to amplify your toolkit, which will help with both in-person communication and in writing.

Develop talking points for a range of situations

When you are preparing for a presentation, advocating for an idea, making a major request, or speaking on behalf of the organization, employ this process. It systematically equips you to speak effectively and respond to questions or challenges. Working with another person or a small group is ideal, but you can use the process on your own as well. Try deploying all your different "parts" to explore viewpoints (spelled out in chapter 4). Here's how to create talking points.

1. Specify the occasion and your goal. Do you want to deliver a presentation? Get a job? Gain something from your supervisor? Sign a new client? Consider who will be on "the other side" and think through your audience's characteristics and style (chapter 5).

2. Brainstorm the most important points that are most likely to accomplish your goal with that audience. Let's say you're proposing that your department invest in new technology and expect a mixed audience of broad-perspective managers, techies, financial types, and technology-averse staffers. To get buy-in, you need to address all of their concerns. Create a list of shorthand-style points. For an event like this one, it might in part read:
   - Proposed system saved Facilities 6 percent in tech expenses last year
   - Can customize to support development of new Product A
   - System incorporates speed, efficiency, and user-friendly features
   - Adaptable to unanticipated future needs
   - Easy to learn, have in-house capability for teaching it

   The one-phrase summaries are intended to spur easy recall of in-depth information.

3. Switch roles to play "the other side." Brainstorm: What questions will the audience members ask? Their probable objections? Vulnerabilities of your position? Speak to all. *Always consider the questions you hope will not be asked*. They probably will be, and you particularly need to be prepared.

4. Create your presentation. Put the talking points in logical order starting with the most important ones for your most important audiences. You'll no doubt have time limits and even if you don't, overkill works against you. So reserve some points as backup.

Voilà—you're ready! Before the event, scan your talking points and recall the substance behind them. Review your answers to anticipated questions. And rehearse what you can. Talking points gives you an excellent way to prepare for job interviews and many everyday occasions as well as those that feel make-or-break.

Techniques to bring people to your side

An important principle of persuasion is to go where your audience is—that is, take account of what they already know, what matters to them, and what they feel will benefit them. Your audience profile-building tools (chapter 5) give you the key for this thinking. Here are nine specific tips to draw on. With suitable adaptation, they apply to just about all media channels as well as occasions like pitching an idea, defending a proposal, or simply sharing information.

1. Believe in what you're "selling"! Theodore Roosevelt said it best: "Nobody cares how much you know until they know how much you care."

2. Focus on benefits—what something does for your audience, rather than *features*, technical specs that define its characteristics. Think what's-in-it-for-me—*me* meaning the other person.

3. Go for proof and evidence: rather than making vague general claims, find data—statistics, graphics, testimonials, reviews, etc.

4. Brush up a bit on rhetorical devices, the use of your voice, and body language to support your presentation skills—watching TED talks is a good way—and rehearse by recording your voice.

5. Work out your message in writing rather than letting PowerPoint or another graphic system dictate it via space or graphic restrictions. Think of the challenge as giving a speech plus visuals that

add another dimension. Keep the on-screen words few and the typeface big!

6. Stick to simple language that works for the spoken medium and be sure to use good transitions between ideas to create a logical flow, both for written and spoken media.

7. Take account of opposing arguments and incorporate them into your presentation. For example, "It's true that until two years ago the best way to do it was with the Goldberg Variation. But now . . ." Or "Diversity has many pluses, of course—but specialization gives our company a strong marketing advantage."

8. Make what you say or write engaging and as interesting as you can. There are few captive audiences these days! People must be enticed to listen or read. Use stories and visuals to bring your ideas to life.

9. Keep your message clear and simple: good persuaders, like good teachers, strive to accomplish incremental understanding and change, not quick revolutions.

Keep in mind that psychologists, neuroscientists, and marketing specialists are coming to agree that *human beings make most decisions on an emotional rather than rational basis*. We often make choices on emotional grounds—the car makes us feel adventurous, the dress helps us feel beautiful, the trip to Mozambique sounds exciting—and then back the decision up with logic: "The car is rated highly by *Hot Gears* magazine," "The dress is on sale," "I can write a blog about motels in Mozambique."

COMMUNICATE YOUR VALUE

In addition to asking targeted questions and delivering specific arguments, we often—whether intentionally or not—communicate messages about our role in our workplace. In a workshop for public relations specialists, Natalie once asked this question: How do you explain your own value to other people, either where you work or in general? Not one person appeared to have given this any thought. They assumed identifying themselves by position—"I'm assistant PR manager for MaxiMal Enterprises"—was enough. Even expanded with activity statements like "I write press releases and help plan events," this approach communicates little and loses the speaker good opportunities to deliver a message about herself.

You will find yourself mysteriously more successful if you think through why the profession you practice matters—and why *you* matter. A thinking structure may help. First consider how your unit fits into the organization. Ask:

1. What is the company's mission? (The answer most often doesn't relate to its official mission statement.)
2. What is the purpose of my department or unit? What does success mean?
3. What do I contribute to that purpose? How do I make a difference?

If you're an employee, you contribute to big-picture mission and department goals, whether you are currently aware of that or not. If one of the PR professionals introduced herself to someone in a different department, for example, she might say something like this: "I'm assistant head of public relations. We help top management understand our customers and connect with them. We create programs to show people they can trust our company and value our products so they become loyal customers. My role is to build good relationships through social media."

If you're an independent contractor of any kind, or an entrepreneur, adapt the questions to what you provide. They're critical for finding your market and speaking to it. An architect, for example, must always be ready to tell a prospect why he should hire an architect rather than a contractor. A contractor must be ready to explain to a client the advantage of hiring an overseer rather than seeking her own plumber, carpenter, etc. The plumber may have to explain why it's better to ask a professional to do the job rather than trying to fix the leak yourself.

No matter how you are positioned right now, you will benefit from being able to explain your own value on a moment's notice. Think about running into the CEO in the elevator, a sales prospect on the grocery line, a new boss who wants to know what you contribute, or the department head who's cutting costs 15 percent. Be prepared, as the Boy Scouts used to say. Here are some questions to consider in assessing your value to your employer or your customer base.

- What drew me to the work I'm doing (or want to do)?
- Why do I feel passionate, or at least very interested, in this work?
- What have I already accomplished and hope to accomplish for this organization? For my team?

- What makes me feel successful?
- What special or unusual skills or experience do I bring? Personal qualities?
- What sets me apart? What can I do that most other people can't?
- How have I progressed during the past year? Five years?

Of course, focus on what fits the situation—if you're facing a cost-cutter, it's most important to get across how your continued presence benefits the company. *Investing some time this way gives you the language to communicate your value to other people, as well as to yourself.* It clarifies where you are now and where you ultimately want to be. This makes it much easier to move in the chosen direction.

This "know your value" exercise also prepares you to tell other people who you are in a tangible way, such as through the "elevator speech." This is basically a say-able version of your personal value statement to use when you meet new people, especially at meetings and industry events. You're aiming for fifteen to twenty seconds of natural-sounding introduction that communicates the core of your personal or business message. Read the following two examples and note the difference that a concrete explanation of value makes:

1. "Hi, I'm Melissa James. I'm a senior CPA with Dafne Buck Miller and Sly. We're a full-service general practice accounting firm. I've been there for seven years; we have seventy-six accountants. My own specialization is in eldercare—I work with clients who operate nursing homes and assisted-living facilities."
2. "Hi. I'm Jack Miller. I'm an accountant. I help people who manage nursing homes operate them more efficiently. I work with them on business decisions and bring them new ideas to run their homes better, so they can concentrate on what they're all about—caring for their seniors."

A good way to gauge your own content is to check what you drafted and ask, who will be interested? Why should they care? Am I provoking curiosity? Geared to an elder-care industry audience, Jack's pitch invites questions like, "What kind of new ideas do you introduce?" or "How do you find them?" or "How do you work with an in-house business department?" *Who you work with and how your work ultimately helps—someone, something—guides your central message.* If you don't think your work helps anyone, keep thinking. An accountant for a domestic violence agency may work with numbers all day, but ultimately he is helping women find new lives.

Here's an anecdote to help you remember this point. When John F. Kennedy was touring NASA in the early days of space exploration, he passed a janitor with a mop in his hand. "Hi," JFK said. "I'm Jack Kennedy, the president. What do you do?"

The man answered, "We're sending a man to the moon."

Dig as hard as you must for your mission. To be valued, you must feel valuable and communicate that effectively.

IMPROVE YOUR WRITING: A MINI-COURSE

How many people in your work orbit know you only by your writing? How many of your opportunities depended at some critical point on writing? Not to mention that more and more employers require job candidates to take a writing test. They have learned how closely written skills connect to productivity, teamwork, efficiency, employee engagement, customer relations, and more—in other words, the bottom line.

If you haven't learned to write well yet, that doesn't mean you can't. Like most people, you've probably been looking at the wrong model. Good business writing today is conversational and straightforward. It's not about grammar, punctuation, and spelling, so forget those drills that kept you from liking to write. The more interesting challenge is to strategize, which requires knowing your goals, your audience, and how to bring them together. This capsule guide shows you how to begin transforming your writing into a powerful tool, and you can use this structure to help you think through any medium and situation.

Use a structure to plan everything you write

We have discussed the need for advance prep in several sections already, so it will not come as a surprise to you that structured planning is also essential to effective writing. This strategic approach works for everything from websites to resumes, white papers, presentations, blogs, social media, and all the rest. It's based on how many professional writers invest their time: *one-third planning, one-third drafting, and one-third revising.* Spontaneous and unedited messages dashed off without thought can discredit you. A professional never sends out a first draft, and you shouldn't either. This applies even when you are writing to a friend (who may be an industry colleague or in a position to refer you someday), and even when you're saying something that seems simple. See every message as a tiny fragment of the image you want to create for yourself, as though it is a piece of a mosaic. Here are the steps.

Step 1:Define your goal and audience

Brainstorm with yourself to figure out exactly what you want to happen after the person you're writing to reads the message. Almost always, you want them to give you something or agree with something. So, what is your "ask"?

Your goal can range from "read my resume" to "fix this problem" to "come to a meeting," "approve this request," "follow this procedure," or "buy my product, service, or idea." Look this way at your e-mails, reports, blogs, applications, and all the rest, and you're ten steps ahead of most people.

You also have a secondary but always important goal: communicating your best self. If you want to be seen as a reliable, level-headed problem-solver, use your writing to support that message. If you want to be perceived as eccentric, creative, and independent, OK—write that way.

Next think about your audience. Here's where the profiling skills you developed in chapter 5 pay off nicely. If you've already done a written portrait of your reader, like your supervisor, you have a ready-to-use blueprint for framing your message. You know what the person cares about, his priorities, preferred communication style, and much more. If you haven't yet done such a profile or are writing to someone new, pull one together. The more important your request, the more depth the effort merits. Asking for more vacation time probably warrants more thought than ordering more pens.

What if you're writing to a stranger? You can figure out a lot of useful generalizations by knowing what position they hold, their expertise, and their probable goals and concerns. A CEO, for example, is very likely a big-picture person guided by the bottom line: saving time and increasing profits. A CFO probably wants more numbers and details. A nonprofit leader is typically driven by a central mission, which you can easily learn.

If you're writing to a group, use the same kind of thinking to create a composite profile. Writing to a group of engineers demands a different orientation from writing to painters or carpenters, for example.

Next, use this goal and audience framework to decide on message content. Brainstorm the ideas, information, and selling points that will make the most sense to your reader and align with her general priorities and interests. And, when possible, give the other person something she wants.

Why should my coworker Hank care about the meeting I want him to attend? Why should my boss let me buy a top-of-the-line new computer? Why should the department head where I want to work grant me an interview? *Draft a message only when you know why the person you're writing to should agree to give you what you want.* And this usually means making what's in it for the other person crystal clear.

Think inside this structure of what you want, and who you want it from, and write a simple list of what to cover. If you have even a little familiarity with the person you're writing to, you already know a great way to shortcut your way to his heart: role reversal. Visualize him, adopt his perspective, and fully imagine holding a conversation about your subject (see chapter 4). This will help you anticipate questions and objections and build answers into your first communication, minimizing the need for a second chance to make your case.

Step 2: Draft your message: beginning, middle, end

Review your list and with your audience in mind, look for your strongest selling point. Move it to the top and shuffle the rest into a reasonably logical order. Decide whether you need an intro statement to explain why you're writing—e.g., "Dear Russ: I am very interested in working on the new project and know I can do an outstanding job."

Always get to the point as quickly as you can, whatever you're writing. No one has the patience anymore to wade through endless material, or even to the second paragraph, to find out why a message was written and why he should care.

After saying why you're writing, move straight to your substance. Start with what you chose as your best point. For example, "Last year I led the Green Space Project, described in the quarterly report as engaging Millennials more effectively than we have ever done before. I believe this know-how will greatly benefit the new project."

That's your lead. Now draft the middle, which in this case consists of the rest of your selling points. Use them in an order that feels natural. Be like Goldilocks—aim to say not too little, not too much, but just enough to make your case. Generally, it is more effective to work out a unified statement that ties your points together than to list bullet points.

When you've done that, it's time to close. Circle back to what you want. For example: "I'll welcome a chance to speak with you in person about my enthusiasm and special qualifications for this assignment."

Now you have a draft and are ready to troubleshoot.

Step 3: Review and edit

Give yourself some breathing space—ten minutes if that's all you have for a simple message, a few days for a major document. Start your review with content: Is my argument good? Did I leave anything out? Any over-kill or repetition? And always: *How will this message make my reader feel?* Am I using any prejudicial language, betraying a negative emotion, addressing the person in any inappropriate way? Relationship building is one of your goals, so this is important.

Every message has a *tone,* a general feeling rather like tone of voice. You can sound sad, angry, happy, critical, or respectful according to the words you choose and how you put them together. Aim always to come across as respectful and preferably upbeat and friendly. Avoid letting any negative emotion creep into your message: no frustration, annoyance, fear, dislike, or sense of rejection. Such feelings have a magnified effect in writing and serve you poorly. Humor is risky, because without expression and tone of voice, it's easy to misinterpret—especially irony and sarcasm.

Beware of communicating your state of mind when you feel that you are justifiably indignant or outraged. Think carefully about how such a message will be received, remembering that you want to retain the relationship, not destroy it. So don't burn bridges in writing.

There's also an intangible characteristic we'll call warmth. The business world is a big impersonal place. Just about everyone welcomes the feeling that someone else cares about him or her personally, even if the acquaintanceship is superficial. Especially if you're writing to an important client, or an angry customer, or a higher-up, try to summon positive feelings about the person as you write—or even just smile. You'll know when a more formal tone is called for—in a job application letter, for example.

Call on the techniques you learned in earlier chapters when you need to write difficult messages and anticipate your reader's reactions. Visualization is especially helpful. Create the person you're writing to in your mind as fully as you can. Then imagine having a conversation with him about your subject, and what questions or objections you might hear. Take account of his perspective in your message and you'll automatically know the right tone and content to include.

Practical guidelines for good business writing

If you reverse roles with your intended readers, you can see how they would define good writing. The same way you would! Some recommendations:

- *Be clear:* Say what you mean immediately and unambiguously.
- *Be concise:* In language and ideas, go for accessibility and speedy reading, cutting all unnecessary words.
- *Be simple:* Take the easiest way to say something and to be understood—simple words, simple sentences, simple structure.
- *Take action mode:* Minimize use of "to be" verbs—is, will be, have been, etc. Use the present tense or simple past tense and active rather than passive voice. Rather than "John was called to the CEO's office," write "The CEO called John to his office." Use the most active-feeling verbs you can find: "Sales leaped upward in March" is better than "The March sales records got better."
- *Minimize descriptive words*—adjectives and adverbs. Usually they add little or nothing.
- *Instill good rhythm:* Read your writing aloud and wherever you stumble or take on a singsongy cadence, edit: you have too many difficult abstract words and complicated sentences. Build a rhythm that pulls readers along by alternating short sentences with longer ones that use two or three commas.
- *Cut back prepositions*—the little words like "on," "to," "of," "and." They usually produce clumsy sentences—read them aloud and you'll hear it. One per sentence is plenty.
- *Change abstract words to concrete words:* Abstract words often end in -ly, -ing, -ion, -ious—use them sparingly, no more than one per sentence each when possible. Prefer the basic one- and two-syllable words that you use in conversation. In the English language, they're the old Anglo-Saxon words and we all trust them.
- *Avoid industry jargon:* People may not agree on its meaning as much as you think. Also give a pass to trite phrases and colloquialisms, especially if writing to nonnative English speakers.
- *Use short sentences:* Readability research says that sentences that are fourteen to eighteen words long *on average* are most easily understood by the most people (on average means that some sentences can be a few words long, others twenty-five, for example). This includes sophisticated academics—they don't like ponderous writing that needs to be figured out either!
- *Write short paragraphs:* Messages with short paragraphs are easier to read and more likely to be read. That means three to five sentences each. This helps bypass organization problems.

In general, aim for writing that *looks* accessible—most of us shy away from dense material with scant white space. Subheads, short paragraphs, and deliberate use of empty space or graphics, if appropriate, further this cause.

And write to *sound good*. Reading what you write aloud is a sure-fire diagnostic technique for what ails it. And to hold your audience, always write for speed readers. We are all impatient, over-messaged, and selective. We read only what targets us directly and maintains our interest by staying concise and on topic. Interesting is even better.

While professionals try to follow guidelines like these as they write, the post-draft editing part is essential to implementing them. After you've done your content review and made changes as necessary, and fixed the message's tone, order, language, and visual impact, proofread. Your spelling and grammar need to be basically correct. Always print out important documents before delivering them and edit on paper, then transfer the changes to your computer. You'll find it much easier to spot problems and mistakes.

Write your way to better thinking

The written word is also a first-rate tool for understanding yourself and for channeling yourself into logical thinking. Our minds are naturally lazy because thinking consumes a lot of energy. So when we give our brains a break and think through a problem without making a written record, we tend to keep circling around and often don't progress much beyond the starting point.

Developing your ability to think through writing echoes the way mankind has used the written word since its invention by various cultures. From pictograms on, the written (or engraved) record has served as the foundation upon which we base our pursuit of knowledge. Writing enables scientists, engineers, and master chefs to work together and advance the sum of knowledge in their fields, step-by-step. A biologist was once asked why the octopus, suspected to be perhaps the smartest animal of all, failed to build a civilization. Two reasons, he replied: the octopus has a short life span and does not possess a written language.

Use the writing process we capsulized to clarify your thinking. Your brain shifts into a different mode when required to work things through and express them in specific words instead of general feelings. You're channeled to develop your thoughts step-by-step. That's why we recommend doing this book's activities in writing. Record keeping also helps you chart your own progress, which will reinforce your motivation.

Note, too, that while most of us use the computer and smaller devices for writing these days, researchers find that handwriting has a different value. Lecture notes taken by hand have the longest staying power. A surprising number of professional writers still handwrite their material because they're positive it helps them think better.

MONITOR AND CONTROL YOUR ONLINE PRESENCE

Your workplace may or may not use Facebook or other social media for everyday communication. A growing number of businesses adopt the idea that employees are best reached through the media they prefer. If so, remember that when you use a channel for business purposes, it's mandatory to stay businesslike. Don't relax as if you're talking to friends. Also, while social media gives you access to an astonishing number of people few of us could even dream of reaching a decade ago, this power must be used responsibly. When you reach out to someone via LinkedIn, Twitter, or any other medium, be sure to create the good impression you want.

A big challenge with social media for many people is separating personal life from the professional. Unless you have reason to think otherwise, it's not a good idea to friend your boss or other managers from your company. Almost definitely, they don't want to friend you. Of course, they can check you out via social channels without your permission or awareness. You can count on this when you're applying for a job or someone investigates your suitability for a role they're filling. Your online life is pretty much an open book.

This suggests two principles. First, relentlessly *monitor yourself and post only things that do you credit*—and won't terrify you to see on the boss's screen or the front page of your local newspaper. If you think the latter is unlikely, what about the future? What if you run for office, are up for CEO, or your part-time business hits the big time? Today's carelessness, whether on social channels, e-mail, or another medium, may live to haunt you. If you read the news, we don't need to prove this. It's demonstrated every day. Pushing the delete button doesn't erase everything politicians and business leaders would like.

Doing yourself credit also means never, never posting anything that is personally derogatory about another person or is outright unkind. Anonymity seems to tempt some people to cruelty. Online bullying is still bullying. If you are tempted to say something mean, reflect on how you would feel about it if you were the other person. If you're tempted to toss off a joke or snide remark that might conceivably be interpreted against you, or labels you as the kind of person you don't want to be, remember that careers are lost that way. Stop to think.

Second, since your social media life is your public presence, think about using it in productive ways. *Make your social media use part of your career strategy.* What skills, capabilities, and personal qualities do you want others to know about? What expertise would you like to demonstrate? Smart entrepreneurs determine their business mission, audience, and competitive advantage to guide them on deciding what to post and publish. Many enterprises hire marketing specialists to build social media programs that support their selling and customer contact. You can do the same. Decide whom you want to reach or connect with and figure out what they care about and want to know. And determine to always be your best self when you communicate in writing, even on social media. Strategize how Facebook, Twitter, LinkedIn, Snapchat, Instagram, and perhaps a website and blogging fit into your own big picture.

Don't overlook media you might not naturally gravitate toward if your potential employers, clients, or colleagues use it. LinkedIn, for example, though not a favorite of many Millennials, is a primary tool for connecting among professionals and for hiring.

Finally, we recommend using your best writing skills with everything you post. Remember how infinite the audience can be. Even when few people see something, what if they include your current boss? Or a prospective new one? Make it a rule to never undermine your best self.

INTO ACTION

1. *Think: How can you change one thing about how you communicate that will help you change a relationship?* Write a plan based on that.

2. *Write your elevator speech, read it aloud, record it.* Then edit and rework it so it sounds natural. Then practice it many times. Try it out at home—and take it somewhere when you need to introduce yourself!

3. *Write an e-mail to your supervisor asking for something he or she will be reluctant to give you.*

4. *Take something substantial you wrote and review it against the guidelines and criteria in this chapter.* What might you change if

you were writing this material now in terms of content, style, or writing technique?

5. *Write a sincere thank you to someone who deserves it, finding ways to frame your appreciation in ways that are meaningful to the recipient.* Try writing a sincere apology to someone as well. For both, identify someone either in your past or the present that you would like to have expressed your feelings to.

6. *Identify opportunities at work where more thoughtful communication would benefit you, both in writing and in person, for both everyday interaction and important occasions.* Collect such possibilities and think about how *Genie* strategies in this and other chapters can help. Write a plan and include any supplemental training that would benefit you.

Chapter 7

MANAGING UP: IMPROVE YOUR RELATIONSHIP WITH THE BOSS

Do you have a great boss? We rarely hear anyone respond with an enthusiastic "yes!" We tend to focus on the boss's deficits and all the ways in which he or she fails to lead well or support us. More often, however, we do hear "I *used* to have a great boss." Do managers improve in retrospect, like good wine?

Probably the contradiction comes from our lack of perspective on the immediate. A former supervisor may settle out as a positive force in our minds over time, but the boss we see every day tempts us to criticize. We tend to take his good points for granted and chafe under all the behaviors, attitudes, and decisions we don't like. This prevents us from noticing how our own role may contribute to interactions and outcomes we don't like, and leads us to overlook opportunities to improve the relationship by taking the lead.

Suspend disbelief if necessary and accept that your boss has strengths as well as weaknesses. Most bosses are well intentioned and want their subordinates to succeed. Certainly there are also more than enough bosses from hell—we'll get to them in the next chapter—but here we'll focus on the kind of boss who offers plenty of scope to create a better relationship. Wherever your boss falls on your personal ratings scale, *Genie* techniques can help you improve your work life.

Instead of focusing on your problems, take a minute to consider the boss's perspective and our own expectations.

FIND EMPATHY FOR MANAGERS
Pity the poor boss, if you can.

He or she is caught somewhere in the middle between the higher-ups and a crew of diverse people with different functions, talents, personalities, and needs. To satisfy the first group, a manager must achieve set goals by orchestrating what the second group does. And this supervisor probably lives with many of the same or similar problems as his staff members in trying to meet other people's expectations without enough resources, training, or time.

If you're already a boss, you probably know this in-the-middle feeling. If you're an independent worker, the story isn't a whole lot different. Every client is in effect "the boss," and you must constantly assess each one and adapt how you interact. In extreme cases, you might fire a "bad client"—but more often, you must make your best effort to work with those you don't overly like or respect.

Regardless of our specific position, we all have a set of expectations when it comes to leadership. See if you agree with the following roster of ideal qualities you want from a boss. Add any missing traits that matter to you.

WHAT CHARACTERIZES A GOOD BOSS?
We want our supervisors to be:

- Fair
- Honest
- Empathetic
- Kind
- Respectful
- Reliable
- Appreciative
- Knowledgeable
- Well organized
- Supportive
- Good listeners
- Good mentors
- Good communicators
- Good conflict managers

We ask that in relating to us, they also:

- Set clear expectations
- Make good decisions

- Act with integrity
- Encourage different opinions and perspectives
- Promote risk-taking
- Establish a positive atmosphere
- Promote good teamwork
- Hold negative and unproductive people accountable
- Understand the work we do

We also pray that our boss is able to motivate us and protect us from any negative influences including, in many cases, her own imperfect superiors. You want her to be a leader as well, so add the ability to set a vision, inspire us to higher levels of achievement, and exemplify positive values. If you prefer to be managed by someone with a sense of humor, add that, too.

Is this so much to ask for? Well, yes. If you've ever worked for someone with more than a few such attributes, hold onto that memory! Knowing what it takes to be a good manager may help you improve your own boss's capabilities, at least a little, and certainly your relationship with him or her. The above checklist may also help you to more objectively assess the boss you've got and appreciate qualities you take for granted when you dwell on what you don't like.

It may also highlight how rarely first-rate supervisors are found. Throughout the working world, from corporation to nonprofit to government agency, many managers seem inadequate to the role. This creates disengaged employees, absenteeism, high turnover, and ultimately a monumental drag on the bottom line.

Consider your own experience. If you go to an office, do your interactions with the immediate supervisor make or break the whole experience? When you think back over your work history, is your relationship with each of your immediate supervisors the first thing that comes to mind? If the relationship matters so much, why do so many organizations seem not to care about it enough?

Gallup, which does massive surveys of the workplace, says that poor managers flourish because of misplaced company values that lead to inadequate training, shortsighted promotion programs, and counterproductive policies and reward systems. Instead of investing in creating good managers like those we all want, companies may value technical skills more highly, or the ability to "get things done" and churn out good numbers in the short run. At the same time, most managers feel they must produce more and more with less and less.

This may not always be obvious. Typically, supervisors are responsible for a lot of under-the-surface work beyond the actual product or service: managing budgets, writing performance reviews, dealing with a bureaucracy, and so on. And the fact that a supervisor enforces a policy, promotes a project, or makes a cut doesn't mean she agrees with it. Managers are expected to implement and enforce all kinds of things they may not like. These kinds of challenges are important to keep in mind when you feel frustrated with the relationship between you and your boss.

WHAT CHARACTERIZES A GOOD EMPLOYEE? FLIP THE PICTURE

It may surprise you that we first addressed *the boss's* problems in some detail. But understanding them goes a long way toward your ability to build a better relationship.

Equally important is understanding what your boss may expect of you. Individual personality, the nature of the work, and company culture all count in the full picture. But we can safely define that a manager appreciates and values the employee who is able to:

- Self-motivate and stay on track without more guidance and encouragement than he is able to give.
- Produce reliably: on time, efficiently, and without fuss.
- Take the initiative to find and suggest solutions.
- Grow and welcome chances to sharpen her existing skills and learn new ones.
- Contribute ideas and suggestions while understanding that they may not be adopted.
- Show commitment to the job, give it 100 percent, and pitch in at crunch times.

Beyond this checklist is a whole set of desirable personal qualities that may not be expressed, but underpin expectations, especially when hiring practices are well formulated. Preferred candidates for both hiring and promotion demonstrate:

- An even temperament that takes ups and downs in stride.
- Willingness to commit to the company and department mission.
- Good attitude that contributes to positive group morale.
- Team spirit in working well with others across gender, age, and cultural differences.

- Tactful behavior with VIPs, clients, collaborators, senior executives.
- Strong written and spoken communication skills.

From this perspective, how do you think a manager feels, and reacts, when a staff member prompts discipline issues by coming in late or missing deadlines, wastes staff energies by squabbling with coworkers, complains he doesn't get the best assignments, brings interpersonal office (or his own) problems to the boss's office, shows up with a chip on his shoulder, needs constant oversight and support, gossips, loses his temper often, bullies others, resists guidance, or argues against policies or initiatives beyond the manager's control?

When you see a problem from the manager's perspective, you can decide more effectively which issues to pick, when to stand up for yourself, what you can and can't change, and how to strategize for what you want.

FOUR USEFUL GENERALIZATIONS ABOUT SUPERVISORS

Before we move on to talk about specific challenges and strategies for improving your relationship with your supervisor, here are some underlying principles of organizational life to bear in mind that are rarely articulated but apply just about everywhere.

1. A manager *wants* everyone who reports to her to succeed. That's the only way she can succeed in turn. So most managers, except the minority who are truly negative spirits, want you to like your work and be happy in your job. This gives you a lot of leverage if you prove your value. No supervisor wants to lose a good worker who contributes, makes her work easier, and acts as a positive presence. This gives you power, but use it carefully, preferably when you need something important.

2. The higher the position someone holds in any organization, the broader his perspective must be. The boss's wide-angle view must be more inclusive than that of anyone reporting to him. He's in charge of deploying his forces and resources to accomplish the mission. This mandates a whole set of priorities, decisions, and actions that differ from those of an individual staff member.

3. Your role—whatever the nature of your work—is always to help the boss succeed and make her look good. Embarrassing or un-

dermining your manager in any way, to anyone, in any circumstance, will not endear you. Accept that in many organizations, taking credit for a subordinate's work is expected, all the way up the line. This isn't really unfair. Ultimately the CEO takes the credit—or the fall. Success or failure happened under his banner. However, smart managers provide appropriate recognition.

4.   Managers require respect from subordinates in order to do their jobs. You can instantly alienate your boss by saying or doing something that shows a disrespectful attitude. Moreover, someone you visibly disrespect will not respect you. The bad feeling colors all interactions. Even if you feel this boss hasn't earned respect, why undermine yourself by making it obvious? A new boss, or a younger one, or an ex-friend promoted over your head is especially sensitive to even subtle signs of disrespect. This is also true of a boss who is insecure in any way, which includes many of them.

Can you act respectful if you don't mean it? Yes, you can monitor yourself, but it's much better—in line with *Genie* principles—to find something in the other person that you can genuinely respect. Practicing empathy helps a lot. So does adapting specific strategies discussed earlier: creating a profile, role reversal, and reframing your perceptions, for example. Now we'll add some new ideas to what you already learned in previous chapters. We can't cover all possible challenges, so review these approaches with imagination to interpret what will best serve you.

WHEN MEETING THE BOSS: FIND YOUR BEST FOOT

Many people are finding that a constant reshuffle in their organizations brings a musical chairs atmosphere to the workplace. You may in the future need to welcome many new bosses because they move often, and you may move around as well. This makes it important to apply your relationship skills to interacting with managers who are new to you.

First, remind yourself to reserve judgment. As you know, a new position is challenging and calls up insecurities in most of us. You might not see the person's best side right away. And try not to classify the new boss instinctively—he may look like your Uncle Joe, but he is not. She may be filling the same role as the last boss, but she is a different person and will accomplish it differently. She may look judgmental or distant, but the book is not always the cover.

On the other hand, it's essential for a new supervisor to size up his team. Early in the learning curve he needs to know how the human pieces fit together, understand each one's responsibilities, and very likely, begin framing new routes to the mission. He may even arrive with a charge to make change happen.

It's easy to imagine that a new manager's priorities include learning what "is"—how the unit has done things and how it works. She also needs to establish herself as worthy of respect, find out whom to trust and rely on, and identify problem spots. Adding to these pressures, the new role probably represents a promotion with more responsibility, or a larger staff, or new skills to master. She probably has her own new boss to understand and please.

In dealing with any boss, it's necessary to constantly balance your priorities and aspirations, risks and benefits, leverage points and vulnerabilities. Aim to know yourself as well as the other person. Chapters 2, 3, and 4 help you gain insight on both, especially in conjunction with the profile-building techniques in chapter 5.

But when you report to someone new, you're at an especially important juncture. Prepare to take the broadest view of what you do and why it matters. Decide how you want the new person to see you. How forthcoming should you be? There's no one-size-fits-all answer to many dilemmas you may face. Each time, assess your own appetite for risk, as stockbrokers put it, especially when you don't yet know how far to trust someone or what their marching orders may be. Here's how one person judged the risks and planned accordingly. See if you think he handled it well.

Mark had been working nearly ten years for an appliance manufacturer, codirecting dealer relations programs. Market shifts prompted top management to realign departments and relocate supervisors. Mark got a new boss and blithely assumed the importance of his role and his own quiet efficiency would be recognized. So he saw little reason to think the change would affect him.

But after a month, he found himself faced with reconciling two concurrent demands. The new department head—Martha—scheduled him to present his goals for the year. And he learned that bonuses would in the future be tied to achieving specific goals.

"I certainly don't want to lose bonus money because I fail to meet goals I set myself," Mark reasoned. "And while I'd love to suggest a major new project I've had in mind for a long time, implementing it would be almost impossible because it requires cooperation of half a dozen department heads who are on my level, or higher. I've had trouble getting everyone aligned on smaller projects in the past. So experience tells me I'm unlikely to get it now." His conclusion: "I'll be conservative and set small goals I can be sure of meeting."

His codirector took a different tack and proposed a new initiative—less ambitious than Mark's new idea, but good enough to ensure that Mark would henceforth report to him.

The conservative approach proved ineffective in this situation. Mark didn't take account of the new department head's perspective and drives. Martha's role was to evaluate him "from scratch" in context of new company imperatives. She may have been on the lookout for staff to reassign, consolidate, promote, or trim. From that perspective, this was not the time to present as a small thinker with small, safe goals. Mark risked being identified as someone who can't be expected to contribute a lot beyond the established routine. His approach set an unpromising tone for the relationship and didn't promote his own success.

But if he had chosen to explain his ambitious project and gotten the go-ahead, what if his fears about pulling it off were justified? He might have strategized to minimize this risk.

Option 1: Mark describes the major goal he aims to achieve, then presents a relatively modest, achievable goal for the year as a first step toward accomplishing the ultimate one.

Option 2: Mark presents his full ambitious goal and paints an alluring vision of what will change for the better once it's achieved—and then explains that full participation by six department heads is needed.

Option 3: Mark combines both options: Here's my vision, here's what can realistically be accomplished this year. I can direct an accelerated version if the relevant people cooperate.

If Mark presents his idea effectively, he has a good chance of securing Martha's support for the accelerated version. It doesn't cost her much—perhaps a memo or phone calls to the department heads saying their cooperation with this project is important. But of course, she'll do this only if Mark's idea aligns with the company's current vision and priorities as well as Martha's. Any old big idea won't do.

Mark's cautious approach ended up giving his colleague the chance to rise above. Just as unfortunate, he missed the chance to accomplish a project that would have given him great personal satisfaction and probably would have enabled him to stand out. Sometimes it's best to have confidence in your own ideas and the courage to take a chance.

Of course, challenges may persist or arise regardless of how you present yourself in the beginning of your relationship. The following sections will address some of the common problems and offer long-term solutions for collaborating with your boss more effectively.

BE A FRIEND TO YOUR BOSS—BUT BE APPROPRIATE, TOO

Because it is often difficult to speak up at work, we often swallow our reactions. Negative attitudes build up over time, often on both sides. *Genie* recommends that in many instances where a relationship isn't going well, *you* take the initiative. Whether a problem is long-standing or involves a new supervisor with whom you don't immediately relate, there's often no need to resign yourself to feeling unhappy or to jump ship. First assess the possibilities for improvement.

To start, consider: What do I know about this person? Might there be ways to relate to her that I haven't tried? Have I communicated respect and openness to her viewpoint?

To open up your perceptions, look for face-to-face opportunities. We don't get to know other people by writing memos or texting! Here's an informal "law" of human behavior: we come to like people we spend time with. That said, how to go about claiming more of your supervisor's time without becoming a nuisance?

First of all, make the effort to think of him and treat him as a fully dimensional person, not just a cog in your work life. Here are some specific ideas for how to approach this goal.

- Notice what he's interested in and what he values—do you see a family graduation photo? Golf trophy? Vacation keepsake? Award? Tune in to chances to express interest and a suitable degree of curiosity.
- Offer a meaningful compliment that you believe in. Rarely does a subordinate tell the boss she's doing a good job or express appreciation.
- Identify interests that align with yours in some way, even indirectly: a passion for a sports team, interest in music, or love of travel, for example. But be careful about politics and religion!
- Behave as if you're happy to have the job and work in this office.
- Introduce "How am I doing?" conversations at suitable intervals.
- Show appreciation for advice, constructive criticism, guidance, and anything else you want to happen again.
- Watch for chances to lighten his load at crunch times: "I know you have a lot on your plate right now, how can I help?"
- Ask to buy him a cup of coffee: probably none of your peers do.

- Stay within bounds: don't friend him on social media, burden him unnecessarily with personal problems, share personal life details, ask for favors, act like a buddy, or expect him to.

KNOW THE BIG PICTURE AND ALIGN WITH IT

In addition to improving your personal relationship with your boss, think about how you both fit into the larger organization and adjust your behavior accordingly. To accomplish your work most effectively and be valued as you wish, it is important to be in line with the basic mission of your unit, department, and organization and to demonstrate this alignment to your supervisor. This sounds like common sense, but a surprising number of people fail to do this, especially if they are new to the workplace. To echo John F. Kennedy's famous line, think not just what the company can do for you, but what you can do for the company.

Alignment takes knowledge and thought. On the largest level: What are the organization's goals, beyond making or raising money? What are its biggest challenges? How is it organized? What can you figure out about how and why decisions are made, and by whom? Understand the organization's big picture and see yourself as actively contributing to that. Observe, research, ask. Notice what company leaders are saying on the web, in memos, in press releases. Check out your personal networks. If the company does not communicate expansively, ask good questions. See chapter 11 for specific ways to decipher company culture.

Also analyze the department or unit you work for. How does it fit into the company mission? What are your supervisor's main responsibilities? Main challenges? Priorities? And think seriously about how *you* fit in: What are you depended upon to produce or contribute?

A reality check on how well you are aligned with your immediate unit and beyond may be in order. Sometimes we make inaccurate assumptions about what other people value. This is easier to see in a common experience from our personal lives. For example, one partner may feel he is constantly catering to the other person's needs, but not realize he is performing based on his own perspective rather than hers. He has not checked with her about what she wants. So despite good intentions, misunderstandings blossom and the two people find themselves at odds. And both feel unappreciated!

Such situations develop even more easily in our work lives, because we're less apt to raise the issues and discover the mismatch until it's late in the game. We may work hard at pleasing a supervisor by doing what we think she wants, but this effort might be wasted if we have incorrect assumptions about what she values.

Therefore, take pause to be sure you're on the same track. At home, you might suggest, "Let's talk every night" to understand how each of you sees things. At work, try to listen objectively to other people's viewpoints to understand their perspectives as separate from your own. One good way to clear up misapprehensions is to ask direct questions. What are the priorities? What do you expect from me? What's most important for me to contribute? How else can I help? Rather than fully immersing yourself in immediate responsibilities, find ways to see the fuller dimension.

Here's a cautionary tale about someone who didn't give the alignment principle its just due despite holding her position for many years.

Norma headed the publication office of an agency that created marketing materials for nonprofit clients. She liked her job and got along well with her superiors on the top level. However, one day they summarily announced that she was to stop outsourcing all print jobs. Instead, all client publications would in the future be produced on an in-house machine.

Norma was shocked: she hadn't been consulted, and she disliked the in-house system. She shared this with everyone concerned: "I said over and over again that it's slow and it does a bad job; it doesn't print all the formats—we'll never be able to keep up our standards! All I heard back was 'we'll work it out.' I was very angry and showed it. I even yelled at my boss. But I didn't get any support.

"So I wrote a memo saying I felt like I'm all by myself on a sinking ship and no one would come to rescue me! My boss, a fair person whom I liked a lot, was very unhappy with my reaction. He said it was inappropriate. But to this day—years later—I can feel my frustration and still feel let down at not getting backup. I was the only one who cared about quality."

Showing anger in person was clearly harmful to Norma's good relationships. Putting it in writing further scuttled a lot of positive feelings built over years. But worse was the misalignment Norma demonstrated to her superiors. She assumed the decision was a money-saving tactic, which it probably was, but didn't see the goal as valid. Had she attempted some dispassionate fact-finding, she might have learned, for example, that the agency was concerned about keeping costs down for its nonprofit clientele. In any case, she was unwilling to look past the conviction that her own focus on quality was more important.

The challenge so often is not in what happens, but how you react. It's never helpful to present yourself as inflexible and narrow. It's even more alienating to support a personal belief by expressing a strong negative emotion. Norma failed to align with her company's mission, culture, and systems despite her long-term tenure on the job. Further, faced with a decision she didn't agree with, she didn't investigate the reasoning behind the edict.

She stayed at her job a while longer, but was thereafter treated as someone with limitations. Eventually she was invited to retire early with the sentiment "You've been great, but it's time for new thinking."

SPEAK THE BOSS'S LANGUAGE

Investing in a broad perspective of the company's mission and your department's responsibility sets the stage for talking the same language as those you report to. You don't want to be like Norma, spouting "quality" when to the decision-maker, it's about "saving money." When you're on the same wavelength, there's a happy side benefit: you own a good technique for equalizing the relationship at times when you need it.

A built-in challenge of interacting with a superior is the power differential. After all, one person—you—is accountable to the other. You must ask for things rather than allocating them at will, carry out decisions you may not like, and perhaps feel at the mercy of someone who underrates or overburdens you. The boss's opinion carries more weight than yours. The words of an in-charge person are heard differently. Subordinates probably monitor what he says and act on it more often than he realizes. And, of course, his personal opinion of you can have more impact on your future than vice versa.

Given these challenges, how can you equalize the relationship?

Think about your value as a partner rather than a supplicant. When you hit a dead end on an assignment, for example, or confront a major roadblock, your first impulse might be to say: "I have a problem meeting this contract deadline because I just can't get an answer from Purchasing." See if this sounds different: "We want to get this contract out by the fourth and this needs an answer from Purchasing today. Can we talk about how to move them forward?"

The second version presents the challenge as a mutual one to be solved together—*we*—rather than as a complaint in terms of an *I* who needs help and can't solve a problem on his own. Think about working *with* your boss, rather than working *for* him. Your whole self-presentation changes. It puts what you need in context of a common interest, rather than a hopeful or defensive ask. More examples:

1. "I'm completely overwhelmed!" versus "I've got competing priorities—can we talk about what needs to be done first?"
2. "I just can't use this new system—why did we have to change the software?" versus "I'd do this assignment a lot faster with some coaching on the new software. How about I ask IT to give our office a few hours of training to bring us up to speed?"
3. "You know I'm really interested in projects like this one. Why can't I work on it, instead of this routine stuff which any intern could do?" versus "I'm not slated to work with the team developing this project, but I'm very interested in it. How can I demonstrate I would be of value?"
4. "I've been working here for almost a year and haven't gotten a raise. When will something be done?" versus "I've been working here almost a year now. Can we talk about how I'm doing, and what else I can contribute?"

When you see yourself as helping to accomplish the same mission as the boss's, you naturally present yourself as capable, resourceful, mission oriented, and dedicated to becoming more valuable. You're a problem-solver rather than, let's face it, a whiner with grievances or challenges you can't meet. Speak from this perspective and you may find yourself behaving differently and thinking differently. And you will elicit a whole different set of responses.

WHEN DISAPPOINTMENT LOOMS, TAKE THE HIGH ROAD

One of the biggest challenges in communicating with your boss comes when you are dealing with disappointment. Being bypassed for opportunities is a complaint often heard from people who work hard, build their skills, and feel dedicated to their jobs. When you don't get that promotion, transfer to the new department you requested, or the raise you were counting on, how do you react?

Here, too, remind yourself of the big picture. You'll want to take stock of how your career is doing, but remember that the world, or your career, doesn't end with even a major disappointment. You may never know why a decision was made. The higher-ups may have faced a hard choice—or not. They may anticipate your disappointment, or be oblivious. What's certain, however, is that you should expect that any observable response on your part will very much be noticed. A show of temper and visible resentment don't speak well for you.

Many of the techniques we've talked about, such as choosing to pause and manage your emotions, will help. Here's an example.

Janet, a successful salesperson, brought more money into the company than most of her colleagues. So she was very upset when an administrative position she wanted was awarded to her friend Calvin instead. His sales record was less impressive than hers, and he had been with the company a shorter time. Janet suspected that the promotion was gender influenced, making her even more angry and resentful. Her immediate inclination was to charge into her boss's office and let him know how she felt. However, she had the good fortune to find that he had left for a long weekend. This gave her the time she needed to think through her reaction more clearly and strategically.

She later reflected, "Telling my supervisor how mad I was would have felt good in the moment. But the more I thought about it, the more I realized how shortsighted that was. I would absolutely not get the result that I wanted and would probably make my boss angry at me while achieving nothing." With effort, Janet dialed down her anger over the weekend. On Monday she walked into her boss's office with a smile on her face.

Her approach: "First, I congratulated him on recognizing all of Calvin's good qualities and emphasized how much I thought that in his new position, Calvin would help us get better results. Then I told him that I really appreciated his foresight and wanted to discuss with him some of the gifts that I brought to the company. I was careful to be modest, but covered lots of territory. Then I thanked my boss for making all my successes possible by having confidence in me." Janet also made a point of congratulating Calvin and offering full support for him in his new role.

Within three weeks, she was called into her boss's office and offered a new supervisory position, one that was much more appealing to her than the one that Calvin had assumed.

ASSESS YOUR SUPERVISOR MORE OBJECTIVELY: MAKE A PRO AND CON LIST

This advice is especially important in situations that provoke disillusionment or resentment, but it is good strategy to apply in all situations. Often, we are so consumed by the immediate, and entrenched in our own narrow perspective, that we can't tell an elm tree from a maple. A competent, generally considerate manager might snap at you on occasion, vent, or give you too many assignments and too short a deadline. As discussed in chapter 2, we may reflexively apply a label like "bully" or a phrase like "he's impossible to deal with." Once we have planted such labels in our own minds, we limit our perceptions and ability to strategize.

Focusing on the negative is a human tendency. One rule of thumb you may have heard is that it takes five good experiences to move us past a single negative one. When it comes to people, we may fasten onto someone's less stellar qualities and narrow our vision so it's hard to see past what we don't like and create a balanced view. But we can choose to break that pattern.

We're not implying that there aren't plenty of difficult people in the workplace, people who challenge our relationship-building efforts. But most people have both strengths and weaknesses, moments of confidence and moments of insecurity, good moods and bad moods. It's often helpful to break out of the immediate circumstances and our own feelings of grievance.

A straightforward way to help you assess your supervisor more objectively and keep you from falling into a negative trap is to create a simple "pro" and "con" list. First, list what you dislike about your boss and/or the reasons for your immediate frustration. You'll probably find this list comes easy because you've put the negatives in front of your mind! Then create a list of your supervisor's good qualities, attributes, and accomplishments. If this takes effort, welcome it, because the challenge is pulling you past your emotions toward more objectivity. Now look at both lists. How do they compare? Do the positives outweigh the negatives—if not in quantity, in degree of importance to you? Any surprises?

If you do this exercise conscientiously, you may lead yourself beyond the annoyances and surprise yourself by identifying solutions. Here's how this worked for Stephanie, a marketing director.

She was so exasperated with her organization's CEO, Stan, that her resentments kept her up at night. "I had already lost my temper more than once while trying to explain, for the twentieth time, that I felt really tapped out, overwhelmed by the effort to maintain my constant work flow and add new projects as he dreamed them up. I'd asked over and over again for more resources to handle the bigger workload—a new assistant in particular. But he kept evading my request and just said vague things like 'maybe another budget cycle.' I was biting my tongue when we talked and worried about the effect of my next explosion, which I felt was bound to happen."

Stephanie drew up a list of complaints about her boss and came up with this:

- He doesn't listen to what I need.

- He doesn't value my department's work, marketing, as much as he values program development. (He increased *their* staffing!)
- He withholds information I need until the last minute, then surprises me.
- He takes for granted the ton of extra hours I work.
- He even expects that the young people who report to me should sacrifice their personal time—which is so unfair I won't ask it of them.
- He's never there! He travels a lot, and I don't get to talk to him when I need to. At times, this slows everything to a crawl and makes it even harder for me to keep up.

Stephanie then drew up her list of Stan's good qualities, assets she likes and respects. She had reeled off her complaints in a rush, her voice vibrating with emotion. The grievances that kept her up at night obviously occupied her mental center stage. Composing the "pro" list took more deliberative thought to work past her negative screen. In the end, though, the list was substantial:

- He's led the organization to become bigger and much more successful.
- He's promoted a positive office atmosphere that's far more congenial than it was under the last director.
- Many of his ideas are good.
- He trusts me to make the right decisions on how to accomplish what he asks for.
- He clearly cares about the quality of our work and values my good results, though he rarely says so directly.

Just the act of writing this list moved Stephanie toward taking a more analytic view. When she scrutinized it side by side with the "con" list, her balance shifted. The problems created by Stan's habits didn't disappear, but she saw that when looked at more objectively, he was a good person to work for. The list of cons was slightly longer, but she quickly recognized that the positives were more important to her. She was especially reminded that he had improved the work environment and that it compared favorably with other places she's worked.

Stephanie emerged from the list-making with a renewed appreciation of her job. She remembered that she's doing work she loves, to her own highest standard, and is valued. Under this director's leadership, the organization is thriving and she is part of his team. Even more: the list generated some potential solutions.

For instance, might the communication problem be alleviated by regular or periodic Skype conversations? Would her on-the-road boss agree to that? Very likely, if Stephanie explains the advantages and accommodates his schedule. If he is traveling in a different time zone, she might offer to talk in the evening, for example. And rather than once again telling the boss that she can't do more work without more help, what if she takes the initiative to suggest a new project herself, excites him about the benefits, and then explains the resources she'd need to carry that out and more?

Stephanie was able to break the pattern of expectancy. The boss *expects* Stephanie to resist additional work and complain that she is understaffed (which may be part of the reason he talks to her less than she'd like). Stephanie *expects* to be brushed off. But instead of maintaining her defensive posture and repeating her complaints, now she's the one suggesting a new project, though conditionally.

Also, she's integrating what she perceives Stan most values—program development—with her marketing function, which is in fact realistic: a new program requires marketing support to succeed, a point her actions will implicitly make.

In sum, reviewing the pro and con lists energized Stephanie to take the initiative in a few directions, with a positive demeanor that anticipated positive results—always more successful. The process led her to challenge her assumptions: that the boss deliberately withholds information, for example, and doesn't sufficiently value her role. She was shocked to realize that probably in his eyes, she was becoming someone who resists new ideas.

Note how in this case assigning labels or ideas to someone else—for example, "he's insensitive," "he's oblivious," or "he doesn't care how much work I have"—can short-circuit the creative thinking that leads to a productive path. The obstacles you erect also blind you to your boss's perspective and ability to make a compassionate connection. Consider that there is often an "also," an additional factor that you might be overlooking. For example, "He works a very hectic, over-committed schedule himself." "He's trying to overhaul the system and move us in new directions." Or maybe "Donations are down 3 percent this quarter, and he's concerned with how to make up the difference—maybe I can suggest some new ways to support fundraising."

Stephanie moved forward by framing the situation as resolvable rather than escalating it into ever more negative territory, and by responding to the fuller picture. Try this strategy in a wide range of situations where you may be limiting your perspective, and use it to counter the temptation to act intemperately or in other ways contrary to your interests.

HOW TO GET A BOSS TO LISTEN

Genie gives you a number of resources with which to plan and carry out important conversations. Draw on them to strategize interactions with your boss. When you're about to ask for something important, pitch an idea, or broach a difficult subject, try running through the toolkit. Some possibilities:

- Use a role reversal to put yourself inside her head and frame your thinking (chapter 4).
- Build a profile of the individual taking personal characteristics as well as company position into account (chapter 5).
- Apply the "what's in it for me" idea when you want buy-in or agreement: articulate how the manager and the organization will gain (chapter 6).
- Prepare talking points to organize your ideas and brainstorm the questions or issues likely to come up (chapter 6).

Also, review any negative assumptions about both your own capabilities and your boss, tap into your confidence, use a relaxation technique that works for you. A number of options are covered in chapter 3.

And try to perform frequent reality checks. Before an encounter that matters to you, ask yourself, *What do I want to achieve?* What is the probable outcome of what I intend to say and do? Does it match the outcome I want? Consider whether you're thinking in big-picture or short-sighted terms: there's no point in gaining a tree and losing the forest. For example, don't use tactics or language that might damage a relationship unless your goal is very important to you and you've consciously decided the risk is worth taking. Norma, who fought her boss for the sake of "quality," lost something much more important than she might have gained when she refused to support a high-level decision.

But often, you want to present your own viewpoint, idea, or request with the best chance of success. Here are some tips based on effective pitching to draw on.

Ten ways to persuade a boss

1. Frame your pitch to this individual's self-interest.
2. Adopt an enthusiastic but objective tone, whether you're delivering the message in writing or in person (always choose in person when you can).
3. Focus on benefits (what your proposal will accomplish) rather than features (e.g., technical specs and descriptions).
4. Cite examples of where else your suggested approach has worked and what it achieved or improved.
5. Brainstorm the "con" arguments as well as the "pro."
6. Acknowledge the opposition and surround it: "True, early experience with the Brown Paradigm was not 100 percent, but the new model . . ."
7. Prepare to answer questions, especially the one you dread most.
8. Adapt your language to mesh with the other person's perspective.
9. Organize a persuasive argument in a logical way and start with what's most important—to the other person, not you.
10. Show, don't tell: use evidence, stories, demos, visuals to bring your idea, recommendation, or request to life, as suited to the case.

Learn from your own experience

Here's a helpful technique for connecting with a manager who is not giving you the support or approval you need.

Review your past experience with this person and think of a situation where he *was* supportive. What did you say? How did you say it? Visualize as fully as you can how you presented the successful request—your mood, tone of voice, the language you used, how you felt. Can you now re-create or echo that in the current situation?

Visualize the boss as well. Did any point you made seem to clinch his positive reaction? If you recall a time when he enthusiastically endorsed a measure that saved 7 percent on an expense, for example, can you translate your current "ask" into a similar bottom-line benefit? Generally speaking, saving time or money is a winning argument with most managers. So is solving problems.

Another way to use past experience is to review a situation where you found him *not* supportive. Perhaps he rushed you out of the office midway through your spiel. Re-create the moment: Where did he lose interest? What could you have said that would have elicited a different response? Could you have stated different benefits, spoken differently, provided more evidence of what could result from a "yes"? Reality check: Looking back, was your idea a good one? Could you have increased your chance of success by approaching him when he had more time or would be more receptive? (Studies show that the best time to sell anything to most people is after lunch.)

Use the "thanks-for-the-great-idea" strategy

We like this quote, attributed variously to Harry S. Truman and Ronald Reagan: "It is amazing what you can accomplish if you do not care who gets the credit."

And here's a favorite story told by the head of an engineering lab about someone who uses this approach masterfully. On occasion, a young researcher, Neil, drops in on Al, the lab chief, and the conversation goes like this.

Neil: Hi, Al, if you have a minute, I was hoping you'd help me with a problem I'm having.

Al: Sure!

Neil: I'm trying to figure out why when I use the Model A wiring approach for the new instrumentation, the result creates a lot more heat than I want. I had a small thought. Maybe I could try using the platinum option to divert the current to Point B rather than A. What do you think would happen?

Al: Well, let me think. I'm not sure, but maybe it would be useful to take the compression factor into account.

Neil: That's an interesting idea! If the platinum worked and I amped the energy up even more the connection might work smoothly and bypass the problem completely. Do you think that would result?

Al: It might.

Neil: And if that doesn't work, what do you think about trying a G-class circuit interrupter?

Al: Sounds worth a shot. The results might suggest other options you could bring into play.

Neil: Yes! I see what you mean. So if this gets the response we want, we'll learn something and might be able to improve the circuitry and solve the roadblock in the whole system!

Al: That would be great!

Neil: Wow! Thanks so much, Al. I'd like to follow up on your idea and work on the problem next week, is that OK?

Al: OK!

Al's comment: "Every time Neil does this, I realize that all along he has an idea he wants to go after. It doesn't matter what I say, he'll arrive at the conclusion he has in mind. I also know he is very smart and sometimes ten steps ahead of me. When he asks me to authorize a project this way, we both feel good."

What if you don't want the boss to take credit for something you did? It's actually her prerogative to do so. However, you are entitled to feel appreciated and rewarded. A smart boss will thank you and share the good reaction other people—probably her own superiors—accord the idea or project or accomplishment. She might recognize you within the department and praise you to coworkers when everyone is together. Or she might do nothing immediate but award you interesting assignments in the future and a good formal review.

However, if you feel that acknowledgment has not been fair, bring it up in a tactful way—one more reason to understand your own manager as thoroughly as you can: it helps you figure out what you can reasonably request. You might ask if it's possible for people beyond the immediate department, or the higher-ups, to be aware of your contribution. You might cite the good outcome as an example of your capabilities in requesting something you want or need. You definitely might bring it up when discussing your performance for the period. People have short memories! So plan a cheerfully expressed reminder.

Avoid a resentful or critical tone. In fact, it's often a good idea to begin such a conversation with something like, "Thank you for the challenging opportunity that gave me a chance to show what I can contribute." If you want to hit the whole chord, add, "I hope you agree that I'm ready for more responsibility. I would love the opportunity to contribute more." What rational boss could not love you?

INTO ACTION

1. *Ask for something you wanted yesterday.* Think of something you once wanted but didn't ask for. Taking account of the ideas in this chapter and strategies from previous ones, how would you frame your request now? Suggestions: try a quick profile of the other person, find a self-interest match point, create talking points, plan the conversation, and decide on how to present yourself and speak.

2. *Ask for something today.* Think of something you want now. Start with a reality check: Is your request reasonable? Do you deserve a yes? Is it within the boss's power to give it to you? Next, do the rest of the steps outlined in 1. Then rehearse. Start with a confidence-building exercise (chapter 3) and try a role reversal activity like the Empty Chair technique (chapter 4) to explore your supervisor's perspective and possible responses. Consider how a reframing (chapter 3) might help. Try recording the conversation and listen to how you sound, as objectively as possible. Would you grant the request if your roles were reversed? If not, back to the drawing board! Once you're completely prepared, decide whether to go for it. If you say no to yourself, figure out the reason for hesitating, weigh the risks and benefits, and redecide.

3. *Try the pro and con experiment.* Visualize your immediate supervisor and make up your two lists: everything you don't like about him and everything positive you can think of. Then analyze the results to see which list weighs more heavily in assessing your job satisfaction and what you're learning or gaining under his direction. Do you respect or like him more than your top-of-the-head reactions suggest? Does this process clarify any sticking points and hint at any problem-solving approaches to try? It's also enlightening to use the pro and con technique to evaluate former bosses.

4. *Experiment with Neil's approach.* Can you think of a way to use Neil's strategy—get buy-in by presenting your idea to the boss and convincing him it's his own?

Chapter 8

MANAGING UP:
WHEN THE BOSS IS DIFFICULT

So far, we've talked about managers who are basically well disposed, reasonably open to new ideas, and behave in generally encouraging ways. They may have limitations, blind spots, and bad moods, but you can take account of their strengths and weaknesses and learn to bring out their better angels. But what about the mean-spirited bosses: the ones who, unlike Al, are not OK with feeling a subordinate is smarter; who give you few if any positives to cite on a pro and con assessment; who appear to dislike you, limit you, ignore you, undermine you, or treat you unfairly?

Such managers may be in the minority, but their misuse of power can totally ruin a job and confront you with difficult decisions on how to respond. Dealing with bad bosses can deplete your energies and cast everyday issues into constant crisis. When the interaction is truly hostile, it can literally make you sick.

We'll tell you outright that when someone falls toward the extreme of the spectrum—as in "bully"—your best option is usually to get out from under. We know this isn't always possible. You have rent to pay, an ongoing investment in your career and perhaps the company, an industry you are part of, and a reputation to preserve. While we can't resolve this kind of dilemma for you, we can show you options for maintaining your confidence and handling yourself well until you're able to make a graceful exit. Controlling your own timetable can be critical.

PERFORM A REALITY CHECK

It's wise to first question the conclusions you've already come to about your boss. As earlier chapters explain, our own assumptions and patterns of behavior play a big part in determining how someone reacts to us and treats us. To assess your immediate supervisor, use the pro and con strategy in chapter 7 to see what positive traits you might identify to balance the negative ones. Build a profile, as described in chapter 5, to better understand where the person may be coming from: the pressures, insecurities, and stresses with which she lives.

Make an educated guess about what drives him—how does he measure success? What keeps him up at night? What matters to him? This may make you more empathetic and able to distance yourself from reflexive emotional responses. For example, when Cassie opened up her perceptions of her boss (chapter 5), she realized that the older woman felt surrounded by disrespectful, mean girls. This insight enabled her to shift her own behavior so both women could interact more comfortably. See yourself through your supervisor's eyes using role reversal (chapter 4). And take some time to analyze the situation with the following questions. Answer in writing, because this will help you see more connections.

1. When and how did the bad relationship start? Can you pinpoint a specific incident or occasion?
2. What sustains the negativity of this relationship? Why does it appear unresolvable? Describe subsequent occasions that illustrate the problems and reinforce your sense of the relationship.

Review your answers to the two questions above: Do you see how any of your own actions may have played a role in the poor relationship? Does the manager have any reason to question the quality of your work or how you interact with her, or with others? Have you paid attention to any guidance or criticism she provided? Continue:

3. Do you think your boss feels that *you* support *him*? That you respect him?
4. Do you compare him, in your mind, to a previous boss you liked and respected more?
5. Does your boss know you are unhappy with how you are treated?
6. Do other people have similar problems with this manager? If so, a few, or everyone?
7. Have you ever initiated a direct conversation with this person to clear up misunderstandings?
8. Are some people able to interact more effectively with this person? Can you learn from them? If you see other people also being mistreated, can you learn anything from that?

If you feel you are a particular target of ill treatment, consider asking your coworkers if they have the same impression. And think, as objectively as possible, if you can pinpoint any aspects of the poor relationship that stem from your quality of work, attitude, office interactions, communication style, and so on. Try to identify the triggers that provoke the behavior you don't like.

Working through this set of questions may orient you to see a potential for a reset. If you can identify a way to generate a change, give it serious thought. If you feel there's been a misunderstanding or misperception, for example, you might entertain the idea of a straightforward conversation. If your work has presented problems, strategize how to improve your performance and how to shift the boss's perceptions of you. If you suspect that your tone and attitude give away a lack of respect, or antagonism, figure out what might counter that. Exploring an access point such as a shared interest, or offering a sincere compliment, are ways to do that.

Don't overlook your own negative patterns. Know what triggers *your* insecurities and negative response when interacting with this supervisor.

None of this suggests that it's all in your mind! Many varieties of bad bosses may confront you during your career, irrelevant of your value, dedication, and accomplishments. Sometimes it's the positive attributes that trigger mistreatment when managers are insecure about their own abilities. However, it is always important to perform a reality check to get a more accurate assessment of where the problem lies.

HOW TO HANDLE YOUR BAD BOSS

To misquote a famous line from literature, all bad bosses produce unhappiness in their own way. We can't cover every kind of poor supervisor, so we will give you a set of examples that relate to the situations we hear about most often. Read them with imagination for ideas you can adapt. We'll start with the milder forms of bad-bossism and work our way down to bully hell.

The micromanager: ask questions and more questions

Micromanagers and their close cousins, perfectionists, can drive you crazy. Even if well meaning, they seem impelled to oversee every step of a task and may demand that it be done over and over again. This is not only unpleasant. It also undermines a subordinate's sense of engagement and makes it hard to move forward in any meaningful way.

One strategy for alleviating the micromanager impact is to ask direct questions—far more than you need to carry out the assignment if left to your own judgment. Inviting them to tell you exactly what they want makes them feel in control and undercuts their opportunities to criticize. Attending to their fixation on detail beforehand, rather than ceaselessly trying to figure out how to please them, can help them feel understood and builds trust. Andrea, who took a job managing the practical side of life for a wealthy couple who operate their own business, used this strategy.

The job, which involves tasks from managing both partners' appointments to shopping for the household and coordinating their personal and work lives, was a much-needed opportunity for Andrea at this point in her career, but the first month drove her crazy.

"No matter how hard I worked I couldn't make Karen happy," she says. "I did everything she asked, meticulously. But she always found more I should have done. One day I worked ten hours to do everything on her list and expected a thank you—instead she said, 'OK, but next time do it *this* way.' I was falling short on all the marks and worn to a frazzle. The odd thing was they trusted me with handling money but didn't trust me to make even small decisions on what to buy and where to buy it from."

Unwilling to continue this way, Andrea saw that if she couldn't manage Karen, she'd have to quit. So she decided to employ the many-questions technique.

"Every day I ask a ton of them. Not just what do you want done, but how do you want it done? What do you want to see out of this? What's most important to get done first? Karen is happy to tell me, and I write it down. This gives me a structure, which I appreciate, and Karen's criticism started to lighten up." Andrea also began carefully observing what Karen did herself and how. For example, she noticed that her boss redid parts of her work, such as how appointments were recorded. She asked questions about that as well, and when Karen told her specifically what she preferred, Andrea changed her approach to match.

Andrea accidentally came up with a second strategy. Given all the criticism, she'd been afraid to ask her employers how she was doing. But after two months, in frustration, she requested that input. To her surprise, both expressed strong satisfaction with her performance. Even more surprising, they offered support for her future career hopes, which she had shared when applying for the job, and offered useful contacts.

The "question" strategy can be borrowed for many types of very demanding people. Try to keep in mind that in many instances, unrealistic expectations and micromanagement reflect a supervisor's own insecurities or personal issues, more strongly than her perceptions of you. A micromanager may in fact approve of the job you're doing—at least, relatively speaking: perfectionists usually have long histories of employing workers short-term. If, however, asking for input just elicits more criticism, take the opportunity to ask more questions toward understanding her viewpoint. Can you depersonalize the relationship by reframing it as a learning opportunity?

Like Andrea, you may find over time that your directness and questioning builds more trust, which improves the relationships to at least some degree. However, don't expect to "cure" a micromanager. Use good self-management strategies to help you live with such a situation more easily when it's necessary.

The boss who has no time for you: align with primary needs

A complaint we hear surprisingly often is at the other end of the spectrum from micromanagement: undersupervision. How do you deal with a boss who gives you too little attention and fails to provide enough guidance?

The most promising way is to closely assess *his* challenges. If you understand how he perceives his goals, where his stresses are coming from, and in some cases his weaknesses, you can position yourself as a supportive ally and may gain his support in return. Therefore, use your chapter 5 profile-painting techniques and look at the company culture (chapter 11). Notice what makes him uneasy and pinpoint the department's problems. Then figure out how to act on your knowledge and communicate your value inside his own framework.

Emily was faced with an impatient manager who resisted giving her any time and then blamed her for falling short. She'd been thrilled to obtain a social media management job in a multinational brokerage firm but knew it was a distinct leap with a steep learning curve. She had never worked for a large organization, was unfamiliar with company-specific policies, and needed to take on unfamiliar work. This included coordinating in-house resources and outside vendors. Things went well for a few months, and she was beginning to find her feet. Then her supportive supervisor was promoted out and Charlie, a few years younger than Emily, was transferred in to fill the role.

The change was difficult for Emily: "My job requires that I know what's happening so I can keep complicated projects together and make sure everyone is staying on track. But Charlie doesn't share information.

He rarely has time for me, and when I do talk to him, he's distracted, takes phone calls, and ends up cutting me short. Then when things go wrong—all sorts of loose ends and tangles—he blames me, sometimes in front of other people! My coworkers get the message, and the vendors have also learned not to respect me. I'm everyone's scapegoat."

Emily wondered if there was a way to turn the situation around. Our advice: start with a reality check. What did she know about this new supervisor? What might be his problems and pressures? Could she identify any motivation for his behavior, which would help her decide what to do? Emily's best interpretation was that Charlie had, like her, made an upward leap and found himself with an unexpectedly challenging job. He appeared to be well liked but she deduced that an engaging personality had helped him succeed in earlier roles. The new job demanded much more. He may have been disappointed to find that as his chief assistant, Emily was still in her own learning curve and not ready to bear more of the burden.

Under Charlie's erratic direction and with Emily's fading authority, the department began falling behind on major projects. Charlie's own supervisors noticed this, no doubt spurring his need to blame her. Since Charlie had come to the job with a ten-year track record in the company and she'd been there only four months, Emily knew she didn't have the credibility to appeal over Charlie's head.

The question for Emily: Does Charlie know what you do and its value to him? Emily said no, he hadn't taken the time to fully understand her role and what she could accomplish. Might Charlie be threatened by her apparent loyalty to her former boss? That was possible. Did she think Charlie was trying to force her out so he could replace her? Emily didn't know. She might simply be the most convenient scapegoat, or he disliked her personally, or he was so immersed in his own transition problems that he wasn't thinking about how his actions affected the department. Probably all of the above.

It's often necessary to take the initiative without knowing the "why" of someone else's behavior. Reasons might emerge as events unfold, but they may not matter a lot. Here is what we suggested to Emily.

First, she should protect herself as much as possible in written form: take meeting notes, write careful e-mails confirming decisions and requests for input, keep in-house people and the vendors on track with written deadline reminders, and copy in all relevant people. Emily should also do her best to build alliances with coworkers and people in other departments with whom she interacts.

And she should take a carefully planned action—make an appointment with Charlie and initiate a conversation in a pattern like this:

1. Thank you for taking the time to talk with me briefly last week. I want to follow up. (This opening puts the last aborted meeting in a good light.)
2. I appreciate the sense of humor you bring to the office; it helps us all lighten up under our times of stress. (A sincere compliment.)
3. I have a plan to address some of the tangles we're having right now by putting a system of checkpoints in place. (A big-picture enticement, no details.)
4. To get this working, I need timely and full information about . . . (a list of what she needs to achieve results that will benefit her boss).
5. I also need your support for working with the vendor in a different way. (A nudge toward giving her the credibility to perform on his behalf.)
6. I'll always keep you fully in the loop and we can lay out the points of concern and decision-making together. (An assurance that he stays in control insofar as he wants to.)
7. And by the way, if at any time you are disappointed with my work, I welcome constructive criticism, so please bring it straight to me. (A soft reference to the blaming syndrome.)

This approach can be adapted to a range of situations where the supervisor doesn't give you enough time or blames you for his own shortcomings. Here, Emily positions herself to become valuable to Charlie by helping to solve the department's major problem, which appeals straight to his self-interest. Since she's still new to the job, she must center on potential, rather than proven, value. Instead of complaining, she communicates exactly what she needs to be successful in context of benefit to him. And she indirectly puts him on notice that she's aware of the scapegoating and he needs to do some repair work for her to be effective.

If you plan to engage in a conversation like Emily's, remember that your tone is critical. It must be cool, upbeat, positive but low-key. Try to bring solutions—not more problems—thereby creating a chance to shift the boss's perception. Emily aimed to show Charlie that she was a can-do person, or at least, someone worth trying out. Taking account of his short attention span in her presence, she painted the picture quickly and avoided a descent into detail. Note that if Emily gains even a partial acknowledgment from Charlie, she can use it to strengthen her authority.

In this instance the jury is still out, but Emily is still on the job. Every month she remains at the company puts her in a better position to apply elsewhere with a helpful new resume credit. Rather than feeling undermined, she is also developing more confidence. Analyzing a hard-to-win situation gives her better perspective on it, and she knows she's taken the initiative to improve the relationship and keep her own self-respect.

The mean-minded boss: treat him as if he were a better person

While it's true that we all make mistakes, we tend to make them more often when dealing with people who seem always to be on the watch for them. Another proof that we tend to meet expectations! You can use this powerful principle in reverse: set positive expectations for someone who is mistreating you, or calling you to account in a demeaning manner, in such a way that she must meet them. The heart of this technique: *when you feel at a disadvantage with someone and can't identify a better side to call forth, speak to her as if she's the person you wish she were.*

This approach can work wonders in a wide range of situations when a difficult person confronts you. Communicate that you expect someone to treat you well or with generosity, and they rise to that expectation more often than you may think. This is not really at odds with common sense. When you act like you expect to feel berated, you may unconsciously egg on a bad-tempered person and bring out his bad side. Sometimes adopting a positive demeanor in itself can shift the atmosphere. If you can talk to an unsympathetic person as if he were someone you like, or expect good things from, you can improve the atmosphere still more.

We all like to think well of ourselves. We're naturally inclined to go along with being addressed as good, or thoughtful, or ethical, and are likely to act more in line with such qualities when another person attributes them to us. Investing trust in someone else is much more likely to bring out trustworthiness. Expecting to be treated well makes it more likely that you will be. Here's an example where the technique worked well.

Jane, chief of business services for a large nonprofit, found herself working for a CEO of classic retro leadership style—she found him dictatorial, judgmental, easily displeased, chilly, and egotistic. He heard only his own opinion and rarely changed his mind. Her job required her to work with him closely, so she felt her days were like walking on eggshells.

Part of her role was attending board meetings. At one session, another department head presented a new initiative that Jane hadn't been told about. Listening, she grew increasingly upset at being left out of the loop. At the end, a board member asked for the project numbers so they could evaluate the investment. The CEO answered, "Yes, of course. Jane is working on that right now, and we'll share it with you shortly."

But Jane had worked herself into a silent frenzy, knowing that the presenter had deliberately bypassed her because they'd had disagreements. In the moment's heat, she totally forgot herself and said, "No, actually I'm not working on that. I'm afraid no one thought about how important it was for us to analyze the idea financially."

She had contradicted her boss in front of his own superiors, the board to which he reported, and in effect accused him of lying. After the meeting, the CEO told Jane frigidly that he was going on vacation immediately and would talk to her the moment he returned.

In the painful weeks that followed, Jane pondered how to handle the unappealing conversation. She didn't think the affronted CEO would fire her, but a deep humiliation loomed. She could try to explain why she'd been angry—but this would make her look incompetent. She might grovel or cry—but this would damage her own self-respect and permanently disadvantage her with this unforgiving person.

She consulted Susan on how to mollify, or neutralize, her boss's anger. Susan led Jane through the reality check: Why do you think your perceptions are valid? Could you be biased? Are you over-ascribing negative qualities? Overlooking good ones? Does the person not have a better side?

Jane acknowledged that the CEO had a charming side that he exhibited with a select few, and that he was quite intelligent. She could see no other saving graces. Susan's ultimate advice: "If you can't find a person's good side or truly believe he doesn't have one, talk to him as if he were the person you wish he were."

Jane worked at translating the strategy to her case. When the CEO returned, she presented herself, sat down, and preemptively began: "First of all, I want to thoroughly apologize for my thoughtless remark. I assure you nothing like this will ever happen again. However, I know you are too fair-minded and generous a person to hold it against me in the long run."

After a long pause the CEO blustered a bit but couldn't find much to say. He came up with a "punishment" that barred Jane from executive team meetings for a period of time. But the dreaded conversation ended up brief and nearly neutral. Here's why Jane succeeded.

First, she began with a full acknowledgment of her "crime," a sincere apology that was mandatory—she had in fact committed a real offense. Her comment violated the basic work commandment to help your boss succeed and look good. Her heartfelt apologetic opener disarmed an abusive lecture.

Next, describing the CEO to himself as "fair-minded and generous" presented him with a dilemma. He could either disagree—"Actually, I'm mean-minded and I like to humiliate stupid subordinates"—or accept the high-minded characterization. If he accepted it, acting in contradiction would be hard.

Jane gauged her audience well. The strategy depended on his intelligence and his ego. He decoded his dilemma instantly and was unwilling to admit to being a bad leader and vindictive person. In the end, Jane succeeded because she broke the boss's expectations. He likely expected a shame-faced, intimidated supplicant. Instead, he was faced with a cool, calm, professional person who took the initiative and owned her mistake. This inherently forced him to reconsider his own position.

Navigating a difficult scenario enabled Jane to feel more confident in her ability to manage herself and therefore control future situations. Her relationship with the CEO became viable, if not cordial, and in the end, she remained on the job longer than he did.

In applying the strategy to your own challenges, you need not necessarily say something close to Jane's words. *The magic comes from the difference you generate in your own behavior.* You can consciously switch your negative expectations to the positive side. For example, if you find your manager closed-minded to new ideas, think through how you would talk to a previous "ideal" boss about a problem or request, expecting a positive or at least open response. You would feel more confident and anticipate a good conversation, right? Might it work to approach your current boss in that spirit, also taking account of her own informational preferences, priorities, and personality?

The insecure or envious boss: recognize the pattern

When the ultimate cause of mistreatment by a supervisor emerges, personal insecurity is often the culprit. Insecure bosses often seem to begrudge their subordinates time or energy. They may be hard to please, set impossible standards, or even seem resentful of their most capable employees. Such people present a special challenge because we can be slow to understand the situation. When you perform in a way that reflects well on the boss, for example, why should she resent you? Why so much insecurity?

Some company cultures breed it from manager to manager on down the chain. Managers assuming a new role are especially apt to feel insecure. The job usually involves a leap in responsibility and demands new skills. There is also strong pressure to perform. A culture shift may be another factor if the person comes from another organization or department.

When the insecurity is situational, it can be at least partly addressed. You might reassure a new boss that you have her back with a statement such as "I just want you to know that I'm glad you're here and will support you one hundred percent, in any way I can." Follow through by educating the newcomer into the ways of your department, tactfully. Try "over-reporting": give this supervisor frequent updates on what you're doing, unasked. This may help her get acclimated and feel reassured that you are acting in her best interest.

If the boss is younger than you, or a first-time supervisor, demonstrate a scrupulous respect, while maintaining your own confident air. It may help to remind yourself that people need time to get used to one another. Keep your mind open; try not to compare the new person with the predecessor you loved working for; respect her learning curve.

But there are many insecure people who can't be "cured" so easily. Like some people we've all met in our personal lives, they need constant reassurance and put us on edge lest we displease them or otherwise trigger their insecurities.

One friend calls them "the soft bullies": they don't seem to be bad-natured people and may not lose their tempers often, but in worrying about their own positioning, they variously micromanage, interfere with work processes and relationships, rarely show appreciation, and provide undermining rather than constructive criticism. Frequently, these people don't take time to explain what they want and may even take pleasure in their subordinates' consequent failures.

To respond effectively to such managers, first recognize what you're dealing with. It helps to *think about what the person does rather than what he says.* Are you often left holding the bag—doing the job and not getting credit? Does he somehow manage to make you feel inadequate in front of other people? Do you "accidentally" get left out of the information loop or meetings? Can you identify anything in the relationship that could bring out his insecurities? Once you see the pattern, you can decide on your best response. That was the case with Jake, working as the number-two manager in the human resources department of a midsized firm.

Jake knew he was doing a good job and that Jenny, the department head, depended on his organizational and people skills to keep things humming. She welcomed his ideas about how to improve services and implemented them. Jenny was pleasant, soft-spoken, a "nice" person. But after about six months, Jake realized that his job was harder than necessary. He explained, "Somehow I wasn't included in some of the meetings, and I realized this was persistent. It made me seem unprepared at the meetings I did go to, and always scrambling for information. I never got acknowledgment for the ideas that made Jenny look good. She kept me away from senior executives and somehow I was always needed when a professional association meeting was being held. It dawned on me that I was getting more and more responsibility but no opportunities to grow."

Jake decided to take a direct tack and found an opportunity for a serious conversation. He made three points: "I can do my job better if I have access to the meetings and information. I'd feel more encouraged if the increasing amount of work I'm doing was appreciated. I'm happy to have earned the department some nice recognition with the last project, but a thank you would have meant a lot."

Jenny listened and thanked him for the "frank input." The result wasn't quite what he'd expected: "The next day she presented me with a gift card to Starbucks! Which was so way off the mark, I took it as a signal to find another spot in the organization or move on out." Jake, with versatile skills, was able to transfer into a management role in another department within a few months.

Not every encounter succeeds in accomplishing what you hoped for. But evaluating the signals can be just as useful. If you learn that the boss is unwilling to give you what you want now or in the reasonable future, you need to consider the importance of your goal and calculate your leverage. If you state your need more strongly, or issue an ultimatum, are you prepared to live with the results or leave if you're denied?

In strategizing, Jake didn't fully take account of how Jenny might view him. He assumed she knew he was capable, reliable, and creative, based on the amount of responsibility she gave him. So where was she coming from to misinterpret what he asked for and withhold appreciation of his value? Why would Jenny act against her own self-interest? Asked to profile his forty-eight-year-old boss, Jake, fifteen years her junior, perceived her as successful in her career with a secure position in the company. As far as he knew, she enjoyed a good personal life.

An outside view suggests under-the-surface tensions. Though generally competent, Jenny nevertheless showed classic symptoms of insecurity. In subtly undermining her own best support she undermined herself, but her resentment of a subordinate's skills overshadowed her rationality.

Talented people of any age may provoke envious feelings among those they report to, or among some peers, exactly because they are perceived as superior. But it's surprising how many young people don't recognize that some older people are geared to resent them. What the young person interprets as general meanness or grumpiness or impatience may be rooted in envy.

UNDERSTANDING AND HANDLING GENERATION TENSIONS

If you're relatively young, try a role reversal with a supervisor. You may be surprised to glimpse that someone a generation or two older might see you as automatically more attractive or fortunate. You have your whole promising future ahead of you, while she may only envision a future much like the present. She may be the boss, but you're in the same place she is right now and though you are currently a subordinate, you may move far ahead to a better place in the long run. If she feels stuck where she is, she may envy your ability to move on more easily, as well as your presumed lack of responsibility.

Even people new to the workplace may come with a more confident demeanor than many Baby Boomers recall having at their age because they were far less nurtured and encouraged while growing up. Your life may feel unsettled and uncertain to you, but perhaps in an older person's eyes, you enjoy an enviable social life, great freedom, and a limitless future. Watching a promising young person reminds some older people of their own mistakes and life disappointments.

So in their eyes they hold the power . . . but you hold the life cards. How to deflect this?

How to defang older-boss envy

1. Frame older supervisors to yourself as people to learn from, and treat them that way. They know more about life and their insights are valuable.

2. Bring out their nurturing qualities by asking, judiciously, for mentoring and explanations.

3. Look for legitimate opportunities to make them feel valued: "That was a great presentation," "I appreciated how you fielded that tough question."

4. Ask for company culture advice: "What do you think is the best way to present a new idea at the next meeting?"

5. Take opportunities to credit them when they support you: "Mike gave me the missing piece on this idea."

6. Find reasons to see them as interesting and follow up in conversation (e.g., remark on artwork in their offices, a photo of them playing a sport, a child's drawing, a souvenir baseball, or other signs of individual personality).

7. Avoid a condescending attitude toward any shortcoming in technology know-how; perhaps offer tech support in a low-key way in exchange for some mentoring.

8. Ask about their vacation, a child's graduation, the family Christmas.

9. Offer to buy them a cup of coffee and talk about something they can share that will benefit you, like company history or systems and processes.

10. Ask the favorite question good salesmen use to draw someone out: "How did you get here?" (In other words, "What was your path to this lofty level of achievement?")

We don't mean that if you are relatively young, it's necessary to assume that every older person envies you. But few people's lives are exactly as they would wish, and the feeling of if-I-had-to-live-my-life-over-again is not rare. It's also true that most older people are ready to like younger ones and feel empathy for those close to their children's age. Regardless, the suggestions on the list are productive when your boss is older, and they are also useful when you encounter any negative emotion from your superiors. If you are the junior person, they are basically good manners. You genuinely can learn a lot from higher-ups and older peers. Why waste the opportunity to learn and build better relationships in the process?

How to interact with a younger boss

More and more often in today's workplace, you may find yourself reporting to a supervisor younger than yourself. This may seem natural if you are a specialist who doesn't expect to perform managerial functions, but at other times it may feel like someone less qualified was hired or promoted over your head. The idea of injecting "new blood" is attractive to many executives because they assume new thinking comes with it.

Many organizations also feel a need to reach young audiences through members of their own cohort, which is perfectly reasonable. And especially in technologically oriented companies and departments, younger people's "native" adeptness is an asset.

If you report to a younger person, be supercareful to show deference. Avoid projecting a condescending air. As always, it is your role to supplement your supervisor's skills and savvy and support the common cause. Look for the good. A young manager may lack the experience you might expect, or possess yourself, but may well bring other skills that are equally or more important. Be open to any new ideas that materialize.

Resist seeing the age differential as a negative reflection on yourself—it's an experience we'll all have sooner or later. Regard the situation as sharing a mutual learning curve in which you can each grow. It's especially beneficial to communicate a supportive attitude at the very beginning. To minimize possible surprises with the young manager's communication and decision-making style, consider the generational differences spelled out in chapter 5.

Also take the trouble to see inside his or her reality with *Genie*'s tools—role reversal and visualization are helpful. Even though you are senior in years but junior on the hierarchy, you can choose to think of yourself as a mentor, but with an extremely tactful voice. Never lecture on how things have been or should be done: be an available, encouraging presence and understand that your young manager needs to sense this spirit, even though he or she may appear to be very confident.

THE INCOMPETENT BOSS: STAND BACK

We are the first to tell you, give people a chance. If you have a new boss, remember that assuming a new role disconcerts most people and they may be less tactful with staff members than they could be. You can start off your relationship with him on a strong note by letting him know, tactfully, that he has your full support. If you are the new person on the team, give yourself time to know and adapt to the boss's style, expectations, and strengths. Don't rush to judgment.

But sometimes, despite your best effort, you may come to the conclusion that the problem in your relationship with your boss comes down to his incompetence. He might make shortsighted decisions, reject advice, or even lack the skills necessary to do the job well or understand your work. In such cases, assess your options. Every situation is different, but standing back is often a good one. Refrain from protecting the incompetent boss and he will usually expose himself sooner or later. If this approach doesn't work, do you want to live within the unsatisfying pattern indefinitely? Your decisions should take account of the job's importance to you, availability of other opportunities, whether you can carve out your own niche of responsibility, and so on.

Our acquaintance Laura was once faced with such a boss. Marta was senior to Laura in length of time with their employer but had previously worked elsewhere in the nonprofit organization. She'd been assigned to the public relations department only a few months before Laura was hired. While Laura came to the role as an experienced specialist, the type of work was new to Marta. Her performance was scattered and ineffective. She was not comfortable with teamwork and rarely consulted with Laura. Instead of stepping back to learn about the department's mission and its work, Marta competed with Laura and routinely took credit for her successes.

Marta was her supervisor, so for some months, Laura deferred to her. She supported projects she didn't agree with; reinterpreted Marta's initiatives in ways that made more sense and promised better results; and when possible, quietly reviewed and edited her communications to other staff members as well as the larger community the department was charged to reach. She didn't protest Marta's consistent process of appropriating every success. But feeling very unhappy with how her job had turned out, she took stock of her options. She was not in the senior position and could not push back directly. So she decided to do . . . nothing.

She explained, "I realized that if I stood back, Marta's ineptness would speak for itself. So I stopped protecting her. I stopped doing all the extra work which she hadn't even asked me to do and didn't appreciate. I let her e-mails and letters and reports go out just as she'd written them. I helped her on projects exactly insofar as she asked me to."

It didn't take long for the program director to notice Marta's small but numerous missteps and put himself on alert to monitor the department's output. Then Marta, in his presence, flubbed a presentation to a major donor. He quickly concluded that the errors and misjudgment were hers. She was soon transferred to another department with limited decision-making opportunities.

WORKPLACE BULLYING: KNOW THE FACTS AND IMPACT

Know right off that if you are bullied by your boss, or have been in the past, you are far from alone. The statistics are depressing: 27 percent of Americans have suffered persistent abusive conduct at work—a basic definition of bullying—and another 21 percent have witnessed it. That's more than 65 million people! And watching others being bullied takes an emotional toll that is similar to that suffered by the targets.

These figures come from the Workplace Bullying Institute of America, which builds public awareness of the problem, advocates for national laws against bullying, and sponsors extensive studies every few years. They also research bully identity:

- In 69 percent of cases, they are men. They target women 57 percent of the time.
- In 31 percent of cases, bullies are female. They target other females 68 percent of the time.
- In 56 percent of cases, bullies occupy the boss's seat.

Rationally, you might expect that the cost of workplace bullying from employers' viewpoint is so high that no organization would tolerate it. Bullying produces high turnover and absenteeism, poor morale, and a disengaged workforce. But the research indicates that only 28 percent of employers acknowledge, condemn, or seek to eliminate bullying. Others even deny its existence, defend it as routine, or even claim it's necessary for a competitive organization.

On-the-ground experience confirms this indifference. Recently, talking with a man who had held a high position in a federal agency, one of us asked whether he'd had any experience with bullies under his tenure. "Yes," he said immediately. "There was someone I remember well, a supervisor who transferred in from another branch where they evidently have a different approach to managing people. I didn't like it."

"What did you do?"

"Well, I took him under my wing and tried several times to help him tone down his approach, but it didn't seem to do any good, so after a while I stopped trying." What was the bully's impact on other members of the department? The man considered for a moment, then shrugged. He had never thought about it.

Bypassing all the complexities associated with bullying, the problem continues because perpetrators are not held accountable. Maybe they're doing "the rest" of their job well and the numbers look good, or higher-ups simply accept that this is a person's "style." An important research finding characterizes *who* gets bullied. Typical victims are not people who provoke high-handed treatment, but rather, people described by others as talented, kind, helpful, cooperative, altruistic, agreeable, and considerate. A substantial number of abused people, however, perceive themselves as vulnerable—in effect, unable to defend themselves. "Niceness" can attract this kind of mistreatment and not counter it, unfortunately.

The maneuverable bully: take charge of your self-respect

When victimized by a bully, we are often extraordinarily slow to recognize the experience. It feels unique to our own circumstances. This prevents us from handling interactions more effectively, accessing possible help, or charting a way out. We feel like we're being subjected to one unhappy surprise after another as the bully dreams them up. We first blame ourselves—a tendency that may be more common to women. Once we recognize the symptoms, we can start to remove ourselves emotionally and consider our options.

Therefore, assess the person who's giving you a hard time thoroughly. Is he a true bully, or just someone who is at times grumpy, stubborn, short-tempered, abrasive, rude, or mean, based on temperament or situation? The distinction is important because different sets of responses are indicated. You can manage someone who isn't always nice with the various techniques demonstrated in *Genie* and even establish yourself as a trusted member of his circle, though you probably can't change him very much. But when someone's goal for all practical purposes is to make you miserable, these techniques don't generally apply. However, one good *Genie* technique described in chapter 4, role-playing a super-confident person, can work very well. Here's how one person used it to improve his own ability to handle a bully.

Michael, a soft-spoken man in his late thirties, was employed as a bookkeeper in a large manufacturing company. He was very competent, worked hard, and was well liked. But a promotion brought him to a new department and new supervisor, Ned.

Ned soon issued a steady flow of criticism. When Michael asked questions relating to his new role, Ned answered with disparaging comments. He directed Michael to do parts of his work over and over again and rarely found it acceptable. Michael's attempts to hold a reasonable conversation with his boss were dismissed arbitrarily. Michael tried to tell himself it was just because he was new to the department and didn't yet know Ned's ways. But over time the ill treatment worsened.

He consulted Susan. Hearing about Ned's behavior, she understood that he was not someone who responded to reasonable requests, or kind words, especially from someone who worked under him. Ned was a bully. And he sounded like a bully who responded only to strong authority and people who didn't reveal intimidation. Michael, with his quiet competence and "niceness," might particularly draw such a person's ire.

Michael needed direct experience with feeling his own power. Susan suggested a special kind of role reversal.

Michael was asked to think of someone in his life he looked up to, a strong no-nonsense person. He quickly came up with a teacher from his first year of high school. When Mr. Andrews walked into the math classroom, everyone immediately quieted down and began paying attention. This teacher projected a sense of calm and self-assurance. With no apparent effort, and never raising his voice, he was able to manage a rambunctious class and lead his students to learn a subject uncongenial to many.

Michael was able to bring up an image of Mr. Andrews standing in front of his class. He took careful note of his posture, the calm and self-assured expression on his face, the no-nonsense look in his eyes, the confident way he held his shoulders, the accompanying easy smile. With that picture clearly in mind, Michael visualized himself reversing roles with Mr. Andrews—standing tall and proud, in that same blue suit, the same horn-rimmed glasses, wearing the same look of confidence on his face, the same proud shoulders, the air of quiet expectation.

Michael followed the experience through and assuming the same body posture and expression as Mr. Andrews, looked at the class through the teacher's eyes. He felt the firmness of his neck and shoulders, the easy pattern of his breathing, the steadiness of his gaze. He gave himself this message: "I am now standing in front of this unruly class, and everyone knows I am the boss. Most important, *I* know I am the boss. I expect to be respected!"

Michael was encouraged to walk around the room as Mr. Andrews, glance down at the students, feel the confidence in his body, and repeat the words. He also visualized leaving the classroom and walking down the corridor with the full experience of "being" Mr. Andrews and then returning to the room, calm and confident.

Michael then began connecting this experience to work by visualizing his next encounter with Ned. The goal was to bring his sense of power to that interaction by facing the boss directly with that same feeling of confidence in his breathing, the way he held his head, the sense of becoming the man he knows himself to be. He would communicate this without words.

Michael continued to practice visualizing conversations with Ned in this way. Gradually, the feeling of self-respect, and confidence in his ability to handle the exchanges, became more natural. He was able to take that sense to work with him. It enabled him to adopt a more positive demeanor instead of a self-effacing one. He prepared himself for conversations holding his "Mr. Andrews self" firmly in place. He found that there was often little difference in what he said, but his manner of delivery changed. Michael developed a different sense of who he was and how to communicate it, and Ned began responding to him more neutrally, if not quite respectfully. This reinforced Michael's reenergized sense of self. The relationship never became a good one, but his supervisor began turning his combative personality in other directions.

The relentless bully: coping options

Unfortunately, many bullies can't be managed by adapting your own behavior or responses. It's usually impossible to deflect them from their apparent mission—to make your life miserable by implementing an unceasing pattern of words and actions to humiliate, isolate, and undermine you. While you are unlikely to know what shaped a personality that enjoys this process, *recognize that in many cases, the bullying is not only an expression of personality—it may have a strategic purpose.* The tormentor may have a goal like forcing his target to resign or creating a graphic example of what can happen to anyone who displeases him. If you know or sense that such a rationale is a partial motivation, you are unlikely to shift his attention away from you.

A relentless bully aims to undermine your confidence and ability to do your job well. The emotional impact of workplace bullying is not unlike that produced by domestic abuse: the targeted person feels that if only he does things "right" and stops provoking his tormentor, all will be tolerable. In fact, expect such situations to escalate. Accept that the work goals you want to pursue don't align with the bully's goals, and achieving your own goals is no longer possible. It's unlikely that you can perform so well that a relentless bully will stop the persecution. She'll erect new obstacles.

We're explaining this in some depth because the best way to help yourself emotionally is to end the worry about what you're doing wrong and stop twisting yourself into knots of acquiescence. While it's quite possible that the bully has intuited vulnerabilities in you—like pride in your own performance—they may relate more to your good qualities and values than any faults in your work or personality. This was the case with Lorna, an urban planner in her forties.

Lorna was happily engaged in a civil service job in a suburban government planning office. In eleven years, her good performance paved the way to advancement and she became director of the five-person department, reporting directly to the mayor. Then the political winds shifted and a new mayor took office.

Her new boss, Jerry, called her in for an explain-your-value conversation. He listened with apparent neutrality to her program summary and the atmosphere seemed fairly relaxed. But he posed one ominous rhetorical question: "So that's what your department does for our investment of a million dollars per year?"

Lorna's account: "A few weeks later, Jerry called me into his office, one-on-one this time. He said really abruptly, 'What's your plan for the year?' I told him we have a number of plans that would move a big batch of ongoing projects forward, and I'd be happy to talk about my new ideas—speeding up our project review process, working more closely with the community. But, I said, of course I felt an overall new plan must support his goals and priorities, and looked forward to his sharing that with me.

"He exploded. 'What! You're the planning director and you're waiting for *me* before you have a plan? You're running an important department without a plan? You want me to do your work for you?' I was speechless! I thought my view was what a new top person would want. Was I wrong? Anyway, how could I oppose a brand-new boss, and tell him what he said didn't make sense. He told me, 'Come back when you have a plan.'"

Lorna pulled out all stops to create the most comprehensive plan she could—a formal integrated fifteen-page document with ambitious goals, specific tactics, and full logistical backup. The day after she delivered it, the plan was back on her desk with a scrawled note: "This isn't what I call a plan!"

Without direction, Lorna tried again, but floundered. Jerry dismissed every hard-wrought plan she gave him. He spoke to her scornfully at executive team meetings. While arbitrary with all department heads, he reserved his real venom for Lorna, belittling her contributions and her work. Her colleagues sat by trying to keep a low profile and rarely disagreed with anything their new leader said. One or two even took the opportunity to blame her for shared projects that hadn't gone well. Jerry found ways to embarrass her in front of the town board several times. And then he placed a summer intern in her office without consulting her. It was his daughter.

This situation made Lorna feel completely alone and disoriented. She recalls, "I've always been known for outstanding work! I had all kinds of awards and fantastic reviews every year. I kept trying to please him. I was so nervous all the time I started to make mistakes. There was no one to talk to; they were all hustling to reestablish their own positions. It took me five months to understand there was no way to ever make the relationship better or please Jerry. He didn't want me to. He wanted me to leave." As a town worker, Lorna was legally protected from dismissal without cause, so Jerry was deliberately forcing her to resign. This would cost Lorna a job she had loved and felt invested in, and probably damage her future career.

"But driving to work every day, half the time I'd have to pull over to the side of the road because I felt so panicky or just plain nauseous. Then I'd be late, more provocation. Once he called me in when I was ten minutes late and talked about me in third person to his deputy: 'Today she was late again. Why do you think she has such trouble being on time?'"

Through it all, Lorna believed that ultimately her good standing for all those years and familiarity with board members would "save" her. Surely as time passed, influential people would realize Jerry was ineffective and disliked by the whole staff. She tried to project a tough front and calm attitude. Then she got a tip from a colleague in HR: things were about to get really bad. "Finally, I found a lawyer. He negotiated terms of leaving for me. I didn't get much, but I signed the release documents they needed. I was out less than a week later."

Subsequently, Lorna searched out other people who'd had similar experiences and came to understand her own better. While her suffering was uniquely hers, she realized, the bullying pattern was all too typical. Recognizing the pattern sooner would have dashed the hope of keeping her job but saved her from the extended nightmare of humiliation and self-doubt. Recognizing your bully is a critical step to handling the situation the best way possible. Here are some strategies to help minimize the damage if you find yourself facing a Jerry.

Practical guidelines for handling a bullying boss

1. *Figure out the abuser's goals.* It is probably his nature to vent his own anger, frustration, and feelings of insecurity this way, and most bullies visibly relish the destruction they wreak. If in addition your bully wants to maneuver you into giving something up, or leaving your job, or particularly dislikes you or something you represent, you are unlikely to shift his direction.

2. *Don't count on help from colleagues.* According to the Workplace Bullying Institute, only in about 25 percent of the time do coworkers come to an abused person's defense. Most people are concerned about the risk of becoming targets themselves. Bullies are well aware of this effect and use it strategically. Cowed people don't disagree or raise opposition.

3. *Don't count on help from higher-ups.* They are less familiar with you and more familiar with the bully, with whom they have more contact. They see a different face during their interactions with your boss. By virtue of his higher position, in their perspective, he is more important to the organization's success and this trumps personal feelings. Also, bullies take care to poison the well. Lorna saw the board members turn against her but never found out what Jerry told them.

4. *Try the HR office for support, but don't be shocked if you get little help.* The people may listen sympathetically and may want to help, but supporting you actively may require them to buck company culture. They may report to the bully themselves. And many see their role as implementers for company leaders rather than employee protectors. If you do complain to HR, or any other formal entity, or engage a lawyer, be sure to document your experience. Record everything you can meticulously, including the bully's communications and your responses, plus your own notes on conversations and incidents.

5. *Avoid giving a bully ammunition that enables him to justify the persecution in other people's eyes.* Show up, do your work as best you can, meet deadlines. Resist attempts to provoke you into emotional displays that can look irrational to bystanders. Never put anything in writing that might hurt you if an impartial review is conducted. Be equally careful about people in whom you confide and what you say, even in your own office. We know bullies who plant surveillance equipment!

6. *Keep reminding yourself that the world is bigger than this experience and actively work on your future.* Reach out to your friends and supporters for perspective. Reaffirm your nonwork life commitments and their importance and build your professional connections outside the office. Maintain a big-picture view of who you are, where you've been, what you've accomplished, and where you want to be in future.

7. *Don't underestimate the emotional and physical impact of bullying.* Sustained ill-treatment can lead to chronic illnesses including cardiovascular and gastrointestinal problems, autoimmune disorders, neurological changes, chronic fatigue syndrome, diabetes, and more. Emotional harm includes anxiety, panic attacks, severe depression, and post-traumatic stress. Recovering from the experience of being bullied, with the attendant feelings of injustice, insecurity, and self-blame, is hard. If you've suffered a bullying boss (or coworker) in the past and remain affected by the experience, check out our "Ghostbusters" activity in chapter 12 for a recovery approach.

8. *Plan your exit strategy!* Figure out your next career step and how to get there. Balance your needs—financial, emotional, health—and make the wisest decision you can. Even if embarking on a new path is not immediately possible, thinking about it will help. If you can achieve a graceful departure at a time of your choosing, typically, everyone will treat you very nicely. In job interviews, it's usually best not to talk about your experience as a bully's target.

How did Lorna ultimately fare? After a few months of shocked disbelief at the state of her career, she threw herself into a whirlwind of professional activity, made contact with new collaborators, and broadened her horizons with classes in business management. In less than two years, she established a successful consultant practice in a related industry. The need to re-prove herself galvanized her to success. As always, living well is the best revenge (and the only one you're apt to get).

Should you speak up or shut up?

Michael approached his bullying boss by learning to stand up for himself. Would it have worked for Lorna? You need to evaluate the nature of your boss's bullying and know yourself: how well you can hold up to an extremely hostile exchange. Calculate your leverage: if you can't be fired outright, you have some options. The hard question is how much you can anticipate improving your situation by directly resisting a bully.

Lorna recalls that at one meeting, her nemesis began needling another department head, Bob. After a few minutes, Bob said in a calm but slightly annoyed tone, "Oh, Jerry. Stop it." And Jerry did. Lorna wonders if she would have fared better by speaking up, rather than concentrating on a poker face. It's hard to say. Lorna is a different person than Bob, a different gender, and the bully in her case had a goal—to replace her with "his own person."

There are times when facing a bully down can achieve a retreat. A friend, Ginny, was hired as a personal assistant to a prominent lawyer working on a big case. The first day on the job she watched him humiliate another lawyer to the point of tears. "I went in and said, 'If you ever speak to *me* like that, I'm out the door. Get it?'

"'Oh my goodness,' the lawyer said. 'Someone intelligent. Can I take you to lunch?'"

Ginny concluded, "I learned that the minute you see it, speak up. You show you are someone who will not suffer the behavior." Some people, like Ginny's employer, are "incremental bullies," who prod people as a way to vent their ill temper or evaluate the person based on their response. When they elicit a defensive posture, they'll continue the habit and may escalate it. You may be able to face this kind of bully down, but always consider your basic need to remain healthy against the importance of staying on the job.

Nonetheless, you may want to speak up. Some ex-targets later regret not confronting their bullying bosses or coworkers. It probably would not have changed the result, and it might even have sped up the finale. But knowing you responded to the treatment head-on can make it much easier to regain self-respect and confidence. It can be hard to escape the feeling that you let someone get away with unjust, inhumane behavior that damaged you.

Perhaps over time, current efforts to stop playground bullying will produce fewer workplace bullies. Meanwhile, here's one more option: check out the Workplace Bullying Institute and support its efforts to enact laws that make bullying at work illegal.

INTO ACTION

1. *Define your good boss.* Look at the list of good-boss attributes at the beginning of chapter 7. Pick out the three qualities most relevant to what you would love to bring out in your current boss. Create a plan to do this, drawing on the various strategies presented in the book.

2. *Write to the "bad" boss.* Draft a detailed letter to the boss who makes you unhappy, expressing what doesn't work for you in his management style, way of communicating, how he critiques your work, etc. *Don't send it!* This is a tool for analysis, to help you sharpen the reasons for your gripes.

3. *Review the letter you wrote.* Do you see any possibilities for helping your supervisor come closer to being the person you want or giving you what you need?

4. *Try your own meeting of minds.* Review the talk-to-your-selves ideas in chapter 4.

5. *Bring to mind a present or past way in which a supervisor disappoints you or leaves you feeling wounded.* Think about how different parts of you can react to the experience. There may be a wounded part, a part that doubts the value of what you asked for or suggested, an angry part, and so on. Try to find a part that feels empathy for the boss and might suggest reasons for the treatment you didn't like. Find a part of yourself that looks more analytically at the big picture and the longer range, and suggests ways you can succeed in your goal with a different approach. Another self might frame the interaction as a learning opportu-

nity. After finding as many parts of yourself as you can, visualize a conversation among them. See what balanced view you can emerge with. Then consider if this experience suggests a possible way to move forward in your current situation or a process to handle future ones.

Chapter 9

MANAGING LATERALLY: COWORKERS AND COLLEAGUES

The coworker who noticeably covets your job, award, or skill . . .

The mean-spirited office mate who constantly snaps at you . . .

The underminer who looks for chances to turn others against you . . .

The teammate who sticks you with the work and then grabs the credit . . .

Such people can make your work life miserable. In fact, they comprise the second most common reason that workers leave their jobs, right on the heels of bad bosses. In some ways, it's easier to deal with annoying peers because you're not challenging superior power. On the other hand, you're challenged to influence people on your own level, or higher, without authority.

When bad behavior is more than occasional, it suggests a deeper problem: the supervisor, for whatever reason, may not hold people accountable. She may not value a congenial environment or may feel that employees should work out their problems on their own. It's also possible that the mean-spirited person shows a different side to superiors. Whatever the story, take account of the fact that the difficult person is for some reason tolerated by the person in charge and the company. This makes it hard to address your issues with toxic people. The best option, as with a bully, is to remove yourself from the person's vicinity as best you can.

But the good news is that many negative coworker situations result not because of hostile personalities, but from misunderstandings, territorial issues, competitive circumstances, and mistakes. This gives you the opportunity to take the initiative and change patterns of behavior that are damaging or simply uncomfortable. So start by assessing the nature of the problem, the causes of friction, and your own possible contribution to both.

PERFORM A REALITY CHECK

Do other people have a similar problem with the person? If not, or if your reaction is much stronger, examine your own style of relating. You may bear at least some of the responsibility for a negative relationship, and once you acknowledge this, you can probably come up with ways to improve it.

To assess your motivation as well as the nature of the situation, ask yourself:

- How important is this person to my work life?
- Do this person's attitude and actions really affect my work? My long-term plans?
- Can I distance myself to be less affected by this individual?
- Is my reaction more extreme than it should be?
- Might one of my personal patterns be triggered?

Once you begin distancing yourself from the emotional overlay the problem person generates, you can develop a more accurate awareness of how much she really matters in the scheme of things. Then you can assess your options. If you can reduce contact with the source of irritation without meaningful consequence, why not do so? If that isn't possible, the challenge is to abstract yourself emotionally and remind yourself often of the larger perspective. Appealing to higher authority is generally a last resort, but at times it's necessary. But before taking any definitive action, put some energy into understanding the individual.

Try a little empathy

Consider the other person, moving past labels like "meanie" or "credit thief" or "grump" to understand more impartially where the bad spirit comes from. Many of the strategies covered in earlier chapters, such as those for understanding your supervisor, are equally productive when applied to your coworkers. As with bosses, distinguish between a chronically sour or angry person and those who occasionally throw a tantrum or vent their ill humor. Practicing some empathy and extending the benefit of the doubt to someone cost nothing. We're not suggesting that if you discover your difficult coworker is having health problems, or a hard time at home, or leads a lonely personal life, you can make up for whatever he feels is amiss. But it's a ton easier to rein in your auto-response patterns and not take it personally when you have this kind of awareness. And a sympathetic inquiry, as opposed to a gruff dismissal, can help someone feel a bit better, and perhaps, in turn, act better.

It's much harder or even impossible to mitigate the sour spirit or relentless sniper who seems to draw from an endless reservoir of ill will. Still, it's useful to remember that angry people are usually unhappy. Reminding yourself that "it's not about me" gives you ways to respond less emotionally.

Abstract yourself and review the big picture

Abstracting yourself also enables you to see more clearly how your responses or personal patterns might contribute to problems or even create new ones. This was the case with Terri, a twenty-five-year-old architect in her first career job. Although she was succeeding professionally, she became emotionally trapped in her strong dislike of Alicia, a peer holding a parallel position. "I get everything I have by working really hard," Terri complained. "But Alicia flirts and maneuvers her way into the best assignments and then gets other people to do the work. She's done this to me on a few projects and then she tries to steal the credit. I'm the kind of person that won't stand for that!"

An escalating anger at Alicia led Terri to an uncontrolled outburst that was witnessed by other coworkers as well as an executive. Justified as she felt, Terri worried that the next explosion—which she anticipated—would interfere with the promotion she wanted. So she sought advice. We led her through a reality check, and the essentials boiled down to:

- Does any success Alicia achieves really affect your own prospects or path? "No."
- Is it important to change your own behavior? "Yes. I see that losing my temper again could be very bad."
- Can you recognize your own hot buttons—what sets off your anger?

This last question took some thought, but Terri acknowledged that the situation echoed her previous experience with women in her cohort whom she perceived as threatening her own accomplishments. This recognition—coupled with admitting the importance of mastering herself—led Terri to begin monitoring her own emotional triggers. She reminded herself to pause before reacting when she felt provoked. Terri was also able to act more strategically: she took herself out of Alicia's sphere by looking for different project assignments and found a neutral reason to request a physical relocation. These seem like commonsense approaches, and they are—but when we let emotions cloud our perspective, we often fail to see them.

Analyze relationship patterns with a metaphor

It can be notably hard to see the obvious when our perceptions are mixed, people behave inconsistently, and our emotions superimpose themselves. A useful way to rise above this confusion is to view a relationship through the lens of metaphor. This strategy can crystallize your experience and tap into your intuition. It makes it possible to break through to better understand a relationship or even predict someone's future actions.

Many executives act on this idea by playing golf, or a team sport, with a job candidate or business rival. Their presumption is that an individual's behavior in the sports realm parallels how he will behave in business: Is he a good team player? Does he follow the rules or bend them, or even cheat? Does he grandstand? How does he react to setbacks, winning, losing? How does he interact with the other players between rounds? What does he talk about?

Visualizing a relationship as a dance is a good way to experiment with metaphor without venturing onto a playing field. It can illuminate the structure and pattern of your interaction with a coworker and also give you some insights about your own role in how things play out.

To set the mood, take some quiet time and relax. You can do a full visualization and watch yourself dress in your favorite dancing clothes, arrive at the venue, hear the music you choose, and find the partner you choose. Or you might just try going straight to the main event.

Imagine you are dancing with your problem coworker. Watch the dance:

1. Who is leading? Who follows? How is this decided?
2. Is there a struggle for control? How is it expressed on the dance floor, and what can you learn from this?
3. Is the movement smooth or uneven, or even jerky?
4. Do the two people move in unison, adapting to each other? Or do they move in opposition? Does one get in the other's way?

Watch for a pattern in how you and the other person interact as dancers, and think about whether that pattern in some way represents the pattern of your work relationship. Visualizing your experience in a physical form can illuminate what's happening and how you might act to change direction. Here's how one person, Anita, learned from this metaphor.

Anita and Marilyn were program supervisors in a small nonprofit for disabled children. The organization encouraged friendly competition and for the most part this made for a creative environment. But in Anita's eyes, Marilyn began to increasingly dominate decision-making that should have been done jointly. She appeared to feel that she was entitled to chart direction for both programs, and Anita felt sidelined by Marilyn's takeover style.

Anita decided to speak up to Marilyn. But to prepare for the hostile conversation she anticipated, she needed to clarify her experience. Anita thought the "dance" technique could help.

Anita pictured herself at the year-end holiday party, where everyone danced with one another in a relaxed environment. And she saw herself asking Marilyn to dance—which she could never imagine doing in real life. The first thing she noticed in her visualization was that although she was the one to ask Marilyn, she automatically assumed Marilyn would lead. And she was unsettled by how automatic her expectation was. For a moment, in her visualization, she saw herself as a mannequin, standing frozen as the other woman made elaborate twirls and turns around her. But the anger she felt quickly morphed into an "aha" moment, as she allowed herself to take in a recognition of her complicity in the little drama. This realization inspired her to visualize an alternative scene.

Anita visualized herself saying to Marilyn, "Let's take turns leading in a dance." Then she offered to let Marilyn go first. Anita immediately realized that by making the offer, she felt much more cooperative about this arrangement than before. And as she further visualized the scene, she realized that Marilyn then became more open to her as well.

It did not surprise Anita that given the choice, Marilyn preferred to take the leadership role, and she assumed that in this visualization Marilyn would try to take the lead from her periodically. What Anita didn't expect was her own negative response. She discovered that she was actively thinking about how she could throw Marilyn off course in the dance. And she began to wonder in what ways she was doing that in their work relationship as well. The idea that they were both participating in behavior to undermine each other was a real surprise to Anita, who often tended to see herself as the underappreciated victim.

This set of insights did not magically change everything in the relationship between the two coworkers. But by facilitating Anita's awareness of both women's behavior patterns, it allowed her to become increasingly mindful of her own responsibility for their communication problems. On this basis, she planned an entirely different conversation than the confrontational one she had expected. Instead of assuming that working together well was not possible, she made an important decision: she would talk out her concerns with Marilyn in a collegial way. She invited her coworker to lunch. Marilyn responded enthusiastically, and knowing that they were both interested in developing a better relationship enabled Anita to plan a productive conversation—and feel confident in taking the lead.

The dance metaphor is particularly revealing in regard to patterns of influence between people. Some people discover that they are always following rather than leading, or that the dancers are out of sync, or even that one person tries to trip the other. One person complained that his partner was standing on his feet for a free ride. You might see a way to improve the relationship by taking turns at leading, like Anita. Or you might in other situations decide to avoid depending on that particular dance partner.

COOL A COMPETITIVE SPIRIT

Competitive feelings can arise from rivalries that some industries and organizations promote. Sales forces are often managed that way. In any industry, when people hold oppositional roles, it is equally easy to fall into personalizing a negative interaction. For example, our acquaintance Toni, who managed a communications department, was often at odds with an editor, Tom, who worked in the production office and proofread the materials she and her staff produced. Arguments about what was "correct," and whether it mattered, led to uncounted small power struggles. The two thoroughly disliked each other.

After five years of coexisting in this manner, they found themselves seated together during a social occasion. They were forced to converse with each other politely through a long dinner and both ended up cautiously enjoying it. Thereafter, the tension dissipated and they were able to disagree amicably rather than with reflexive hostility. Could they have found common ground as workmates and avoided years of unnecessary stress? Quite probably. If either Toni or Tom had taken the lead and suggested that cup of coffee we keep recommending, their interactions could have been a lot more congenial.

BE THE BEARER OF OLIVE BRANCHES

Sometimes, as we've said in the chapters on dealing with supervisors, a common personal interest or experience can help you relate to someone with whom you don't naturally get along. It's a good idea to actively scout for these access points among all your coworkers because this strengthens positive relationships as well as your ability to weather negative people and events. See it as building your own team, whatever your position or type of work. Research affirms that reliable relationships are a key building block of resiliency in both our everyday lives and times of crisis.

But in some instances, there seems to be no common ground at all. You may need to work closely with someone who dislikes you, or vice versa, or who may even be an outright enemy. When negative feelings are firmly entrenched, can you remedy the relationship upon need? Here too, you might be able to accomplish marvels by taking the lead to bridge the impasse.

We can't control other people, but by acting strategically ourselves, we can reshape how they behave to a degree that may prove sufficient. It requires working past your emotional convictions about a person—no matter how justified you feel they are. Assume they have a better side and speak to that part. And give them a chance to save face. That goes a long way in many, many situations and usually costs you absolutely nothing. You may be surprised to find how often other people are happy to grab your olive branch, whatever the rationale behind it: a shared interest in achieving the goal, an expression of support, a way to make amends even if you feel no responsibility for a transgression.

Often a small, but carefully targeted gesture is enough to bring the other person onto your track or at least run in parallel. This was the case when Gwen, a project manager, was assigned to collaborate with a hostile colleague, Dan, on a major presentation. Dan held a position equivalent to Gwen's and made his dislike of her clear. He actively opposed her recommendations to management as often as he could. Gwen had no idea why Dan built up such enmity toward her, but in turn, she had come to see him as narrow-minded, egotistic, and hopelessly old-fashioned.

The project was a milestone opportunity for Gwen, so she thought carefully about what to do. She saw three options:

1. Complain to the supervisor-in-charge that she can't work with Dan. But this would make her look childish and unprofessional, and might cost her future opportunities as well as the immediate one.
2. Do her part separately, without reference to Dan. This route was sure to produce an inferior result. The project required integrating two different skill sets.
3. Find a way to neutralize Dan's enmity and improve the relationship for the occasion.

Despite recognizing the logic of the last approach, Gwen found herself resistant. "He's worked against me for years. He's paranoid, sulks endlessly, and won't talk to me. If I try to reach him, he'll just get angry and make it worse."

Gwen needed to deal with her own sensitivities as well as come up with an initiative to create a functional relationship. She buoyed her motivation by reminding herself of the high-stakes goals and envisioning what she would gain by co-delivering a dynamite project. This helped her begin to look at the challenge more objectively and shift her mindset to "How can I accomplish this?"

"Actually, at that point the answer pretty much hit me in the face," she recalls. "What would work for me was taking account of our common ground—the need to perform outstandingly on a joint project. He had as much at stake as I did and might welcome a truce."

Gwen decided that a face-to-face meeting or telephone call might raise both their backs, and too fast a response from either of them could make it even harder to work together. So she whittled down her olive branch to a brief e-mail:

Dear Dan:
   I'm looking forward to working on our project and I know we'll do a great job. Would Wednesday at 2 be convenient for our first planning session?
Best, Gwen

The minimalist wording offers no chance for misinterpretation and raises no issues that would trigger Dan's ire. It ignores his bad behavior and allows him to score psychological points because Gwen did the reaching out. Taking the high road cost Gwen nothing. The two of them worked the project through in a carefully respectful manner. Early into the work, Gwen found opportunities to let Dan take the lead in small ways, and to praise his contribution, further lightening the atmosphere. Both were happy with the project results, as were the higher powers.

What if Gwen's emotional assessment of Dan was right-on and he had no "best side"? Here's the beauty: it doesn't matter—when you extend the peace offering, you are likely in many circumstances to achieve reconciliation.

PUSH THE RESET BUTTON

Sometimes an olive branch is insufficient to the challenge. You may be involved in a confrontation that you can't win, or an impasse that seems unbridgeable. In such cases, a useful strategy is to aim for a reset—a back-to-the-beginning move that's common in worlds where confrontation is the norm. Smart politicians, for example, remember that no matter how bitter the feelings involved in a hard-fought election, the parties will need to work together after the event. Effective union leaders refrain from burning down all the bridges even during the most hostile negotiations. Mechanisms to rebuild relationships and move past the disagreement are essential.

An interesting use of reset on a lofty level is demonstrated by an anecdote that journalist Tom Brokaw shared at Nancy Reagan's funeral. In covering Ronald Reagan's years in the White House, Brokaw developed a good relationship with the First Lady. However, he infuriated the fiercely protective Nancy when he wrote an article criticizing Reagan for an election campaign tactic. When a state dinner approached, knowing he would have to face her in the receiving line, he tried to think of something adequate to say toward mending fences. When the moment finally arrived, he said simply, "Nancy, back to square one." She laughed and echoed the thought: "Tom, back to square one."

The next day Brokaw received a photo of that exact moment, inscribed with the same words. He observed that the incident demonstrated Nancy's ability to stand her ground, get her message across, and move on. So when there's no perfect resolution, you too can bring out "back to square one." Here's a workaday example of using this technique well.

Mallory was in charge of a small unit in a state education department, and the three people reporting to her included Mac, an administrative assistant (once known as a secretary). Mac was the department's most junior person in the role. The most senior person by longevity and influence was Jackie, who worked for the department head. Except for newcomer Mac, the assistants had for years worked smoothly together under Jackie. One day, Mallory arrived at work to find Mac's desk empty and Mac "disappeared." She asked what was going on, and Jackie abruptly announced, "I'm sorry, but I had him transferred. I just couldn't stand having him around our office any longer. He's rude and uncooperative. I'm sure there are some good people available to fill his spot if you check with HR." She then turned on her heel and marched away.

Mallory was speechless. Jackie had transferred her own assistant without consulting her. She thought about complaining to the department head but realized he would support Jackie. Angry and resentful, she retreated into a chilly silence and ignored Jackie. Jackie reciprocated with apparent indifference.

Mallory felt disrespected and justifiably angry but could find no productive outlets for her reaction. "I knew for certain that Jackie had the top honcho's complete support, right or wrong, so complaining to him wouldn't help and would identify me with a losing battle. Complaining to HR might make sense because as a unit chief I was higher on the company totem pole than an administrative assistant. But Jackie had a long, respectable track record and, I was sure, examples of Mac's inadequacy and uncooperative spirit—I'd never claim he didn't have weaknesses." She also saw that making an official complaint was sure to get a negative reaction from the whole close-knit office crew because they were not just loyal to Jackie, but also wary of crossing her. "I couldn't imagine what having the whole support staff mad at me would do to my office life."

After two weeks of retreat, Mallory wanted to end the hostile face-off. But she definitely did not want to apologize. So the next time she encountered Jackie, she said in a neutral, even, but assertive tone: "Jackie, I don't like what's happening here. Let's just move on."

She then told us what happened next: "Jackie looked at me, nodded once, and said simply, 'yes.' That was the entire conversation, no smiles. But after that everything went back to normal and comfortable. We never talked about it. Jackie was actually especially nice to me for the rest of the time we worked together—and to my new administrative assistant."

KNOW WHEN TO APPEAL TO HIGHER AUTHORITY—AND WHEN NOT TO

When should you go to the boss with a complaint? If a truly toxic person is the problem, and you believe the supervisor is unaware of his impact, you might consider explaining the situation—carefully. But as a general rule of thumb, reach over someone's head as seldom as possible. Most managers intensely dislike being asked to intervene in personal relationships and will not think better of you for passing the burden to them rather than resolving things yourself like a grown-up.

Especially if a grievance derives from your individual experience with a coworker, rather than from a feeling shared by the group, think hard before appealing to a higher authority. Play the possible scenarios out in your mind. For example, say you are annoyed that someone you share an office with spends so much time making personal phone calls. Will you tell the boss that it's hard for you to concentrate because of all that telephone chatter? Because the behavior has a work impact, he'll need to address it. Even if he wants to be tactful, it will be obvious that you are the tattler. How will that affect your office life? Here's a cautionary tale along these lines.

Dianne, a technology specialist at a Fortune 100 corporation, often worked on projects with a peer on the same level, Alison. "But Alison wasn't doing her fair share," Dianne says. "So I went to our mutual supervisor and complained. He obviously spoke to her about it. She stormed into my office and confronted me: 'Why did you go to him? Why didn't you come to me to work this out?' I realized she was right, I should have done that, and apologized profusely. And I kept apologizing. From then on she did her share—exactly half the work each time. But she never spoke to me again—just communicated in writing."

When Dianne passed Alison in the hall, she would smile and say hello, but Alison ignored her. "Eventually I was reassigned to another office and saw her infrequently. But it still took a lot out of me that someone should be so hostile that I felt uneasy about running into her." Mistakes like this are hard to remedy, especially if the other person proves to be an unforgiving type.

If Dianne had taken the better route and addressed her colleague frankly, but the unfair behavior continued, what then? In that case, talking to the boss might be an inevitable option. When someone else's behavior impairs your ability to perform well and you can't resolve the issue with that person, your supervisor needs to know. But use your best planning skills before that conversation.

Tie complaints to the bottom line

If you do go to the boss with a complaint about a coworker, avoid vague statements like "He's just so hard to get along with" or somewhat more explicitly, "She does as little as she can and then tries to take all the credit for my work." They sound like personal laments. As such, they disinterest many managers, and your complaint may be held against you. After all, you're asking the boss to have a difficult conversation on emotion-laden terms. He may decline to address the issue in which case you will likely feel embarrassed. Or he might issue a perfunctory order to the offender, like "Try to get along better with Harriet, she's unhappy working with you." This will not help matters.

It is far more effective to adopt the *we* rather than *I* communication approach. Frame the conversation as a sharing of information that's of mutual concern: "I have concerns about how our office is getting this project done. I see us falling behind schedule because the team isn't distributing work well. Marty, Jen, and I are handling 90 percent of the workload. If Catherine was asked to handle a bit more, we could stay on track." Or "I see the office wasting a lot of time on personalities. The gossiping creates bad feelings that get in the way of our group energy."

Notice that if you imagine how your voice would sound saying things like this, it sounds even and neutral, rather than whiny. Here's an example of a strategic way someone allied himself with the bottom line and positioned himself as a contributor rather than a complainer.

Sean joined a small investment firm as a junior partner and reported to Harry, who did similar work but had been in place several years. Sean was immediately successful—more so than Harry. Apparently resenting this, Harry used his seniority privilege to review Sean's deals and pore over every item, looking for small errors and discrepancies. He would bring these up at team meetings that Sean was not yet invited to attend. Even worse, Sean knew that Harry sometimes made disparaging comments about him to colleagues. Sean realized that Harry was deliberately trying to provoke and belittle him. He was careful to never take the bait. But over time, the constant need to counter Harry and hold his temper took a toll on his work life, which was by nature already stressful.

He needed to free himself from this underminer. He had worked to establish himself as a creative and reliable producer, and he knew that complaining about another member of the group would set him back. So he assessed the higher executives in the group and his existing relationships with them to determine which of them thought in ways similar to his. He decided to reach out to a particular senior partner, Chuck, for whom he had great respect. In addition, Sean sensed that Chuck was not altogether happy with Harry's performance.

"I didn't want to just make a direct complaint," Sean says. "I realized that this kind of approach comes across as personal, just one employee griping about another. Why would an executive want to get involved in that? I said nothing at all about how I was being treated and kept it very dispassionate. I talked about the work, what was being accomplished, and in the process, referred very neutrally to a stumbling block or two. I mentioned how our follow-through could be better and how the whole team would benefit."

Following the conversation, Sean learned from colleagues that Chuck began countering Harry's criticisms of him when they were voiced in his presence. Sean was soon invited to the team meetings and Chuck saw to it that he had chances to offer input. The senior partners responded to Sean's sound thinking and also to the good opinion of him that Chuck clearly held. Harry, noticing this turn of events, shortly transferred to another part of the firm.

Sean's successful strategy was to identify someone on a higher level with whom he felt a natural affinity and who would be a strong ally. But this strategy only worked because of several additional factors.

First, he steadfastly resisted Harry's bait to attack him. Had he failed to resist it, he'd have handed Harry more grist for his negative mill and communicated to other people that the situation was personal—in which case, as the newer hire, he probably would have lost.

Additionally, his work was genuinely superior to his critic's. The issues he raised caused the higher-up executive to observe both people's effectiveness and judge their relative performance, which defines who is more important to the common cause.

Finally, he addressed, essentially, the obstructer's impact on the bottom line. When you frame a need in those terms, you speak your manager's language. Then what you say is taken as valuable feedback—not personal resentment, whining, or failure to relate well to others.

PREPARE A FAST AND READY RESPONSE

What is more annoying than being struck speechless on the spot by a mean-minded remark or action? Unlike many negative situations that involve a superior, interactions with coworkers can often be resolved by the right spontaneous comment. We have all thought, "If only I'd said that at the time!"

Consider that the right response need not necessarily be exactly spontaneous. You can think out the possibilities in advance when dealing with a persistent problem person. Here are some examples toward building a repertoire of "instant" responses when a coworker oversteps or offends. Note that these are coworker-specific rejoinders, and most are not recommended for use with a manager. Absorb the tone and general content of these examples and adapt them to your own needs. Using first names helps set a good tone.

Delivery is important: you can be righteously indignant if appropriate, or even a bit angry, but assume the higher ground and use a controlled, even, slow-paced, but nonjudgmental inflection and tone of voice. The right delivery enables you to challenge what someone is saying or doing—rather than sounding like you are attacking her personally—and puts the ball in her court. Think about how your favorite cool TV or movie hero would deliver the lines! And it doesn't hurt to rehearse.

If it is someone who whines to you all day about the boss, the company, getting less than he deserves, or his personal life, you might try the following response: "Sandy, I like talking to you, but I'm having trouble concentrating on my work and I'm on deadline. Thanks for understanding."

For someone who gossips about coworkers: "Jennifer, I'm not good with talking about other people, so please keep me out of the loop, all right?"

When someone treats you disrespectfully and ignores what you say at meetings: "Joe, I feel like I'm not being heard. May I repeat the point I'd like to get across?"

Someone is repeatedly rude to you: "Richard, have I been inconsiderate in some way? I'm wondering why you're behaving this way to me."

Someone is bad-mouthing you: "Ellie, have I offended you in some way? I was surprised to hear that you're saying critical things about me to other people. If you feel we're at odds about something, would you come directly to me from now on?"

Someone systematically unloads his responsibilities onto your desk: "Pat, I'd be happy to help with this, but I won't be able to get to it for a few weeks. So if it's due Friday, best to take it back." Or you might try: "There's been some kind of misunderstanding, this part of the work isn't my responsibility, it's yours."

Someone belittles you in front of others while pretending playfulness or affection: "Hank, I really don't like nicknames—please call me

Bonnie from now on, not Bon-Bon, including when you introduce me to people. OK?"

Someone tells dirty jokes or makes unwelcome comments: "Marty, when you say things like that, I feel very uncomfortable. Off-color jokes have that effect on a lot of people, that's why there's a company policy against it." Or maybe: "Jean, I don't appreciate jokes like that. I'd much rather not have to go to the boss about it, so can we agree that you'll give it a rest when I'm around?" Or just: "Oh, Fran, knock it off!"

Company cultures differ. Try to take that into account with your responses. If telling off-color jokes or talking about X-rated movies is the norm, which may be the case no matter what the industry, you'll probably not make much headway by communicating that you're offended. You may need to look away and ignore the conversation as best you can, abstract yourself, or leave the room. If the offenders are deliberately trying to get a rise out of you, foil them by maintaining an even, neutral attitude. They may tire of the effort. If not, and you can't let it slide, consider whether you're living in a culture mismatch and should look for another job. If you consider talking to the boss or HR, weigh the likelihood of gaining the outcome you want against possible repercussions.

INTO ACTION

1. *Build empathy for a coworker you don't like.* Identify someone at work for whom you feel no natural affinity. Scan through the numerous techniques introduced in previous chapters and choose several that you feel might help you understand the person better, and could enable you to figure out how to improve the relationship. Consider:
   - Building a profile of the person (chapter 5)
   - Trying an Empty Chair Role Reversal (chapter 4)
   - Creating a pro and con list of the person's good qualities and assets, and the negative ones (chapter 7)
   - Tracking your own personal triggers: Are they part of the dissonance? (chapter 2)
   - Reframing: Can you find a different perspective on your relationship? (chapter 3)
   - Adjusting your communication style: Can you find a way to change how you communicate with the person? (chapter 6)
   - Identifying a common interest or other access point (chapter 7)

2. *Explore and assess your motivation for improving a coworker relationship.* Take stock of what you lose by maintaining a negative interaction pattern. In addition to producing a personal discomfort with the individual, does it cost you time? The good opinion of others? Emotional distress? Opportunities of any kind?

   What might you gain by taking the lead to improve the relationship?

3. *Write an analysis of the relationship at issue:*
   - Where did the bad feelings start?
   - How are they manifested?
   - What sustains them?
   - What is it costing you?
   - What role do your personal triggers play, as well as those of the other person?

4. *Apply this chapter's techniques to shift a coworker relationship in a more positive direction.* Identify a specific person you don't like, or with whom you have an issue. Can you think of a way to take the lead and improve the interaction?
   - Try the dance metaphor to see if it opens up your thinking about the nature of the problem and your role.
   - Consider the olive branch: Do you see a way to normalize the relationship by finding common ground or extending a hand, even in a small way?
   - Might the reset option work: signaling a readiness to move past the obstacle for a fresh start?
   - In light of the specific nature of the problem you have with this person, can you plan some conversational rejoinders that will calm the waters rather than roil them?

Review all your answers to the above four activities and write an action plan for improving the coworker relationship you identified.

Chapter 10

MOVING ON UP: HOW TO THINK LIKE A MANAGER

M anagement at heart is about people and relationships. You can easily bury yourself in tons of good advice that is strong on theory, technical aspects like financial analysis, and nitty-gritty guidance like how to run a meeting. But if you are now a manager—even if only one person reports to you—or aspire to management, never lose sight of the core reality—managing is about relationships. As *Genie* has shown you in previous chapters, understanding other people and, most of all, yourself is key to forming and sustaining good relationships.

This chapter shows you how to apply many of the strategies you've learned from this book to manage people more effectively; it is also a resource of on-the-ground ideas from the many people we've talked to. The business world uses "people skills" or, rather depressingly, "soft skills," to denote the nontechnical set of qualifications it values. Unfortunately, given the large numbers of ineffective managers, these skills haven't been sufficiently valued in practice. But this is changing rapidly because more organizations are recognizing how closely workplace relationships and communication connect to the bottom line.

More than ever before, possessing good people skills and demonstrating them enables you to succeed. Put yourself into the shoes of an executive, Jeanne, who is about to promote one of two employees to head one of her department's units in the wake of a retirement. Both staff members have been with the company for about the same length of time, and both have received good reviews for their work. Max contributes to team efforts and at times offers good ideas but seems to prefer working on his own. He's reliable and knowledgeable: the go-to person on all technical matters. The second candidate, Nancy, also has a good track record and contributes new ideas. Her reviews particularly note that she is "good with people," communicates well, and thrives on teamwork. Jeanne knows that Nancy gets along well with the group and brings to it a positive, can-do spirit. She goes out of her way to share her own skill set with others. As Jeanne, would you promote Max or Nancy?

Nancy, right? She appears to be already equipped for the most important aspect of the role. Leadership can take many forms—some of the most inspiring visionaries treat their staffs horribly—but in a right-thinking world, relationship skills trump technical qualifications if the goal is to acquire promising managers. See if your own experience validates this: Were you more engaged when you reported to a manager who was nice to work with and seemed to care about you, offered help, and made himself readily available, or one who was outstanding in his technical skill or craft but not so good with people? Under which kind of person did you do your best work? When savvy managers promote, the best candidates are those who get along well with coworkers, appear to be respected, and communicate well. They seem ready to take the helm.

ADOPT A WIDE PERSPECTIVE

The higher you rise on whatever totem pole you contemplate, the broader your perspective must be. Handling wider responsibilities requires a working grasp of everything under your purview. You need not know how to do everything yourself, but want to be knowledgeable enough to oversee all relevant functions, figure out whom to trust for help, and evaluate the necessary specialists. For example, it's hard to run a department without knowing the essentials of how to build and oversee a budget, though you may not do the actual number crunching yourself.

Every manager is a representative and spokesman for the organization, so you need to understand your organization's policies, culture, and mission. Interpreting the mission to your staff, explaining how your unit fits into it, and maintaining their commitment is your responsibility. And you must consciously serve as a role model to your subordinates.

Think like an orchestrator

When you're responsible for the work of other people, you need to shift from a do-it-all mentality, or do-my-little-piece outlook, into the role of orchestra conductor. You're judged by the performance of your team, not your solo part. It's your job to understand the talents, potentials, strengths, weaknesses, and personalities of every member of that team.

Use the tools *Workplace Genie* gives you. Practice profile building and role reversal techniques to delve under the surface and look through each person's eyes as closely as possible. Get to know each person one-on-one. Formally or more casually, interview staff members to assess their capabilities, attitudes, and how they can contribute to your unit's goals. If you're the new manager, this is a must. If you are already a manager, it's never too late. The people you want working under you will welcome your interest.

Use your active listening skills! Ask direct questions in a curious and open-minded way. Brief yourself on the employee's work history before a conversation. A blanket "tell me about yourself" always produces some enlightening information and surprises. Notice what people choose to tell you. Also pose specific open-ended questions that can't be answered with a yes or no. For example:

- How do you see your goal this quarter (or year)?
- What did you accomplish this past year?
- What's been most challenging for you?
- How do you allocate your time?
- Where could you use help?
- What do you want to learn?

If you're interviewing new hires, prompt them with additional questions such as:

- What was a high point in your life (or career)?
- What have you done that didn't turn out as you'd hoped, and how did you deal with that?
- What makes you proud?
- What would be your ideal workplace?
- Who was the best supervisor you ever worked for? Why?

Here's another question for both current or prospective staff members that may yield unexpected answers: Which part of your current work do you most like doing? A magazine editor we know, upon assuming a new position, asked this of an assistant editor long on the job. She hoped to start off on a good footing with her only helper. The assistant replied: "I've been waiting years for someone to ask me that! I love working on technical catalogs. If I never again have to write another article, or talk to contributors, I'll be happy!" The new editor was stunned to hear that her subordinate passionately wanted the work she herself disliked. Without this input, she would have "sacrificed" some of the work she enjoyed most to the other woman, assuming their preferences were the same. The response also told her that this was not the assistant she needed, because editorial backup mattered more than catalog work.

When your staff is larger and allows more flexibility, the question will help you better allocate work and create more enthusiastic employees. People want, appreciate, and value different things. This is good. It gives you more of what you need to orchestrate well. Some corollaries:

- Appreciate and strive for staff diversity of every kind: age, gender, cultural background, specialized skills, personalities.
- Balance individual skills and preferences so people can do what they're best at and like best, insofar as practical.
- Hire and value people who are good at things you're not.

To delegate well, look for strengths, weaknesses, and clues to how much more each person can learn to do and wants to do. When human resources staffers talk about soft skills, "coachability" is high on the list: the ability to learn new skills, hear criticism with an open mind, and learn new things. People have different capacities and levels of interest in improving themselves or their situations. A department chief who had watched a hardworking employee perform admirably for years on organizing departmental files, actually not an easy assignment, wanted to promote him to more interesting work. He called him in and asked: "Marty, what are your goals?"

"To make enough money to feed the cats," Marty replied immediately. His own short story, well told.

With people who are more ambitious than Marty, deploying them well supports team success. We all do our best when we're excited about our work and are much less likely to abandon ship. Giving people ownership of specific areas of responsibility further pushes them to do their best—and so do opportunities to search out greener pastures.

Play to strength and encourage growth

One advantage of knowing your subordinates well is that it's much easier to create a harmonious, well-balanced team whose sum is more than its parts. You can also identify skills and talents that are worth cultivating and will contribute more to the common cause. In addition to closely observing, keep an open mind and watch for clues to potential strengths.

Don't take for granted what people can and can't do—and don't necessarily accept their own self-evaluation at face value. We often don't know our own strengths, and a caring observer can help us recognize them.

Offering a pathway to growth is even better. Encourage your team members to develop new skills, take on challenging projects, and experiment with new directions without fearing failure. Provide what resources are possible. They need not include financial support. Sometimes access to a specialist, a little time to explore, or a learning opportunity that won't break the bank is practical.

Don't lose sight of the basic value of all this: when you generate growth, you generate loyalty and appreciation. These are especially important principles in supervising Millennials. Building an individual's skills can be a good way to resolve territorial issues, too, as in this example.

Lisa was recruited from a similar company by an aerospace firm to fill a newly created position as training director for the sales force. She was surprised on her first day to learn that a relatively low-level staff member had been elevated to become her chief assistant. The woman, Beth, had worked in the department for ten years and had applied for Lisa's job. Beth had no experience as a trainer—her responsibilities had been limited to administrative work—but the department head promoted her because she valued Beth's service and thought she would bring her new boss up to speed faster.

Lisa agreed that she needed Beth to explain the systems and the people. She also saw that Beth's experience with setting up training programs across the country for key people was limited. She introduced a new system for doing the work effectively, but Beth—unable to get past her resentment of Lisa—balked. Lisa looked for a way to connect with her resistant second. "Talking to her and watching her," she recalls, "I saw that Beth cared very much about her work and was very dedicated to the company. So she respected results. I realized that her investment in the company's success gave me a way to bring her over to my way of doing things."

Beth soon did observe that her new boss's methods were successful. Her own interest in becoming a trainer surfaced, and she asked to learn the skill set. But Lisa discovered that her assistant was a poor public speaker and judged that a training program would not significantly change that. "But I also discovered in putting the presentations together that she had a real strength in graphics. I recommended her for a course on presentation design. That was very productive and I was able to put the design responsibility in her hands and focus on content myself. I took her with me to a meeting cross-country, her first business travel, and she was thrilled. After that, we traveled together often and I enjoyed an effective teammate, a good relationship, and mutual respect. I had the best-looking presentations on the circuit."

Lisa wisely found a way to leverage Beth's strengths on several levels. On the "soft skills" side, keying off Beth's genuine dedication to her job and employer, she was able to demonstrate that her "product" was effective and that Lisa herself was an asset in achieving the department's goals—goals to which both were dedicated. Then she identified a personal motivating factor: Beth's desire to learn new skills. When she uncovered in her assistant a hidden potential for graphic work, she helped Beth make the most of it, creating a win-win.

Stay in tune with your people

Practice a curiosity about everyone who reports to you and their personal goals and hopes. Study after study demonstrates that financial reward is not what inspires most people to become their best. More critical are opportunities to learn, grow, and advance. *Working for a supervisor who seems to care for employees and actively mentors them is always at the top of the most-wanted list.* Other motivators include challenging assignments, insight into company thinking, a congenial workplace, recognition, flexible scheduling, a clear career path, low-risk chances to experiment and suggest new ideas, good coffee—any of these and more may motivate different people. Like Lisa, identify what people care about. The best managers understand what makes each person tick and plan for each one's individual job satisfaction. Notice that all these elements are in large part within a supervisor's ability to provide, unless company policy or culture dictates against it.

How can you get to know your subordinates? Many of the strategies presented in *Genie* can help you. Role reversal is especially useful. Build profiles of each person. Look especially for insights into what motivates each one and what triggers his or her sensitivities. It's smart to stay abreast of your staff's presence on social media, not to snoop, but to see what interests them and possibly their wider abilities and thinking. But as always, there's no substitute for face-to-face contact, so build the time for this into your daily schedule. It isn't a distraction from your job: unless your situation is unusual, it's your most important function.

When you talk to a staff member, use your best listening skills. Show interest with good questions and conversational prompts. Don't scan your e-mail, or read something on your desk, or pick up the phone unless it's urgent. Plan for frequent how's-it-going check-ins, rather than formal feedback once a year. Take note of how each person prefers to communicate, and the channels most natural to him. You may need some kind of communal network, like a place on an office intranet, to keep people informed and encourage them to share with one another as well as you. Very likely, you will need to go where they are—for some, this means social media, for others, e-mail. You may well need to hold regular meetings. Everyone complains about them, but especially if your staff goes above nine or so, they're necessary to keep people informed, minimize destructive rumors, and cultivate team spirit. Try to keep them informative, motivating, and short.

You may also need weekly or monthly reports from each employee. In this case as well, people will grouse, but you need to keep track of what's being done and potential bottlenecks. It's wise to train your staff on creating relevant reports and explain their role in decision-making. If your group's overall communication skills are in short supply, you'll benefit from teaching them to write effective e-mails, proposals, blogs, or whatever else matters to your department's success.

ESTABLISH PSYCHOLOGICAL SAFETY

A favorite subject for people who research management techniques is how to create more successful teams. As workplaces move toward team-based organization, or rely on project work, the question becomes critical. Some time back, Google launched in-depth research to find out why some teams accomplished so much. Investigators soon determined that achieving goals does not much correlate with a team's diversity, or personality balance, or variable skill sets. But it took several years of research to conclude that the company's best-performing teams shared one thing: a high level of comfort among members and sensitivity to one another.

On these teams, all team members felt able to speak out, contribute, and make mistakes. The safe environment also made it comfortable for them to share personal aspects of their lives and accept support from the group when needed. Small talk at the start of a meeting, with room for all teammates to report in on how they're doing, helps all feel secure and valued. In this perspective, setting a personal tone is not just "nice" but essential to team success. Some team leaders instinctively took the initiative to create this environment, and now more, at Google and beyond, are being trained to do so.

You may wonder how much personal information is appropriate to share when you're the boss. There's no universal answer. It's true that you establish trust by awarding it. People tend to live up to our expectations, as we have discussed earlier.

Extend trust if you want to be trusted. You will at times be disappointed, but you'll still come out ahead. One point to keep in mind is that it's risky to confide personal matters on a selective basis. Sharing information with one or two individuals rather than the group is rarely a good idea. It creates an air of favoritism and tempts subordinates to take advantage of their privileged status.

Protect your people and watch for signs of trouble

If you've ever reported to someone who vented his own frustrations, grumped about company decisions, or complained about how awful her own boss is, you know the scene. Few behaviors are more debilitating to team morale and productivity. Aim to protect your staff as best you can from the imperfect bosses you may report to and from your own bad moods, inconsistencies, complaints, dissatisfactions, and rants. When Disney hires new employees on any level for its theme parks, they are told, "You no longer have the right to have a bad day." It's a good rule for managing, too.

You are also responsible for protecting your employees from one another. On an everyday basis, this means staying alert to conflicts, negative attitudes, and people who pass their own burdens onto others. It also means being on the watch for any behavioral changes—someone who starts acting in a withdrawn, depressed way or is suddenly late a lot, for example. Your job as a caring and effective manager is to find out why and connect the person with help, if indicated.

Try also to recognize the two-faced individuals we all know: the ones who behave one way to power people, including you, but present a whole different persona to coworkers or subordinates. Notice if you have a toxic employee on staff or someone who for whatever reason appears to be developing into one. Don't ignore this: both anecdotally and statistically, it's clear that chronically bitter, negative individuals ruin work for everyone in their vicinity and vie with bad bosses as the main reason people leave jobs.

Use your observation skills to identify any toxic people. While you don't want to encourage staff members to complain about one another or encourage gossip, you can ask specific, pointed questions to confirm what you've observed, suspect, or have heard from a single source. Not "How do you feel about Pete?" but rather "I get the impression that Pete has been asking other people to do more than their fair share while he does less. Is that your experience?"

If you've built a spirit of trust, people will tell you the truth as they see it and very possibly be relieved that the problem has surfaced. But once it has, expect to act. Find out if the person in question needs help. Try mentoring him. If the counterproductive behavior doesn't stop, try your best to remove the person from your ranks.

Hold people accountable

As one experienced executive shared with us, "You owe it to people to make them accountable!" Feeling that the person in charge cares about how we perform and behave is reassuring. When a manager sets clear expectations and makes sure that we know how to meet them, we feel more comfortable and secure in how we invest our time. This helps most of us do our best and prompts us to overcome our own challenges and take satisfaction from living up to the standards set. If a manager ignores someone who doesn't carry his weight, polarizes the atmosphere, bullies others, or breaks the rules, the whole team can become dangerously disaffected. A "fair" boss does not play favorites, accept excuses, or look the other way. At times, this can mean exercising a "tough love" spirit or hardening the heart to act in ways that few people enjoy. Here's a case in point.

Tamara ran a seven-person marketing department for a substantial retail company. One day her newest hire, a young man in his early thirties named Brad, came into her office very upset. He related that another member of the team, Sherry, hired four months earlier, had befriended him and they often ate lunch together.

"That was fine," Brad said. "It was nice to relate to someone on a new job. But a week or two ago I realized Sherry actually wanted a romantic relationship—though she's married! I'm not at all interested and have been trying to fend her off nicely so we can keep working together. But last night, I got a call from her husband shouting that if I don't keep away from his wife, he'll shoot me! And he's a cop!"

Shocked, Tamara called Sherry into her office. Knowing the matter at hand, Sherry burst into tears, choked out an apology, and sobbed, "I've ruined my life . . . I don't know what I was thinking. I really need this job. I feel so awful . . ."

Faced with a distraught, near-hysterical woman, Tamara was unprepared and ineffective. She said, in essence, "We're all human, we'll get past this. Will you fix things with your husband? Leave Brad alone?"

"Yes!" Sherry said. Tamara told Brad the situation had been neutralized and he need not worry further. She did not discuss the matter with her other staff members, considering it confidential.

Within a month, Brad moved on to another job. Sherry remained. Gradually Tamara's mistake dawned on her. "I let Sherry's emotion reach me and limit my thinking." She hadn't considered that a promising staff member would probably feel outraged at having to continue working side by side with an unpunished Sherry and would leave.

Further, she saw belatedly that Sherry's risky behavior and bad judgment represented more than a brief lapse. They reflected on her character and a failure to respect her job. "Forgiving her was bad for my department, bad for the company," Tamara saw. "Brad probably shared the story with the rest of the staff before he left, so I'm sure there were less visible results as well. I should have fired her."

Sherry outlasted Tamara and ended up heading the department, another cause of regret for her former boss. Clearly, it would have been better for everyone—except Sherry—if Tamara had hardened her heart and acted with more toughness for the team, the company, and herself.

Tamara should not have protected Sherry. Note that if an organization has any HR resources at all, this type of situation calls for bringing in help to handle the interaction or coach the supervisor through it.

Plan out difficult conversations

The higher you rise in an organization, the more likely you are to be frequently surprised by staff conflicts, cliques, and problems. As the person responsible for the psychological safety of your team, you need to be a fair and objective judge, quick on your feet, and ready to protect the unit's comfort and cohesiveness when threatened. But how can you prepare for the unexpected? Here's a structure to use that will help safeguard you against making poor snap decisions and support your own best judgment. It has much in common with the Power Pause idea, introduced in chapter 3, but broadens the scale beyond "you" to the broader responsibility of the team.

1. *Gather information.* What happened? What do I know? What do I not know, and how can I find out? You may need to hold a

preliminary conversation, conduct other interviews, or dig for facts. Once you understand the elements of a situation . . .

2. *Define the problem or challenge.* What immediate ramifications can you see? Is action necessary? What longer-range results might materialize? Who might be affected? How?

    Can these negative outcomes be limited or prevented? Considering the circumstances and potential ramifications . . .

3. *Figure out the outcome you want.* What result do I want to see as a result of this conversation?

    Never bypass this question to clarify your desired outcome, because it distances you from a shortsighted response. You might feel like exploding in fury when someone makes a mistake, for example, or disrespects you, but this usually causes damage, whoever the offender may be.

    Do you really want to burn this bridge? Alienate the person? Be forced to replace him? Or do you want to repair the problem and maintain or even strengthen relationships in the process? If emotions override your sense of control, go back to the big picture and remind yourself what's at stake. Also remember that it's paramount to maintain your own self-respect and the respect of those who might witness an out-of-control attack.

4. *Consider the personalities and options.* As part of your preparation, try role reversals with the principal people involved (chapter 4). Assess their strengths and weaknesses, how they see the situation and will probably react to your intervention, and yes, consider their relative value to you without sacrificing fairness.

5. *Lay out the options.* Choose the one that best limits the damage and benefits the people that count: the team and yourself. Consider alternative responses should the other person take various tacks.

6. *Script and practice.* Restate the outcome you've decided upon. Create a set of talking points (chapter 6), the main ideas or facts you want to communicate to reach your preferred outcome. Scan them to plan your conversational opener, then arrange your points

in a logical sequence. Identify any decision points along the way that might influence your course.

7. *Prepare mentally.* Give yourself some quiet space before the confrontation. Draw on one or more techniques you know work for you: perhaps Square Breathing (chapter 3), calling on your confident self (chapter 4), or assuming the persona of someone you feel would handle the situation especially well (chapter 4).

8. *Carry out your plan.* Determine to look at the person directly and listen intently. Speak with measured neutrality. *If anything catches you by surprise, pause and think. You are not obliged to instantly respond.* If new factors emerge that you need to think about, say so and defer the conversation. Gather or verify more information in the interim and let the issues settle out.

This preparation process equips you to make better decisions and minimizes the likelihood of harmful fallout. It clarifies the issues and you'll find that often, the imperatives settle out sooner rather than later. This can save you endless hours of agonizing over which route to choose and self-justifying arguments that can accompany unpleasant decisions. Had Tamara used this approach, she would have . . .

1. *Delayed decision until she had asked more questions of a calmer Sherry.* Tamara could have shown some empathy without committing to a resolution that left Sherry unaccountable. She could then interview Brad in more depth to check if the stories matched. Beyond helping her verify that Brad told the full truth, this would have reassured Brad that the situation was taken seriously.

2. *Defined the problem more clearly.* A deferred decision gives Tamara space to reflect on her subordinate's series of transgressions and the results. She would anticipate that Brad might leave if unhappy with the disposition. Moreover, he might go over Tamara's head to complain. Other subordinates might be upset and angry, affecting their work and commitment. So the department's functioning as well as Tamara's own reputation are at risk. Not to mention, what if Sherry did not in fact sufficiently pacify her husband?

When the full picture is spelled out this way, the rest of the steps fall quickly into place. It becomes clear that the only real option is to let Sherry go. Knowing this to be the desired outcome, Tamara can easily script her side of the conversation and prepare for her subordinate's probable reaction. Her own certainty would strengthen her resolve and equip her to deliver the message as kindly as she wishes but without granting forgiveness. Had she thought the situation through systematically, Tamara would not have placed herself at risk, and would have only needed to replace a single subordinate.

THINK LEADER OF THE PACK

It's useful to think of yourself as Team Leader. Build your team, encourage your team, protect your team. Offer trust and express confidence in each member. Act as a role model—your hard work and ethical behavior will inspire the same in others. When you are consistent, fair, generous, and hold to standards, you promote team spirit.

Communicate that you believe in what you're doing and that it's important, and other people will do their best. Show you care about people, and they will care about their work and want to meet high expectations. If you're lucky, you work within an organizational culture that fosters this positive environment and people expect to trust one another and work together. If you're not so lucky, you're challenged to create engagement and collegiality despite the negative culture. We'll give you some ways to do that in the next chapter.

INTO ACTION

1. *Define the boss you want to be.* What do you believe are the ideal qualities of a good boss? Scan the first few pages of chapter 7 and the ideas in this chapter to come up with a personal checklist. How many of these criteria do you think you can presently meet? If you now manage other people, or hope to do so, which attributes do you need to improve? Identify specific ways you could undertake this self-development. For example, find a mentor; take workshops; ask a friend to teach you a skill; join Toastmasters; take a course or a degree program at a local college. Many of these options cost little or nothing (except time). Create a plan!

2. *Find a role model.* Pick out the best supervisor you've worked for at any point. Is he or she a good role model? Think analyti-

cally about what made that person so effective. How did he communicate, assign work, provide praise and criticism? How did he encourage you? Express caring? Stay in touch with staff?

3. *Write to your role model.* To help articulate your thoughts, write a letter to the manager you see as your role model, thanking her in a way appropriate to what you gained from the relationship. If practical, consider sending the letter—every teacher treasures the few notes she receives from former students. A caring supervisor similarly deserves your retroactive appreciation.

4. *Assess the managers you didn't like.* What have you learned from supervisors who you did *not* like working for? Don't overlook your earliest experience in the workforce as a sales clerk, ice cream scooper, busboy, or gas jockey. Across industries, good and bad managers have everything in common with their counterparts because the role is the same: to bring out the best in people and lead the team well. What did the boss do to make you feel good about the job and enjoy it? Did he do anything that had the opposite effect and wasn't necessary? Did you understand your role and how to fulfill it well? The less trained a supervisor is, the more glaring their mistakes may be.

Chapter 11

NAVIGATING YOUR ORGANIZATION'S CULTURE AND YOUR PLACE IN IT

Matthew loved his job. He worked in marketing for an aviation company and in seven years worked his way up to the senior manager level. He came to know other people in his industry through a professional association and received an offer to move upward and head a rival firm's marketing unit.

"I was flattered to be recruited, and the move seemed like the natural next stage for me," Matthew recounts. "But after a few weeks at the new place, I felt like I'd landed in hell. People in my former job were genuinely devoted to working together. I was used to so much trust. A conversation was your word. Overnight I found myself living in a world of backbiting and dishonesty. If an agreement wasn't in writing, people would actually lie and say they hadn't been consulted, even though they'd signed off on it in person. I went home depressed and feeling disillusioned every night asking myself, 'What have I done? Why did I leave such a great job?'"

Matthew had fallen prey to the corporate culture pitfall: like most people who haven't experienced several different environments, he was blissfully unaware that every organization has its own culture. "Corporate culture" is slippery to define and broader than it might sound. It lives equally in nonprofits, governmental agencies and organizations, creative enterprises, and every other kind of enterprise. But for our purpose, here's the bottom line: every organization functions by unspoken patterns that determine how people are treated and treat each other. Underlying these patterns are entrenched processes that identify what success means, whom to reward, what behaviors to encourage, and what to measure. These built-ins often bear little relation to the organization's carefully written values, mission, and goals. They are the living embodiment of forces below the surface.

UNDERSTANDING AND ASSESSING CORPORATE CULTURE

You may be able to adapt and feel comfortable in many company cultures, according to how closely you align with them personally or how flexible you are. Problems arise because business cultures are mostly invisible until we move from one to another or companies merge. In both instances, most people are unprepared for how hard it is to mesh different ways of thinking and doing.

Especially if they've been with their companies a long time, decision-makers are often oblivious to their own culture. It just seems like the natural way things are done. New hires are equally unaware until they encounter a culture shift head-on. Not incidentally, an estimated 50 percent to 89 percent of top corporate hires fail within a year because of poor cultural fit. This applies down the line as well, though on lower levels; mutual dissatisfaction is less critical and new people try harder to stick it out.

But like people at the top, new hires may find that decisions are made and everyday interactions are transacted in ways wholly new to them. Instead of shared information and experiences, they might encounter structured and protected silos: differing systems for valuing performance, unfamiliar rules of behavior, and unspoken rules of communication. The atmosphere may feel colder—or warmer; the people welcoming, competitive, or even hostile.

The cultural milieu has a powerful impact on your everyday life and how you get things done. It affects your degree of engagement, your ability to do your best, and the degree of satisfaction you can take from your work. It determines many of the ways you interact with coworkers. So you want a good match.

When this proves not to be the case, is the only solution to leave? Not necessarily. The job may be important to your career path—or to your ability to feed your eating habit. A friend who left a creative field to work in a more structured industry reports that it felt like he'd blundered into alien territory. The people dressed more formally and made decisions in a more multilevel top-down pattern. He felt challenged to prove himself rather than welcomed. But because he had to live with the decision, he told himself, "This is a grown-up job that may not be fun like my old one, but I can learn to make it work."

Matthew did the same. Though still bemoaning the job he gave up, which he retrospectively saw as his personal dream job, he stayed at the new company for a number of years. "I learned to adapt and to protect myself," he shared. He dressed better. He got every agreement in writing and wrote endless memos for the record. He worked to make his own small department an oasis of cooperation and collaboration. Over time, he coached his staff in the behavior he valued, and hired carefully. In effect, he was able to create a mini-culture within the larger one.

In a big organization, long-standing departments and branches often create their own cultures. Combining two departments, which happens increasingly for financial reasons, can be just as harrowing as company mergers.

How do work cultures get so entrenched? It's generally agreed that organizations sooner or later reflect the nature and character of the people who run them. The founders create the footprint, and each generation of leaders adapt to that, filling empty spaces as they arise. Ways of thinking and doing become absorbed into the enterprise's fabric, becoming very hard to change. Today, because organizations need to be more agile and competitive, culture change is often high on the agenda. Business schools teach plenty of courses on it. But there's no magic formula—only a healthy supply of consultants.

Why should you care about corporate culture?

If you're currently employed, understanding the environment you work in helps you thrive best and make the most of what your company offers. It enables you to assess every situation within the context of company culture and make good decisions about what to do and how to behave. It saves you from committing faux pas or more serious missteps in how you communicate, ask for things, and interact. Knowing what is valued helps you choose what to focus on and what to prioritize. You have better guidelines for accomplishing more and getting more from your efforts, whatever your goals.

If you're looking for a new job, inform yourself about the culture so you can know how it does or doesn't suit you. At different points, you need a different fit because specific things become more or less important. If you start a family, for example, stability, benefits, and flex time suddenly rise to the A-list. Know yourself—what you most value at this point in your life, what you want to learn, what kind of environment most suits you, your ultimate dreams—and then balance this against a potential job and possible long-term benefits.

Looking inside corporate culture

Don't expect a manager or HR specialist to explain a corporate culture to you. You'll probably get a blank look. You need to tease it out yourself and peek under the blanket. If you're already holding a job, you can never know too much about what succeeds best in your organization. Treat this knowledge as a high priority. A formal or informal mentor can be a big help. If you're a Millennial, don't overlook the opportunity to learn how things are done, and what is valued, from the older folks. If you're a job candidate, your culture homework prepares you to interview well with both better questions and better answers. Here are some ways to investigate a culture you're part of, or may want to be.

Your best tools: observation, research, and Q&A. It's not unlike how you might have chosen a college: you probably did online research; connected with people to talk to; and once on campus, questioned the recruiter and experienced the physical environment to sense its general tone, how it made you feel. Let's look at using these approaches to investigate company culture.

Do your homework

Start with the tons of available print and online material, all easy to access. Carefully examined, the company website tells you how the organization officially sees and presents itself. Note the mission statement and values, which may or may not have a relation to reality; the style, tone, and content; the visuals with which the organization chooses to represent itself. Analyze for whom the site is written and any underlying messages you can sense in style and content choices. Check out the pages that introduce top company leaders to see who they are and how they talk about the company.

The site's history section is worth attention because it tells you how the culture was forged. This can make a tangible difference. Matthew, who moved from a culture he loved to one that disenchanted him, believes that the "good" culture resulted from the company's founding as a family enterprise. Over several generations, it maintained its personal warmth and sense of caring. A specialist in consumer electronics found a company founded by engineers a chilly place to be, compared to a similar company founded by marketers. One of us once worked for a giant retail chain that was founded seventy-five years earlier by an industry icon who kept secret accounting books and cheated his partners out of their stake when the business grew. All those years later, corporate HQ was a mean-spirited place to work.

Social media gives you a whole other dimension to review. Google the company and see what comes up. Growth projections by outside analysts? Industry issues and projections? Controversies? Reputation issues? Lawsuits? Create a Google alert to stay abreast of possible news. Facebook is increasingly used to showcase "inside" company culture by reporting on events, communicating values, and connecting to the community. Check out how an organization uses Twitter, and what it's saying. LinkedIn enables you to search out company features and identify current workers you might connect with.

Employee review sites can be especially revealing. In some, the content is "employee generated," providing firsthand opinions on each workplace. You can variously find salary information, in-depth company analyses, and ways to contact employees through Facebook or other venues. (Review sites include Glassdoor, Great Place to Work, Hallway, TheJobCrowd, and Indeed.)

Use your observation skills on site
On the premises, look around systematically and for starters, note:

- How space is arranged: Do you see any places for informal interaction? A long corridor with offices running along it sets a different tone than a more circular setup that allows for meeting space in the center.
- Do you see amenities to make life comfortable: coffee room, cafeteria, relaxation space, employee services?
- Who has the big offices, and who works in cubicles?
- How do people dress and adorn their spaces?
- Do people appear to talk to one another? Do they look relaxed and happy, or tense and self-contained?
- Does the atmosphere feel friendly or formal?
- What kind of communication is used, and what does it look like? What's posted on bulletin boards?
- Do you feel you are meeting and seeing people you can get along with and might even like to know?

Ask less obvious questions
The more informed you are through advance research, the better the questions you can come up with. For answers, people close to your age

currently working at the place you're investigating are good sources, as are the people who interview you. Here are some ideas to draw from. Of course, add your own questions to surface what's important to you. If you want a socially conscious employer, for example, ask about opportunities to do company-supported volunteer work or sponsorship for community-outreach programs. If flexible hours matter to you, ask about that. Some questions to consider:

To evaluate fit: What does it take to succeed here? What kind of people are happy working here? What kind of people do not succeed? Who would be considered a "hero"—a highly admired person—by this organization? How do you recognize and reward good work? How will I spend my days at the beginning?

Risk and growth factors: How do you encourage people to contribute new ideas? Is experimentation encouraged? Risk-taking? Is mentoring promoted, and how does it work? How do employees acquire new skills and what learning would I be eligible for? What kind of opportunities to grow are provided?

Big-picture issues: How is information shared? How are people evaluated and how often? How are people promoted? What is turnover like? Is there a lot of overtime?

"Insider" questions (depending on who you're talking to): What is the CEO like? What is your sense of company values? What is the atmosphere like: Friendly, collegial, team-oriented, supportive? Formal and structured? Competitive? Do the people like each other? Are the supervisors competent and fair? What makes you proud or happy to work here? What would you change if you could?

One more important question: Is the organization growing, holding its own, or contracting? Expanding organizations are happier and more optimistic places than those that are losing business, laying people off, or reorganizing for efficiency. To see friends fired and your own workload multiply is depressing. Worrying that they may be next makes people tense. It's been documented that when a layoff is announced, 30 percent of the remaining employees begin to look around for other opportunities. A recruiter may not share such information readily, but you can easily research this.

Look past your assumptions

In evaluating corporate culture, don't make easy assumptions based on the nature of an industry. *Workplace culture doesn't necessarily correlate with the work*. A technology organization can have a positive, warm spirit—Google is known for this, other cutting-edge tech companies are definitely not. NASA is famous for its enthusiastic team spirit, but other government agencies with missions just as high-minded are reported to be terrible places to work. Someone we know was quickly disenchanted when he scored a dream job with a national union—it turned out that he believed in the cause but not the people. A nonprofit or educational institution may have a noble mission but a negative, dehumanizing atmosphere for employees. The reverse can also be true: companies with a not-so-noble mission—like tobacco manufacturing—may invest handsomely in creating a positive, benefits-rich culture to counterbalance the defensiveness employees may feel.

Overall, it can be hard to find a culture that feels like a perfect fit and offers you the right opportunity. A decision is usually a balancing act. You may not want to rule out working for a "bad" culture, however you define that, unless you find it really unbearable. It may offer a way to get a foot in the door, expand your horizons, learn something important, gain a helpful credential, or experience a specific opportunity you'd value. If you know yourself to be a confident, assertive self-starter who can withstand some slings and arrows, a competitive setting can be a good context in which to stand out and advance toward your goals. When you feel secure in your ability to handle yourself and manage your relationships, many more options are open to you. Use your *Genie* strategies!

ENGAGE YOURSELF AND CREATE THE JOB YOU WANT

Despite your best attempts to find a good fit, you might still encounter yourself dissatisfied with your job. As we pointed out in chapter 1, fully two-thirds of employees today report themselves as unengaged. If you are part of this group because you're out of sync with your supervisor, don't like your work environment, feel stuck in place, or for any other reason, can you improve your situation so you can still look forward to work and benefit from it?

One way to integrate yourself more into your team, unit, or organization and like your job better is to find ways to engage yourself. It takes some creativity and the will to be proactive. We're sure you want to find meaning and satisfaction in your work; often, neither is handed to you. Make the effort, take the lead, and you may effect a degree of change that surprises you.

Here are some ways to jump-start your thinking.

1. Look at the big picture and figure out the "true" company mission. Maintaining the larger perspective prevents you from being caught up in immediacies and personalities. Identify ways to make your work more mission relevant.
2. Create your own work balance by juggling tasks. For example, chart a master plan of your job components, tasks, and deadlines, and then figure out how to produce the best daily experiences for yourself.
3. Profile your department's personalities deeper than you have so far to discover something new about each person and develop closer relationships with as many coworkers as possible.
4. Identify what you'd like to learn and explore how you can gain those opportunities. Company workshops, online courses, or even support for outside learning experiences are often available.
5. Join task forces or committees or cross-departmental project teams that are open to you, even if you have to do so on your own time.
6. Identify a potential mentor, in your department or elsewhere, and plan how to make contact and introduce yourself as someone worthy of the person's time and energy. Find role models to learn from as well.
7. Build alliances outside your workplace. Join professional associations and participate actively. You'll get to know significant people in your field as well as peers.
8. If your job is poorly defined or you don't have enough interesting work, create the role yourself based on your own strengths and interests.

Here's how one person redefined his role by taking the initiative. Lars had begun a new job at a brokerage firm. Despite bringing strong experience to the job, he found himself relegated to backup tasks. He repeatedly told his supervisor of his interest in helping with department projects but continued to be sidelined. He suspected that the department head was uncomfortable with his personal fast-paced style. As months passed, he was sure he'd been pigeonholed and would not be given scope to demonstrate his abilities. He found himself with unwelcome time on his hands.

Lars decided to look around the office for people who were understaffed and could use more manpower. He found Ed, an up-and-coming program director working on a complex project with too much to do. "I told Ed I had some extra time and would be interested in offering whatever help I could to put the project together. He took me up on it and working with him, I was not only impressed with what he was doing, I learned some new strategies."

Lars found himself with a valued ally and more insight into the company. When he spotted a chance for a promotion into another department, Ed's recommendation helped significantly. His new position gave him plenty of new challenges and room for growth.

Taking the initiative to handle "extra" work gave Lars the chance to create value for himself. It can be a much more effective tactic than complaining about your situation—which endears you to no one. If you want to use an approach like this, be sure you keep fulfilling the "regular" job requirements and ask for the supervisor's approval if it seems in order. Always offer to do more work for your own department first.

BUILD YOUR IN-HOUSE ALLIANCES

Hannah, a customer relations specialist, was hired as department manager by a midsized organization. The job required her to work closely with other department heads on the same level, but she found that it was harder than expected to get buy-in from her peers. Her ideas were often "overlooked" at meetings, and the others seemed to come to agreement on major decisions with little discussion and remarkable speed. The steamroller effect puzzled her.

Hannah knew most of the other directors had been with the organization much longer than she had. She also realized that as the only woman in the group, she was experiencing a classic male-female challenge: subtle mistreatment that made her feel marginalized. She tried adopting a more assertive communication style with little result. Later on, knowing she was about to leave, one group member enlightened her.

"When I started here about fifteen years ago, John, Phil, and Russ were also new," Bob said. "We were all about the same age and at the same stage of our careers. So at the very beginning we made a pact. Whenever we found an opportunity, we would back each other up, praise each other's work, and promote each other's reputation. It's really worked! We all got where we wanted to be faster than we would have, and now that we're all department heads, we get what we want most of the time."

That, dear reader, is how secret alliances can work—and be used against you. We all know about "old boys' networks," sets of entrenched decision-makers who favor "their own kind." There are also "new boys' networks" and, more often than in the past, "new girls' networks." In Hannah's case, the network included one-third of the company directors, enough for the members to move things their way especially when they chose to hash out a matter before a meeting and come to agreement.

Is a network like this unethical? The group did not appear to use its alliance to undermine other people, but certainly there was a manipulative quality to what they achieved together. Non–group members found it harder to promote their own viewpoints and, no doubt, competitors were outpaced. It's an example of group power that we don't recommend, but it brings home what alliances can do, for or against you. Large organizations especially may breed many such under-the-ice networks. Women have only recently begun to catch up with the value of forging their own.

Work alliances ideally give you a support system, a reality check, a go-to group to bounce things off of and help solve problems. Allies keep you informed of things happening outside your immediate line of sight. This matters because day-to-day life makes us myopic and we may fail to see the bigger picture even when it directly affects us.

Alliance-building guidelines

Look proactively for people you respect, would like to know better, and can learn from. They need not be like you—in fact, there are many reasons to identify people with different skills and perspective than your own. If they are better than you are at some things, that's all to the good. Keep in mind that just as in playing tennis or dancing, the better the other person is, the better you perform yourself. You never need other people to perform badly in order for you to look good—and be good—at what you do. Remember to:

1. Create alliances based on positive goals and aim for a collaborative spirit.
2. Look beyond your immediate environment to build cross-departmental relationships.
3. Act as a resource for your allies whenever you can and give advice—when asked.

4. Share helpful information but stay ethical and don't break confidences.
5. Hold up your end and more when collaborating.
6. Refrain from gossiping or bad-mouthing others—people assume you'll do the same to them.
7. Actively sustain the alliance with regular contact and genuine interest in the other people.

A work alliance does not need to be, and shouldn't be, a secret society. In fact, you'll benefit in many ways from other people's observations that you have friends. Many younger people don't realize that a network's value increases over time and may become instrumental to their future. Certainly, a high-up manager may be helpful when you need a recommendation, or may even bring you along when he or she moves on up. *But your best future referrals, offers, and support will come from your peers.* So it is smart to actively cultivate those alliances, maintain them when you move around, and sustain them into the future.

EXPRESS EMOTION AT WORK: YES? NO? WHEN?

It seems obvious that almost everyone will function best in a warm, collegial atmosphere with low anxiety and stress. At work, you are part of a community, and it's far better to be a good member of it, a credit rather than a debit. Sharing a positive spirit goes surprisingly far in enabling any organization to function well. You might think that every company would consider it high priority to foster this atmosphere and develop an environment of emotional comfort. A growing number of organizations are in fact trying to do this—it's often a "culture change" objective—but shifting from chilly and competitive to warm and caring demands much more than a cosmetic makeover. Moreover, implementation falls to managers. A wise one can create an emotionally comfortable mini-world, like Matthew did in the story earlier in this chapter. But as we have discussed, many managers are not equipped for the human relations part of their jobs.

Most organizations do value self-controlled behavior. Positive emotions—like enthusiasm, happiness, and serenity—are welcome in almost every workplace. Negative emotions are not. People who are often angry, mean tempered, dissatisfied, or apt to burst into tears are disruptive. The rest of us become distracted and upset. And perhaps unhappy ourselves.

As a rule of thumb: determine to check your negative emotions like anger, anxiety, and jealousy at the door. Rightly or wrongly, whatever the provocation, succumbing to uncontrolled displays of such feelings marks you as a loser. Anger is the biggest problem for many people. Know yourself: you may be quick to anger as a defense mechanism or in response to a particular trigger. But other than facing up to a bully, from the organizational standpoint, it's hard to think of many situations that justify the risk. Better to take yourself to a cool place and think through the pros and cons of a strong reaction. What is the risk to you? Your job? Your future? Use *Genie* techniques such as the Power Pause and the Emotion Thermostat visualization to regain perspective. If, in your cooler moments, you judge that you need to address the issue that caused your response, draw on a role reversal technique to understand the interaction and plan the conversation carefully.

What about when your emotion is caused by an extreme reason, such as a major disruption in your personal life? Gauge organizational culture in deciding what to share with the boss or coworkers. It's rarely a good idea to share personal problems and work frustrations. However, if a situation affects your performance and you want time away or to access a special resource, it's necessary to speak to your supervisor. In such cases, there's no need to maintain a poker face—it would seem abnormal, in fact. People find that an honest interaction can create a closer bond.

What about when you're directly faced with someone else's anger? When this happens in the presence of other people, it can challenge relationships beyond your personal one with the angry person. In the case of a boss who loses her temper, office morale is threatened and witnesses may be strongly affected, as they are when they see a bully's attack. For your part, keep your cool, and figure out later how to address whatever caused the anger, and also its aftermath. It's entirely relevant to point out the impact of an outburst on bystanders and how it undermines your ability to perform well.

If a coworker loses his temper or attacks you, be aware that witnesses will form a judgment about you as well as the transgressor. Deal with the situation in a way that preserves your self-respect. For example, you might say, "Let's talk about it when you cool down," and move out of his vicinity. Other people will find a measured response impressive. If, on the other hand, you lose your own temper, you may give credence to the attacker's claims.

A useful technique is one you may find familiar because customer service reps are trained to use it: mirroring. It reassures angry people that they are being heard, as in: "I hear you are upset because your name was omitted from the meeting notice" or "I understand you're unhappy that I was picked for the promotion." No explanations are offered, but if the simple message is delivered in a neutral, sympathetic tone, it typically has a calming effect.

What if you are subjected to sustained hostility by a coworker? Here's how you can strategize and be a good community citizen.

- Take some time, preferably not in the office, to reflect and think things through.
- If you've made a mistake, own it. Apologize if appropriate.
- If you see no specific reason for the sustained hostility, get to know the person's patterns and the triggers that activate them.
- Find ways to work around those patterns and avoid the triggers.
- Work to identify your own triggers so you can refrain from reacting to provocation.
- Write an action plan for yourself with techniques for handling situations with this particular person as they arise. This preparation helps you abstract yourself from the moment's heat and enables you to think better on your feet.

ENCOUNTERING GENDER UNFAIRNESS

Unfortunately, gender bias against women is built into the fabric of many organizations, regardless of their type. This is clearly the case in typically male-dominated industries like engineering and science. But even in fields where most members are female, the upper echelons have typically been populated by men. For example, until recently, nearly all school principals and superintendents were men even though probably 90 percent of educators were women. Businesses like advertising, law, and architecture, even in this enlightened day and age, are for the most part directed by men. Most surprising, perhaps, is the scarcity of women in the higher ranks of dot-coms and startup organizations.

Such scarcities are often attributed to a "pipeline" issue—not enough women choose to qualify for the field or commit to the step-by-step process of rising to the top. The reasons cited for this situation include the absence of high-achieving role models to emulate; entrenched, unspoken policies that favor promoting men; and many women's own sense that advancing in their field is too expensive emotionally or in terms of family priorities.

In response to women's more forceful voices and their own need to compete for talent, many industries and organizations are sponsoring research to find out where the potential female leaders are and how to cultivate them, just as they are with minorities. One consequence of the quest for equal opportunity and fairness: more men are starting to complain that the cards are stacked against them now. So it's complicated for everyone. But men still hold the advantage. It's hard to think of a profession that practices a bias against men. A man who trains to be a nurse, or a kindergarten teacher, may arouse skepticism and be teased by his female cohort, but once qualified, he will have far better opportunities to be hired and promoted.

So here is our advice for women navigating gender bias in organizational waters: recognize that the currents are tricky. Many Millennials, believing robustly in their own value and the idea of inclusiveness, are shocked to discover gender or any other bias in their workplaces. Gen Xers, often the middle managers, are just as unhappy to find that after a certain point they face a glass ceiling, though it may have moved upward since their mothers' experience. And older women may remain shadowed by their own career history.

This is the case with Lois, the first woman to achieve partner status in her law firm, as recounted by another firm partner, Tim. In awarding her partnership, the law group acknowledged Lois's contributions to the common cause and the group welcomed her warmly. "But we found that she constantly complained about how she was treated. When she was accidentally omitted from a group e-mail, she was furious.

"She assumed bad intentions on our part rather than thinking it might be an oversight, which it was. She seems to live her whole life on edge for every occasion where she can say, 'I do the grunt work, he gets the glory.' She's constantly angry and expresses it really well, so it ends up reinforcing her perceptions. She's exhausting to work with."

Tim's account suggests that Lois no doubt has some legitimate grounds for complaint. "We did leave her out of one meeting because the particular client insisted on meeting only with three specific men. Was there a gender bias? Sure, but what should we do? Tell the client he could only meet with people *we* consider our best?"

That's a difficult question. But it's clear that as a result of her simmering resentment, Lois is being left out of more meetings. "It's getting so we don't want to be around her," Tim says. "I avoid her as much as I can myself."

Lois's career history as a woman over forty probably gives her legitimate cause to suspect she's being discriminated against. Women still have an uphill battle to demonstrate that they possess "gravitas" as well as talent and skill. This makes it even more important that women practice strategic approaches to their careers and relationship building.

Lois would be more effective if she suspended her disbelief and framed the incidents that make her unhappy to find other interpretations. This would lead her to resolve the problem in a much better and more casual way ("Hey, Hal, I didn't get the e-mail on the new Waterbird account. Did I fall off your distribution list?"). And taking account of the men's perspective would tell her how dangerously she's undermining herself. Pausing deliberatively before she lashes out would help her respond more advantageously and enable her to improve relationships rather than hurt them.

Behaving as if peoples' intentions are good—even when you suspect they are not—gives you far more control than escalating a problem by acting on worst-scenario assumptions. Remind yourself how hard it can be to know in the moment whether a problem is objectively real, or if it might derive more from your own set of negative assumptions. We like this quote from the writer Anaïs Nin: "We don't see things as they are, but as we are."

We are not in the least trying to minimize gender-based problems and obstacles in the workplace, or deny that there are important differences between men and women. Susan knows from her psychotherapy practice that both sexes experience much the same challenges: a "bad" boss, disrespect, unequal opportunity, undermining coworkers, unpleasant environments. However, how they react to situations can differ.

Recent research validates old observations that women more typically blame themselves when things go wrong, overinflate the importance of their mistakes, and take things more personally. They tend to focus on their "faults" and "inadequacies," which often leads them to underestimate their own capabilities.

In contrast, many men feel they are intrinsically qualified to go after what they want and that they will come up to par once the opportunity is won. They more often possess a win-lose attitude (note that most books on work relationships written by men use battleground terminology and recommend manipulative "power" techniques). Many men are more likely to react with anger when mistreated, whether expressed or not.

Does this sound like gross generalization? Of course, but unfortunately, it's supported by research. Where does all this leave a woman?

Many companies are initiating programs to encourage women to stay and grow through mentoring, sustained support, and accommodation to their needs. The motivation is not usually philanthropic: many women-led companies are recognized as notably profitable, and more companies understand that they need to maintain and develop this half of their talent pool.

Assess your organization objectively to recognize the glass ceilings, if any; look for opportunities extended to women and take advantage of them; and if you are ambitious, work to *be* valuable, by learning and building your skills. Use *Workplace Genie* techniques to *feel* valuable and to communicate that value and your high expectations.

Male readers may take issue with the foregoing focus on women. We fully realize that a number of men feel that their own opportunities become more limited if and when women, as well as minority groups to which they do not belong, get preference for hiring and promotion. The redress period in all such situations poses difficulties for everyone, and certainly individuals can be unfairly treated in the process. If we figure out how to solve this major issue, we promise to write a book about that.

AT ISSUE: SEXUAL HARASSMENT

Nothing feels more personal than being sexually harassed at work, but unfortunately, it's all too common because it's intrinsic to a company culture or, at the least, is tolerated because leaders look the other way. An extraordinary one out of three to four women, depending on the study, report having been sexually harassed in the workplace. As do one in ten men. So this is a reality everyone must be prepared for, outrageous as that might seem.

High-profile cases of pervasive sexual harassment in many organizations and entire industries are coming into the light, though not fast enough for many people. Often it's difficult to pin down what constitutes sexual harassment in everyday office life. Where do we draw the line between acceptable and unacceptable behavior: Does an off-color joke qualify as sexual harassment? Or when someone teases you about how you dress, or walk? Or talks about pornographic materials at work?

Response is very individual. It depends on how you see it and how it makes you feel. Our rule of thumb is that whatever makes you personally uncomfortable in this arena is sexual harassment to you. Also, it makes a difference whether the perpetrator is your boss or a coworker. It can be challenging to chastise a peer for bad behavior, but perfectly possible. When it comes to the boss, trying to change behavior is harder and riskier. Therefore, lines to prevent the experience should be more tightly drawn. It is criminal in every sense for someone in power to extort sexual favors, complicity, or acquiescence to sex-related jokes, innuendos, insults, comments, and so on.

As in other power situations, it is often hard to seek redress. You probably need to worry about keeping your job and not risking your future career by speaking up. And you usually cannot be sure you will find anyone concerned with correcting the situation when it involves high-up people. But here are steps we recommend.

- Make it clear to a misbehaving boss in a neutral, objective way that you do not welcome or enjoy his or her words or actions and wish them to stop.
- Protect yourself by documenting everything: keep those messages, write down incidents soon after they occur, observe when other people are subjected to similar treatment, and take note.
- Investigate company policy. Most organizations have written, explicit definitions of sexual harassment and strict rules against it.
- If the treatment continues, find the best person to talk to in the HR group; bring your backup documentation and talk in terms of the written company policy. Ask what will be done to follow up and when you can check back in.
- Follow up on the timeline specified. If the bad behavior has persisted, make it clear that you do not intend to let the matter drop.
- Consider going up a level or two to bring the problem to the attention of your manager's superiors, especially if you see no action from HR.
- Network around your department to connect with others who are suffering the same mistreatment—and if you feel the situation exists company wide, extend the networking and build alliances.
- Keep in mind that there are government equal rights offices on the local level and on up, but if you go that route, don't expect a cordial reaction from your employer. You will probably not

want to work there anymore. Whistle-blowers lead tough lives. Evidence is very important when you complain to an equal rights office, or to your own lawyer, so keep the documentation going.

We encourage you to address the situation in the way that's most appropriate for you. It's hard to be the first one to speak up, but often, a number of other people are waiting on the sidelines for someone to come forward. In numbers there is strength—and power. Some stellar offenders from the political and entertainment worlds have been toppled off their perches by group action, and wouldn't it be nice if this happened more often, and sooner, in more places?

INTO ACTION

1. *Profile the culture within which you presently work.* Adapt the profiling checklist for individuals, covered in chapter 5, to the organization. Include your best interpretation of the company's mission and values, how decisions get made and who makes them, the general atmosphere, what is rewarded, what is discouraged, and communication style. Write up your summary profile. Did you learn anything that surprised you? Anything useful?

2. *Profile the best culture you've worked in.* What made it a good place to work? Who set the tone? Did the culture encourage you to do a great job, even if it was pumping gas or scooping ice cream? What made you like going to work every day? Could the ideas apply to other kinds of organizations, like the one you work for now?

3. *Formulate your best future culture.* Think about what you ideally want in your next work environment, taking account of your own personality and preferences. Do the preceding exercises clarify what to look for? Write out your goal regarding the corporate culture in which you could flourish.

4. *Create a culture change plan.* Considering your ideas for the preceding two activities, if you could change your current work culture in one particular way, what would you do? Can you think of even a tiny way to start such a change that might help you feel

happier with the environment? If you were in charge, how would your plan read?

5. *Consider your work alliances.* Inside the company, do you have a network of people who mutually trust and support one another, talk to one another honestly, and share information? If so, consider if there are other people who would make good additions to the alliance, or whether it might be of value to build another alliance. If you don't presently have a support network, think about how it would benefit you, who you would like to connect with, and how to start. Create a plan!

Chapter 12

GETTING IT TOGETHER: BIG-PICTURE TOOLS TO PLAN YOUR OWN TRANSFORMATIONS

Workplace Genie has given you a wide range of strategies and techniques to help you see yourself and other people more fully, and act with confidence to transform your relationships. We want to equip you to take an active role in your own growth, improve your work relationships, manage imperfect people and situations, and come to the best decisions.

This special chapter offers several ways to fit everything together for your own big picture. Find here tools for telling your own story, breaking free from bad overshadowing experiences, and planning how to transform important relationships.

Read and use this material with imagination and interpret it to match your own experiences and needs. Many of the strategies shared throughout the book will support these personal journeys.

TELL YOUR STORY TO YOURSELF

Storytelling is today's dominant tool for marketing, online content, organizational development, and public relations. It seems that everyone has discovered the magnetic power of story to illuminate and engage people emotionally. It's also a psychotherapy tool, leading to insights that help people work through problems and move toward change. Psychologists call it "narrative therapy." It frees people to dig beyond the obvious and discover ways to think out what's personally meaningful, what to nurture, what to reframe, what to change. Telling your story connects you with your own inner resources and helps you tap into them on both an everyday basis and to meet challenges.

Your story is a way to understand your own evolution, in which your work history plays a central role. Use story power to find your themes and see how the different stages and parts of your life fit together and have reinforced each other. Here's how the comic and author Tig Notaro put it: "It was through writing that I was able to really understand my story, to really tell it to myself for the first time."

We are different people at different times and the sum total of all the people we've been—our different roles, partnerships, experiences. But we typically immerse ourselves in our immediate problems. Telling your own story can freshen your motivation, reinvigorate your values, and remind you of what's important to you. It helps you clarify who you are and integrate your experience. It also lets you put bad experiences, antagonistic people, and setbacks in a bigger perspective.

Here's the best reward: telling your own story enables you to adjust your own course to head in the direction you choose. You can change your ending! This is more doable than you may think. You already know that your self-perspective shifts with time as well as mood and circumstances. Meeting someone in first grade, for example, takes on a whole different meaning if you re-meet and marry that person twenty-five years later. Or work for her. Being fired usually feels like the biggest tragedy of our lives at first—but if it frees us for a better future than the path we were on, it becomes a lucky break. When you accept the possibility of creating change for yourself, you can adjust your perspective on where you've been, where you want to go, and how to get there.

We'll give you a simple way to go about finding your story. Commit to doing this in writing, because if you try to just imagine it mentally, you miss the threads that lead to new connections. This story is basically for you alone, so don't worry about perfect writing. However, you'll find that self-editing to use language more effectively, and articulate your feelings better, will push you forward dramatically.

We suggest that you don't restrict your life story to work. Aim to tell the whole-person story that covers the important relationships and milestones. You want your work to fit into your life—not the other way around—and storytelling will remind you of this and of what you care about. Give yourself some substantial private time to begin and as many sessions as you need. What could be more interesting, or more productive, to invest in?

A build-your-story structure

1. *Create a timeline.* Start at the beginning with the basic facts—where you were born, family life, outstanding childhood memories, school, work history, all the way to the present. If you want more structure, first make a list of the important stages of your life in any way that suits you. For example:
   A. Early years
   B. Education
   C. First job
   D. Dating
   E. Marriage
   F. Homes
   G. Career stages
   H. Interests and passions
   I. Talents and skills
   J. Biggest influences
   K. Any other categories

2. *Review the timeline, putting yourself inside each stage to free associate.* For each phase or category, identify and note the most important events in your life, the turning points, major learning experiences, achievements, great moments, times of stress. Include obstacles and challenges you overcame in both your personal and work life. Also note disappointments, setbacks, backward loops, and anything that at the time seemed like a failure or difficult personal challenge.

3. *Review your timeline and highlight what seems most important from your "now" perspective.* Do you see any patterns? When you suspect you are glimpsing one, look back through your notes again to see if you can back up the theme. For example, you might notice that you've always spent spare time doing a certain kind of hobby or volunteer work, or you liked working in a certain kind of place, or got along well with specific kinds of people, or always returned to a yet-unrealized goal.

4. *Put it all together in one narrative.* There is no wrong way to tell it, it's yours. Write it as long or as short as you want. Use the first

person—*I*. Let your mind wander in pulling events and people together, or organize carefully, according to what's comfortable. A technique that professional storytellers use (yes, there are such people) is to use the present tense all the way through, as if it's happening right now. This helps you relive the experience more deeply and bring to the surface concrete details that make what happened, and how you felt about it, more tangible. Best starting point? First memory—or anywhere along the line. Alternatively, you can start somewhere in the middle at a pivotal moment, then look back and, finally, forward. When you have your draft, edit what you wrote to improve the language and organization, or not, as you choose.

5. *Put your story aside for a few days or more, and then read it.* Think about what you can learn from it. Ask yourself some questions. How does it make you feel? Any surprises at what you highlighted? Does it give you a different perspective on your accomplishments and your disappointments? Do you see a lot to be proud of? More resilience, perseverance, determination than you thought? More capabilities? Do past nonsuccesses seem less important? Can you see what you learned from them? Did you recollect some resources you used in earlier times that apply to present life? Do you see any new connections between events or people in your life? Any insights into how everything connects to your own motivation and aspirations?

6. *Look at the present as your current "end." Do you want to change this ending?* You have the power to bring about a different outcome, regardless of your age and immediate situation. Just as you can reframe your perspective on a problem, you can reframe the past—your story to date—and understand it from many different angles, all of which have truth. Remember that you unconsciously shift perspective all the time, like when you discover new information you were previously unaware of—for example, a family secret that recasts your understanding of the past or the reason why you lost (or gained) an opportunity.

7. *Think about whether to shift course.* Endings are temporary and malleable. You can change your perspective to redefine where

you are now or follow through on a particular theme. You might find that your career path got sidetracked in a direction you don't like and now you want to make a small, or big, shift in where you're headed. You might rediscover a passion you've neglected and decide to reignite it. You may be able to better define an opportunity you want, or gain clarity on an important decision. You may readjust your priorities and decide to spend less time at the office—or spend it differently. Or you might look at your current manager and coworkers in a bigger perspective and feel moved to nurture some relationships, be more forgiving of transgressors, or overlook small annoyances.

We know your story is a good one. But if you find that it focuses on disappointments, missed opportunities, and mistakes, we encourage a revisit. *This time, consciously begin the journey with a positive perspective because when you expect to see the good, you do.*

An alternative process: If you worry that this job sounds too big, start small. Give some thought to your turning points, obstacles, defining moments, and relationships. Then write one or more anecdotes rather than the full story. Whether from your business or personal life, these focused stories also have a lot to give us. They often become microcosms of our bigger world.

If you find the storytelling experience illuminating, plan to repeat it periodically.

Many people find that as a side benefit, knowing their story is a major business tool. It's invaluable for entrepreneurs because it defines their unique assets and inspiration, enabling them to communicate and market effectively. Many others find it helps them present themselves much better in job interviews, among other occasions.

ANALYZE BAD EXPERIENCES TO FREE YOURSELF

In both of the authors' professional work—psychotherapy and business communications—we encounter people who feel that their entire career, or even life, is overshadowed by a mistake, "failure," or one intensely bad experience such as becoming a bully's target. Moving on is hard. In addition to the psychological and emotional damage inflicted, which can linger indefinitely, they often worry about repeating what happened. And the fear is often justified: our expectations can provoke precisely the responses we don't want, and produce the outcomes we most worry about. To counter this, we created a "Ghostbusters Questionnaire." It's presented as a basis for your own thinking. Adapt it to your own circumstances and needs. This process may take some time if done thoughtfully, but it can help you retrieve your confidence and put the experience in perspective more fully. The questionnaire is followed by two examples of its use.

Bust those ghosts with fifteen questions

If you feel haunted by a situation or interaction from the past, try this analyzer. Answering these questions should provoke more systematic analysis than you've brought to bear before and put things in a new perspective. Write your answers out.

1. Who was involved in the experience or event?
2. Describe the problem.
3. How did it start? If you don't know, make an educated guess.
4. How did it resolve? What were the repercussions at the time?
5. How does it affect you now? Why do you think the situation still feels hard to leave behind?
6. What would it take to get past the negative feelings?
7. What might you have done differently? Include both actions and words.
8. Looking back objectively, as if it happened to someone else, what elements were beyond your control?
9. Can you recognize whether a personal pattern of your own may have been a factor in creating the situation—or reacting to it?
10. Looking back, can you identify whether a personal pattern or personality aspect of the other person was a factor?
11. Can you think of any extenuating circumstances that may have escaped you in the heat or confusion of the moment?
12. What did you learn?
13. What have you done differently since? Have you changed in some way?
14. How would you handle the situation differently today?
15. What positives can you identify that emerged over the long run?

We find that the Ghostbusters strategy produces different kinds of results for everyone, because our ghosts are as individual as we are. Here are two outcomes, capsulized from the writers' responses.

Ghostbusters Example 1:
Escaping a bully's legacy

This example is Lorna's, whose narrative about being a bully's target is recounted in chapter 8.

She was faced with an unrelenting bully who forced her to resign from a career position in which she'd been extremely successful. He was impossible to please, embarrassed her in public, and demeaned her at every turn. She responded by keeping a stiff upper lip and tried to continue her work, assuming that her great track record and familiarity with the powerful board members would ultimately protect her.

She relates: "After I gave up and quit, I found that my confidence was totally shot. It felt like everything I'd done in my whole career—what I had taken so much pride in—was stolen away from me as if it never existed. The fact that none of my colleagues or any board members stood up for me was devastating. It made me question all my judgments, my perceptions about people, and my own worth. I couldn't imagine looking for another job in my field, not knowing what reference I'd get, and felt too old to start over."

But Lorna did look for another job and carved out a successful and satisfying career as an independent consultant. Yet, ten years later she still wondered what she could have done differently and felt she'd never quite recovered her full confidence. She worked through the Ghostbusters analysis and quickly saw the obvious: that most of what happened was out of her control. Her new boss's mind was made up even before he came on the scene, a fact that she learned later. The board members and coworkers were similarly beyond her reach because the bully had more influence with them than she could. More gradually, Lorna also saw that she could have done some things differently. One was recognizing much sooner that she wasn't facing a hurdle she could get past, but a bullying situation from the top, the hardest kind to fight. "This would have given me more cards to play before he did so much damage."

And: "Earlier in my job I should have worked on stronger alliances, which would at least have given me advance information and some emotional support. And I could have stood up for myself—how could it make the situation worse? Then I'd have preserved some self-respect. Most of all, I wish I'd had the courage to ask direct questions and find out what he told other people that caused them to turn against me. I allowed myself to take the rejection personally—which I see is a pattern I'm prone to—and was afraid of what I'd hear. So I was left wondering forever, without a sense of closure."

But the big illumination was that in looking back, Lorna confirmed more strongly that both her life and work became ultimately more interesting and expansive than had she stayed in the job "forever." "I was forced to make a change I wouldn't have chosen—but now can feel proud of myself. It's like the lemon and lemonade idea. I ended up using the awful feeling of loss to energize myself. I can't see myself ever in that situation again, but I've learned to take more care with my assumptions and stand up for myself with more courage. And I take more trouble to find people I can trust to work with. I didn't see how important that was before and I never want to feel that isolated again."

The analysis helped Lorna put her full career in perspective, brought her to better closure, and diminished the emotional hold of her experience. It brought home to her that her career was ultimately better for the change and that she had more than re-earned her confidence through how she handled her new life.

Ghostbusters Example 2:
Understanding a grudge situation

In chapter 9, we talked about Dianne, punished by a coworker who refused to accept her apology for going over her head to complain that her coworker, Alison, wasn't pulling her weight. "After Alison found out and yelled at me, I saw she was right, and I apologized endlessly, but she never spoke to me again. I felt awful: defensive, self-conscious, fearful of running across her. Sometimes I dreaded going to work. It kept me from making friends. I was never comfortable in the job after that. I was really careful around coworkers and worried about making interpersonal mistakes."

After taking herself through the Ghostbusters analysis, Dianne asked herself, "What could I have done?"

"Nothing," she concluded.

How much of the post-incident experience was in her control? "None of it."

Was there a pattern reflected in her behavior, looking back? "I feel bad when I sense rejection. That dominated how I took being treated that way."

We suggested that Dianne try a role reversal. If the situation were reversed and she learned that Alison had gone to the boss and complained that Dianne wasn't doing her share, what would she have done? She surprised herself: "I think I would have said I'm sorry you find I haven't been doing my part of the work—I must have misunderstood what was needed. In the future tell me directly when there's a problem, OK?" So Dianne would have taken responsibility, resolved the problem, and side-stepped a hurtful rift.

Does this give her a different perspective now? "I see that *her* pattern was hostile and aggressive—maybe that's who she is. I might have noticed the clues better. Or maybe I did and that's why I didn't go to her originally. But anyone can make a mistake. It wasn't that big an offense! So it looks like her hostile pattern met my pattern of readiness to feel rejected, and I got stuck in that depressing cycle. She probably enjoyed it, but I sure didn't!"

Anything learned? "I need to respect myself more. I need to take account of the reality of other people and blame myself less if things go wrong. I need to be more aware of my own patterns and try to look at things that happen more objectively. And I have to practice expecting good things from other people—I don't think I'll meet many like Alison, so it would be a big new mistake to expect people to act with such meanness."

REACH FOR A RELATIONSHIP RESET

Genie wants to prepare you for action! If you're reading this book, we suspect you have a specific relationship in mind that you'd love to transform. We further suspect that for many readers, the person is their boss. If not, you can easily translate this approach for use with a coworker, colleague, collaborator, or partner. The approach we suggest has two parts: an analysis of the situation to clarify your goals and challenges, and conversations you can initiate as a result. The book has prepared you for this with numerous strategies and techniques. Draw on those that resonate with you and suggest themselves to your specific case. We'll remind you of some specific approaches as you go along.

Voice your goal and analyze the obstacles

For demonstration purposes, we'll assume the boss is a reasonable and nice enough person rather than a mean-spirited bully. We'll call him J. for John, or Judy, at your preference. There are no wrong answers here, so be honest. The idea is to move you into a cognitive mode so you can better know what you want, who the other person is, and how you can elicit the actions or words you want.

1. *Write down your goal as precisely as you can.* What would a better relationship with J. look like? What do I want to change about how we interact? How would this affect my work life?

2. *What does J. say and/or do that makes me feel dissatisfied with our relationship?* Be concrete. For example: J. doesn't adopt my ideas, gives me too much criticism (or not enough guidance), didn't give me the good performance review I deserved, never talks to me, doesn't smile at me, and so on.

3. *What one, two, or three practical things would I like J. to do (or stop doing) to improve our relationship?* For example: I'd like J. to give me half an hour per week of undivided attention and listen, smile in the morning and say hello, give me more interesting assignments, mentor me more.

4. *How well do I know J.?* Have I built a profile? How to do this is fully spelled out in chapter 5, but among the characteristics to consider are:
    –   What J. is most proud of
    –   What stresses J. might be under, at work and at home
    –   What J. values most—skills, personal qualities, expertise, flexibility, resourcefulness, versatility, and so on
    –   J.'s strong points
    –   J.'s hot buttons and insecurities
    –   People J. is most comfortable with or not so much
    –   Access points—a common interest, sense of humor, sports, hobbies, books, music, movies, television shows

5. *Turn the spotlight on yourself.* What have I learned reading this book about my own negative assumptions? Personal patterns? Limited perspective? Ways of interacting? In what ways might I be provoking responses I don't like? Admit the possibility that you are part of the interaction. Gain insight on this by practicing the Empty Chair Role Reversal, consulting your Wise Future Self, visualizing your typical conversation with J., considering whether strong emotions cloud your perceptions, and so on.

6. *Perform a reality check.* Is your goal achievable? If J. doesn't get along with anyone, or only likes people of a certain age or gen-

der, your road is much rougher. Nor is it practical to expect J. to give you his own job, if that's what you want. Your requests must be reasonable to J. But don't ditch what you want just because it's ambitious—for example, a big promotion. Just know there's no quick fix: you need to visualize a step-by-step approach to winning what you want and cover all the necessary bases.

7. *Review all this data and insight and brainstorm with yourself, or a trusted friend, on how you might take the initiative to achieve your goal.* You might create a list of small gestures that change the atmosphere, like saying good morning or thank you more often. You might practice communicating a relaxed cheerfulness that says you're happy to be at work. Or you might decide to stop resenting other people's great assignments and do a better job on yours. Or go out of your way to learn a new skill on your own time.

Take the conversational lead

Some of the analysis you did in the previous section should suggest direct action: ways to improve the quality of your work or its value in J.'s eyes, for example. But now you are also equipped to introduce your concerns and discuss them productively. A good approach is to plan a two- or three-step process that allows you to build step by step.

The first conversation might start with the obvious: asking direct questions. Unless your profile of your boss suggests she is not open to questions, find an opportunity to converse at a good time of day, and keep an open, receptive mind. *You may hear things you don't like and it's important not to show resistance or resentment.* See yourself as on a fact-finding mission. A preliminary overture can be as simple as:

- How am I doing?
- How can I do better? Do you see an area where I can improve?
- Can I touch base with you once a week (or once a month, or quarter)?

If you need to be more specific, try questions like "Can you give me guidelines for prioritizing better?" or "Can you suggest a way I could have done this better?"

Listen attentively and debrief yourself immediately after the exchange. Observe the clues to how J. judges employees, how he sees you, what *he* wants from *you.* Your openness will show, and it is a rare supervisor who is not pleased when someone wants to contribute more. You're already a step ahead on the road to a better relationship.

What if you don't like what J. wants? Or uncover a major area of conflict? The difference may feel unresolvable—for example, J. wants you to undertake work you hate, or work over weekends, or collaborate with a competitor. Before rejecting whatever it is outright, break down what is asked of you to find aspects that you *can* adjust to. For example, you might be able to use your work time differently, or check office e-mail on weekends, or challenge yourself to work well with someone you don't care for.

Think: What can I live with? What not? If the total picture doesn't work for you, you're still ahead. You've gained a much clearer understanding of your circumstances and can make better decisions about whether to stay on or look to move out.

The second conversation can follow up. If the first conversation goes even reasonably well, you have succeeded in *humanizing the situation.* You may have shifted the relationship—incrementally, to be sure—but enough to improve the climate, identify a harmful pattern, or shift a negative mindset a little. And you've gathered a great deal of information to process. You may now know all or some of the following:

- What J. responded to well
- What was uncomfortable for J
- Where J. got impatient
- What sparked J.'s interest
- Where J. closely focused and where he glazed over
- What questions J. asked and what they tell you
- Your options for follow-up

And, of course, you know how to do a better job in terms of your supervisor's measures of success.

The third conversation can accomplish even more. Imagine what you might gain with approaches like these:

- Ask J. how he mastered certain skills.
- Ask how you can help more at crunch time.
- Tell J. how he helped you with something (which primes the boss to pay attention to what motivates you—like praise, for example).

- Suggest a solution to a problem.
- Tell J. *he's* doing a good job—a supervisor highly values hearing this from an employee.
- Pay J. a sincere compliment about something you can respect or admire: how he handled a difficult customer, how he ran a meeting, how he answered a tough question, how he makes time to talk to staff.

And finally, how radical is this: offer to take him out to lunch. Lunch will give you an opportunity to ask him more good questions, get to know him, and become known. Are you thinking that no one does that? All the more reason. The risk is negligible; the reward big. He or she may not accept, but the offer takes root anyway. If the idea seems really foreign to the culture, stick to buying coffee.

A relationship reset takes time. To keep yourself motivated, remember that when you take the lead to transform a relationship in a manner that's sensitive to the other person, you accomplish a great deal. Just about every manager respects the subordinate who wants to learn, do more, and become better at her work. Your J. may be imperfect in many ways, temperamentally and in management style. Like everyone else, your boss is probably caught up with her own expectations and may not realize that they aren't clear to the staff. Or that people need more training, tools, or other resources to meet her demands. By being a better employee, you help make your boss a better supervisor.

START YOUR BIG ACTION PLANNING

It's time to pull together everything you've learned. Take account of all your thinking and effort, all your notes from the various chapters, and draft a step-by-step plan to transform a work relationship that matters to you. Consider what tools you can deploy to advance this process and make it more fun.

And remember: no matter how dedicated you are to your work, there's not only more to life—the other parts are essential to sustaining your passion and resilience. Your nonwork community is important, whether that community consists of family, friends, professional and personal networks, a religious or civic or social group, athletic team, online communities, coworkers, collaborators, or any combination of these groups. They are your best resources and support. Activate them in times of trouble and when you just need advice or want to learn something. In turn, be there for people. Do your part and more. Treat all people with respect, compassion, and generosity, and they will almost always return that treatment.

Workplace Genie is dedicated to expanding your toolkit of resources, but your own are steadfastly important. This especially applies to your off-hours time where the possibilities are endless and individual: family time, reading, music, meditation, art, yoga, gardening, walking in the woods, playing with your dog, cooking, traveling, sitting in silence, working out, running, cleaning your closets—you name it. We know three people whose favorite leisure activity is ironing. This personal time gives you respite, renewal, inspiration, and perspective. The feelings generated by your personal life go to work with you every day. And vice versa.

We hope you have some fun inventing your own positive mantras to counter the patterns and reactions that can block becoming who you want to be. They can be simple and direct, or more personal. A few we liked hearing about recently:

- "I'll think about this later."
- "I will keep an open mind until I investigate."
- "An angry person is a suffering person."
- "The sun really will come out tomorrow."
- "I'll decide how I feel about this and what to do later."
- "This person is only in his first incarnation, so he doesn't really understand much yet."
- "It's a beautiful world and there's a lot more in it than I'm looking at."

And here's a tattoo we saw on the back of someone's hand to remind herself not to take everything personally: "It's not about you, cookie!"

Or as Merlin the Magician says in T. H. White's *The Once and Future King*, "The best thing for being sad is to learn something. That's the only thing that never fails."

ACKNOWLEDGMENTS

The authors thank Olga Greco, our awesome editor, for believing in *Workplace Genie* and helping us make it a better book.

We also gratefully acknowledge the many people who shared their experiences and helped us bring the ideas to life.

Susan Dowell particularly thanks her colleagues, Jeffrey K. Zeig, PhD, director of the Milton H. Erickson Foundation; and Carolyn Daitch, PhD, director of the Center for the Treatment of Anxiety Disorders, for generously sharing their ideas and expertise for many years.

INDEX